DAN SHEEHAN

Semper Fi, Bill.

AFTER
ACTION

THE TRUE STORY OF
A COBRA PILOT'S JOURNEY

Editorial development and creative design support by Ascent:
www.itsyourlifebethere.com

To all who bear the burden of peace.

PROLOGUE

IF YOU LOOKED around my house, you might never guess I'd been a Marine. With the exception of a small corner of the basement, where some pictures and memorabilia hang on the wall over my computer, there are few clues to my past life.

They are there, just hidden.

A dresser drawer I rarely open contains my Bronze Star, Air Medals and other awards—still hanging on their plastic bars from the last time I'd worn my dress blues. Nestled underneath are three sets of wings—Naval Aviator, gold parachutist and silver freefall. These hard-earned symbols that used to define me sit jumbled in an old Tupperware container along with pocket-knives and broken wrist watches. Their modest trappings don't mean anything—I'm intensely proud of the accomplishments they represent.

There are other souvenirs in that drawer; sweat-stained notepads of radio frequencies and grid coordinates written by shaky, adrenaline-filled hands and love letters from my wife— each one sent without knowing if I'd be alive to read it.

And then there's the cyclic. Just the plastic handle really, sawed off from the metal tube that connected it to the control system of a helicopter. To anyone else it's a piece of garbage. To me it's the last thing a friend held when he died.

A lot of memories reside in that drawer, some good, and some bad. Without consciously deciding to, once I left the Marine

Corps I closed the drawer, eager to move on. My combat tours had been good ones, the kind that end with medals and parties, and I'd convinced myself that I'd escaped unscathed. I wanted them to be part of my past.

I may not have been the toughest Marine ever—but I'd worked with men who could claim that title. I take great pride in being able to call them friends. Most of them think I'm insane for becoming a stay-at-home dad—it's too much work. Those with kids get it though. The birthdays, ball games and dance recitals they missed while deployed often form the only regrets they'll admit to having.

My life looked perfect—on the outside. My last tour in Iraq was five years behind me and I had shifted gears. I had moved into another phase of my life and had no intention of ever looking back.

If earnest desire could make lies true, I would have never had to write this book. I told myself I was fine so often, I almost believed it myself.

I wasn't though.

CHAPTER 1

AUGUST 7, 2009 STARTED no differently from any other day in my new life—a whirlwind of baby bottles, dirty diapers, and getting the dogs outside before they pissed on the floor. The last thing I wanted to do was clean up after two leaky pitbulls.

I got a pot of coffee going and gulped down some breakfast while trying to block my 18-month-old son from eating the dogs' food. I lost. Finger-sweeping kibble out of his mouth, I stuck him in the highchair.

Three little electronic beeps from the coffee maker signaled the official start to the morning.

"Coffee's ready!" I shouted, half to my wife and half in anticipation of the caffeine. I hadn't slept well last night. Again.

Lena mumbled something from deep in the closet where she searched for clothes to fit her expanding belly. Four months pregnant with our daughter, clothes that fit her yesterday routinely shrank overnight.

With a full mug of coffee I gazed out the window, watching the dogs tear around the yard as they welcomed the new day. I tried to submit to the serenity I imagined I should feel amid such domestic bliss. But I couldn't—something was getting in the way.

Goddammit. Not again.

The vague sense of unease was back—or maybe it had never left.

Waiting for Lena I tried to isolate the feeling and, once again, failed. Angrily I pushed it away. I had everything a man could want—a smart and beautiful wife, a blossoming family and time to enjoy them—

So what the hell was bothering me?

My continuing inability to answer that question pissed me off more than anything else.

The unease lingering below the surface of my outwardly contented life wasn't new, although I didn't care to find out when it had begun. Acknowledging that it started shortly after my return from the invasion of Iraq would have legitimized it. That was something I refused to do.

I told myself the disquiet would go away on its own but that argument was wearing thin. If anything, its intensity was growing with time. It intruded the most on occasions when I should have been happiest. Watching my son grow provided a million happy experiences—first steps, pudding sneezes, giggle fits—but I found I couldn't really enjoy them. As soon as I opened the door to thoughts of contented fatherhood, that bitch unease would slip in and spoil everything. I only had one protection, the nuclear option. Unable to enjoy good emotions without suffering bad ones I had to go cold—protecting myself by suppressing them all.

Lena swept into the kitchen in a whirlwind of professional woman. A tantalizing hint of perfume evoked warm memories of last night as she moved past me. I smiled as she ate breakfast, drank coffee and wiped a booger off of our boy's face without a single wasted movement.

Damn, she's good.

I wasn't totally ignorant of my feelings. I just expected them to fall in line and obey. My entire adult life had been spent developing my Marine persona, impervious to pain or stress. Emotions, like muscles, were things to be trained, tools for me to use. I was supposed to control them, not the other way around. And I'd done it well too.

For over eleven years on active duty, the idea of delving into the details of feelings and emotions ranked slightly below a vasectomy with a rusty fishhook on my list of things to do. When something affected me I didn't spend much time figuring out what it was—I either explained it away or buried it. That's what you do in life-or-death situations, and it doesn't get more life-or-death than strapping a helicopter on your back. Controlling my emotions had kept me alive for years.

There had been some things that I couldn't quite control since Iraq, but I figured I could deal with a little emotional weirdness from time to time. The idiosyncrasies weren't a big deal. A little anger here and there, some random tears, maybe some self-medicating with alcohol—nothing to get excited about. The last thing I was going to do was "get in touch with my feelings." I'd sooner camp out for "New Kids On The Block" reunion tour tickets.

I could handle it—I was strong enough to ignore the unease.

Besides, I told myself, it didn't negatively impact anybody else. Only me.

And so, this sunny morning I dealt with it the same way I always had—by shutting down. I'd rather feel nothing than suffer a nagging itch I couldn't scratch.

Lena avoided our son's sticky hands but not mine and I earned a playful smack for pinching her butt as she went to leave. A kiss for him, one for me and she was gone, striding out with a purpose. Released from his high chair, my son babbled contentedly and played with his toys as a comfortable calm fell over the house. I reveled in the momentary quiet.

In a few minutes the phone rang, intruding. Holding the door open to let the dogs in, I glanced at the caller ID.

"Hey Moms and Pops," I answered cheerily, "how's it going?"

There was a moment's hesitation before my dad responded.

"Not too good, Dan." Dad's voice sounded different, strained and flat.

I tensed a little. "What's up?"

"There's no easy way to say this so I'll just come right out with it. Dave was in a crash last night…"

Dad's voice kept sounding in my ears, but my mind instantly accelerated away from our conversation—7000 miles to Afghanistan where my little brother was flying Cobra gunships. My face went numb.

"…in the hospital at Camp Bastion. All Tom could tell me is that he has a broken back and burns on his face and arm, but both he and his copilot are alive."

Tom was the commanding officer of Dave's squadron and an old friend of mine.

Dad seemed to be saying Dave was okay. But something strange was happening to me. In my mind I saw my brother's handsome face melt tragically and images of him—smashed, broken and paralyzed—flashed behind my eyes.

I felt weak and sagged against the wall, stunned. The hand holding the phone shook as I mumbled "fuck" into the handset. No other word could convey the intense shock, hate, and fear that exploded unexpectedly in my head. Confused, I fought back, trying in vain to stem a flood of venomous emotions.

"Fuck is right," Dad answered. The slightest tremor in his voice betrayed the fact that he was struggling to keep it together too.

His tone, and the realization that Dad was close to losing it, penetrated my defenses like they weren't even there. Something broke loose and merciless memories sliced through my suddenly unprotected mind.

The world started to slip away fast. It was as if the kitchen, my boy, the dogs and the whole house ceased to exist. The present disappeared under a torrent of painful images from my past—the cracked and bloodstained helmet of a dead friend, a blackened patch of sand where twisted metal and flesh mingled freely, bodies ripped apart by explosions...Horrific scenes I'd never wanted to see again blasted through my brain, all the more vivid for being sequestered for so long.

I heard my father's voice again and grasped at it, staving off collapse with superhuman effort and succeeding—for the moment.

"Tom asked me for your phone number, so expect a call from him soon."

I grunted something to show I heard and approved. Tommy and I had served together for many years and I knew that Dave was in good hands.

"I've got to go, Dan; I'm heading out the door to catch Mom at work. She doesn't know yet and I'm not going to tell her over the phone."

The familiar steel was back in his voice now. He had something to do, an action to accomplish. I envied his distraction.

"Okay Dad, I'll let you know if Tommy has anything new when he calls." The strength of my own voice surprised me, like it came from someone else.

"Okay Dan." A pause. "I love you son."

Those four words caused a new surge of emotion.

"Thanks Dad, I love you too." The words squeaked out, bypassing the trappings of manliness that usually constrained them. My ancillary identities—man, warrior, Marine—shuffled their feet uncomfortably as the scared little boy within reached out for his dad.

When the phone was back in its cradle the tumultuous feelings surged anew. One particular emotion shot out of the depths of my mind like a bullet. Flatfooted I stood in its path, totally unable to avoid taking it in the chest. A sense of deep, penetrating hatred slammed into my consciousness and left me reeling. Only it wasn't hatred at the enemy for hurting my brother, or for killing my friends in Iraq. It was, inexplicably, hatred of *myself*. In a flash it was gone, leaving me to doubt it had ever been there at all. Confused, I sat down on the floor. Hard.

And then all hell broke loose.

An unstoppable torrent of snarled emotions boiled upward from the depths of my guts. I tried to push them away, to bully them back into submission, but it was no use. They overran my mental defenses, sweeping them aside like toothpicks until none remained. Unprotected, I was powerless before the onslaught.

*...he's in the hospital...*Dad's voice sounded in my head.

Waves of anguish and grief pummeled me as if I'd never see Dave again.

...wounded...

Unbearable sadness rose as if he were dead.

My last reserve of strength left me, and I drowned beneath the flood. My head dropped between my knees and, overwhelmed, I let go.

Time stopped. Vivid flashes of dead friends being pulled from smoldering helicopters and strangers blown into pink mist twisted into a maelstrom of emotions that crushed me like a vice.

A weirdly detached bystander within me noted the intricate grain of the hardwood floor in the instant before tears filled my eyes. Breathing was impossible, but unimportant, and my mouth hung open in a silent grimace. Drool streamed out and mixed with the tears pooling beneath my hanging head. The battle between my physical body and the darkness in my mind raged and my abdominal muscles contracted in one long, sustained crush. It was as if my body was trying to squeeze the poisonous memories out of every pore.

At the same time my rational mind struggled to say "But Dave is alive"—only to be overcome by a more powerful voice in my head. It would not be reasoned with, pushed aside or ignored. Its penetrating, catastrophic message pounded me over and over again: "Your brother is dead, Dave is dead."

This made no sense but the waves of unbearable grief continued their assault. I choked as they swept over my head.

An irresistible order compelled me to breathe. Not a breath really, just a quick equalization of the vacuum in my crushed lungs before my muscles clamped down and returned my body to a state of rigor mortis.

On and on it went, the pain, the uncoiling emotions. I don't really know how long it lasted. Maybe minutes. It felt like forever.

Who was this stranger? What happened to the guy who could hold it all together?

At that moment my dog wiggled her way between my knees and I lifted my head at her touch. Kitty pushed her big, flat, pitbull skull into my chest and held it there, unmoving.

I grabbed her and squeezed as if she were a life ring, burying my face in her warm, soft fur. I felt the intensity of the waves dissipate slightly. She may have only been trying to tell me that I hadn't fed her yet, but her timing couldn't have been better. I don't know how long I sat there like that, sobbing into velvety fur that smelled of warm puppy, but it was probably only a few minutes.

The phone rang again.

I wiped my eyes and mouth quickly before noticing my son standing next to Ozzy, my other dog. Uncertain what was going on, they stood just beyond arm's reach and watched me with weirdly similar, puzzled looks on their faces. Only their outer coatings—fur versus dried milk—were different. I shook my head and cleared my throat to see if I'd be able to talk at all, then answered the phone.

"Hello?" I thought I sounded pretty normal.

"Shoe, it's Hobbit." Radio callsigns had replaced given names years ago as our normal mode of address. The slight static on the line was the only indication my friend Tom was calling from Afghanistan.

"Your brother's gonna be fine," he continued without

waiting for a response. Small talk was never part of our conversations and besides, there was no need to dance around the subject. We both knew why he was calling.

"He's got a fractured spine, superficial burns on the side of his face and on one of his arms, but he is up and walking around, harassing the nurses and making some little Afghan kid in the cot next to him laugh. He's out of his mind on pain killers and making the best of it."

I felt myself smile at the thought of my brother clowning around. The relief I felt at hearing his words spread quickly through me and I blurted out, "Shit, Tommy, what happened?"

"Don't really know yet; I haven't been able to talk to Dave. His section lead said that they were forced to fly low over the river by bad weather and they flushed some insurgents out of cover. Your brother called them out and took tac lead of the section to engage; next thing the lead aircraft saw was Dave's flaming bird skidding across the riverbank on its side. There's nothing left of it now; everything burned in the fire."

"Dave and the copilot got out all right though?" I asked. Something in me needed assurance. It just seemed too miraculous that they could have survived a crash like that. I'd known too many others who hadn't.

"Yeah, the copilot is a little worse but both are in the hospital getting treated. They're both going to be okay."

When Tommy hung up, the silence on the end of the line mirrored the strange silence that filled the house. I looked around quickly to see what my son was doing and was relieved to find he hadn't moved. I smiled at the sight of my little guy pulling a bone out of Ozzy's huge mouth with impunity. Kitty hadn't moved a muscle during the phone call, just kept her head solidly pressed against my chest. Her physical contact gave me such comfort that I'm not sure what I would have done without it.

But in an instant it was upon me again. It wasn't a flood this time, but rather a wildfire of grief that surprised me from out of the darkness. I buried my face in Kitty's back and squeezed her hard as new tears flashed hot down my cheeks. I was already rebuilding my defenses though and the quality of the experience was different.

Instead of getting overrun by the flames, my conscious self hid like a firefighter under an emergency shelter, hoping for the best.

What the fuck is going on?

On the conscious level I knew that Dave was alive. I knew he'd survived the crash and was resting in a hospital—so why was I reacting like he was dead? Why were the parts of myself outside the shelter burning in anguish as though he'd been killed?

For the first time I saw it.

Something wasn't right—*in me.*

Recognition of the disconnect between the reality of the situation and my reaction to it dawned slowly. With it came confusion.

While sobs wracked my body and tears dripped on the floor, the quivering voice under the shelter started to call out. It started meekly but rapidly gained strength.

"What the fuck, dude? He's fine—knock this shit off and get up."

The roar of the flames died down as the voice got louder and more insistent. Finally I listened to it and struggled to my feet, feeling the constricting bands around my chest loosen ever so slightly. The overpowering grief had lost its strength, burning itself out in a cataclysmic eruption.

Over the next several weeks the news from Afghanistan got better and better for our family. Dave returned to California, describing his injuries offhandedly as a bad sunburn and a sore back, and the whole event was poised to shift from a crisis to family history.

Almost, but not quite. There was something bothering me that I couldn't shake. *What the hell had happened to me?*

I wanted to push away the confusion I felt at my reaction, to forget that I'd glimpsed something dangerous inside me and go back to how things were. But something told me that would be a mistake.

While I'd noted little emotional discontinuities in myself over recent years I'd been able to ignore them. I was all right because I said so. I'd come back from war with all my limbs and faculties intact and I was fine. Except I wasn't, not exactly. Although I didn't want to see it, my wild overreaction to Dave's crash shoved the truth in my face. Something wasn't right—*in me.*

In the aftermath of that reaction I regained my footing—but it was different from before, unsteady, tenuous. Now that I knew these powerful emotions lay dormant, I had to wonder when they would come back. And what would set them off. Distrust and fear of my own reactions grew quickly, eroding my self-confidence.

I didn't even think about that weird flash of self-loathing—the contempt had disappeared so quickly that I could deny it ever existed. Later, I would realize that it hadn't dissipated. Somehow, amid the destruction of all my other mental defenses, some part of me recognized how dangerous that thought was and captured it. Locked away in the bowels of my mind it festered, waiting.

Recognition that something was wrong with me didn't sit well. I wanted to ignore it, to double down on "tough-guy" control over my emotions and move on. I was certain I could handle whatever that suppression cost. It was worth it to me to avoid going there, to avoid entering places in my mind where unprocessed memories howled.

That is, until I realized the price wasn't only mine to pay.

It was a dreary October day, the overcast sky producing a slow drizzle that was turning the fallen leaves into a sodden mass in the yard. Our son was chasing Kitty around the house with his fire truck while Lena and I enjoyed our morning coffee and chatted about nothing in particular. Although I maintained enough focus on the conversation to grunt at appropriate times, my mind slipped away from the comfortable warmth of our kitchen and I got lost in some reflection.

Lena continued talking and, a few minutes later, I dropped back into the moment—which is when I noticed that our boy, now 20-months-old, had stopped chasing Kitty to join us in the kitchen.

The sight of him in his footie pajamas hit me like a truck. It wasn't remarkable, him joining us in the kitchen, but what struck me to my core was his posture and trusting composure as he leaned against the cabinet door. Silently he faced me, holding his stuffed monkey, Steve, in a loving headlock under one arm. His inside leg was slightly bent and crossed in front of the outer and his little shoulder held his weight solidly against the wooden door. He had one thumb in his mouth while he absentmindedly stroked Steve's tail with his other hand.

He had assumed an almost perfect mirror image of...me... exactly the way I was standing, leaning against the door jamb with my arms folded across my chest.

I looked down at him slowly, not wanting to break the spell. When our eyes met he stared back at me, poker-faced. Then the edges of his mouth twitched upward and his face broke wide-open. His big, self-satisfied smile seemed to shout proudly, "See, Dad, I'm just like you!"

Just like me. He wants to be just like me.

That should have filled me with pride and love. But I almost felt sick.

That small, innocent gesture made the cost of my continued denial perfectly clear. It spoke directly to my greatest fear.

That adoring smile pushed me over the edge. I finally saw that my stubborn refusal to acknowledge issues stemming from my time in Iraq no longer affected just me. Now it would endanger the emotional health of my son and soon-to-be-born daughter. I was okay if I was the only person who suffered. But pass it on to my kids?

Oh hell no.

That realization launched a barrage of questions that would not be ignored.

What if the example I provided was all jacked up? What if my interactions with my kids were a confusing mix of unprovoked emotional outbursts separated by periods of detached neglect? Would I ignore minor annoyances until my rage grew uncontrollable? Would the first indication of my displeasure be a backhanded slap? If I couldn't trust my emotions how could I teach them how to feel, to love and be loved? What if my kids grow up thinking my erratic and disproportionate responses are *normal*—that this is how they should react too? Am I in danger of screwing them up—for life?

Oh man. This game has changed.

The realization hit hard and fast that my kids would imitate what I did regardless of whether it was right or wrong, self-destructive or positive. On some level I'd known that all along. I just never imagined I'd come down on the 'screwed-up' side.

Fear of hurting my children provided compelling motivation to figure out what had happened to me. I started digging, using writing as a skeleton key to open locked rooms in my mind. What I found in them were emotions and reactions that define the very essence of a warrior—although I'd considered them flaws in my character, symptoms of weakness. This ignorance had planted a kernel of unease that could have ruined my life, or even killed me, if I allowed it to grow unchecked.

Over time I came to understand the most liberating thing—I was not alone. After a little research it became clear that what I'd considered my 'dirty little secret' was in fact a feeling known to warriors throughout history. It's only now, with our modern sensitivities, that we've forgotten this fundamental component of what it means to be a warrior. Our shared lack of comprehension means more of our fighting men and women who survive the battlefield come home to die at their own hands. Our warriors are unprotected by not knowing the price they pay, even in victory.

The casualties don't stop when the guns fall silent. Those who survive bear wounds that sometimes take years to register. For some that realization comes too late—after marriages are wrecked, childhoods spoiled, lives destroyed—and the survivor is buried beneath the detritus. At that point a previously incomprehensible option whispers the promise of ultimate escape.

It doesn't have to be that way.

The intense experiences of combat can turn a warrior's mind into a pressure cooker, locking in caustic emotions like so much steam. We pride ourselves on being able to hold the lid closed, but at what cost? In the face of my son I found a price I was unwilling to pay. In writing, I inadvertently lifted the lid, releasing the steam. I've learned I can't do anything to change the source of the steam, my personal history is part of the burden I carry. But now the pressure dissipates instead of building dangerously with time.

So here you go. This is how I removed the lid. To my brothers and sisters who continue to struggle on battlefields, both internal and external, this story is for you. Please take what you can from it and chart your own way forward.

Just as there is a time when we must hold the lid down to survive, there comes a time when we must take it off to live.

CHAPTER 2

THE PATH MY LIFE has taken is no accident. I didn't wake up one morning and say, "Gee, I guess I'll join the Marine Corps. That sounds like fun."

Like most members of our all-volunteer military I could have done something else. Nobody offered me the "jail-or-enlist" option in a stuffy courtroom; no draft board picked me out of thin air. I could have gone any direction I wanted to after high school, studied for any number of high-paying careers and lived a financially secure existence.

That sounds as mind-numbingly boring to me now as it did back then.

I worked hard to earn my place in the cockpit of an attack helicopter, training for years in the hope that someday I would have the chance to fly it into battle. When I finally did, it felt like I'd won the lottery.

As the son of a Navy pilot, many of my childhood memories

involved airplanes and the adventures I imagined my father had with them when he wasn't home. I recall well the peculiar smell of my father's flight suit when he'd return from a multi-week trip. That reassuring mixture of Old Spice, hydraulic fluid and burnt avgas will always remind me of crushing hugs and the battered flight bags of presents he'd picked up for my siblings and me from places exotic and exciting.

As I grew older I learned that my father had served in combat, providing close air support from the cockpit of his OV-10A in South Vietnam. Knowing that, I projected onto him all the examples of fictional heroism and bravery that Hollywood had shown me.

Dad would speak of events from his combat tour, but the things he left unsaid had a far greater impact. They were what fostered my adolescent daydreams of his life-or-death actions in the air and on the ground. My fantasies of his heroic struggles colored my perception of what made him so special.

For me, my father's combat tour had made him who he was—the man who occupied a mystical place in my life and heart—and at some point I began to desire that same experience. I wanted to face the same trials and challenges of combat so that I could become a man just like him. These thoughts were never conscious but they funneled my personal dreams and ambitions into a path that became clear to me toward the end of high school.

Choosing a military career was not a lark. I knew it would likely put me in harm's way. That knowledge made joining the Marine Corps the best choice for me. It was a foregone conclusion that if I stayed on active duty I would go to war someday. I wanted to make sure that when I did, I would have the toughest, meanest, nastiest SOBs in the world on either side of me.

I know now that the Marine Corps doesn't hold a monopoly on toughness or courage. But I had to make a choice, and to my 18-year-old mind my reasoning was solid.

After I decided to become a Marine, I set out to attain that goal with every ounce of my being. I was enamored with the challenges presented by a life in the Marines and wholeheartedly believed the overused cliché: Anything that didn't kill me only made me stronger. The more I learned of Marine exploits across the globe, the more their grit and determination elevated them to near-godlike status in my imagination. I never considered the dire circumstances that required their incredible acts of self-sacrifice and bravery, only that they had been lucky enough to be in situations where they could demonstrate their valor. Their heroism invoked jealousy in me that screamed "I can do it too, just gimme a chance!"

The training involved in becoming a Marine was difficult, but I thrived on it. It was the transition between who I was and who I wanted to be. I welcomed each additional trial eagerly. My own self-identity became so entwined with being a Marine that the two were inseparable—I didn't need a tattoo on my arm, it was already on my heart. I gladly conformed and took pride in my newly earned identity, specifically, the link it gave me to the strength and honor of Marines past.

Nobody 'joins' the Marine Corps. You have to *earn* the right to call yourself a Marine. It's not an easy process, nor should it be. Men and women from all different walks of life readily sacrifice large parts of their own identity in order to become one of the few and the proud.

But, there is one small price to pay for that right. You must be ready to kill.

The Marine Corps is different from the other services in this regard. It's not hidden in the fine print, buried beneath offers of money for college or concealed behind high-tech gadgetry. No, the price of being a Marine is proclaimed loud and clear in recruiting posters and slogans. It's in the flashing bayonets of the Silent Drill Team, the painful collars on our dress blues, and in the unapologetic contempt of weakness in any form. To look at a Marine is to see a weapon—ready, trained and able to destroy any enemy, anytime, anywhere. The challenge is clear: "Do you have what it takes?"

From the first day of Officer Candidate School, the Corps reinforced the idea of killing so often that the physical act of taking life soon lost its stigma. That we would accomplish the act was just assumed. The program of instruction swept aside lifetimes of parental programming and uncovered our latent aggressions. Destructive capabilities we'd been taught were wrong were now honed to a razor's edge—sharp enough to make us eager to crush another human's skull with a boot heel. There was no consideration of what it would *feel* like to kill—except that we were supposed to revel in it. Spilling the enemy's blood was everybody's career goal.

I earned my commission as a Second Lieutenant in 1996 and attended The Basic School (TBS) in Quantico, VA. I couldn't wait to learn the skills of my chosen profession. I might go on to fly later, but first I needed to learn how to be a Marine Officer.

In the Marine Corps the infantry is king—everything else exists to support it. That concept was clearly visible in the attitudes of the instructors at TBS and I felt palpable pressure to drop my air contract and try for a grunt slot instead.

I held out though. My dream—scarcely admitted to myself, so remote were the chances of attaining it—required that I remain focused on attending flight school.

I didn't just want to fly anymore, that wasn't enough. I wanted to be the guy the grunts loved, the guy whose arrival overhead meant the situation was no longer in doubt.

I wanted to be a Cobra pilot, the guy who ruled the battlefield.

Of all the aircraft that the Marine Corps flew, none sent shivers down my spine like the venomous lines of the AH-1W Super Cobra gunship. The powerful, concussive beat of its heavy rotor blades invoked images in my head of overwhelming strength and barely contained mayhem at the fingertips of the two pilots in the tiny cockpit. To fly that helicopter, to be master of its incredible firepower and use it to support my brothers on the ground, became aspirations that made my heart race.

There were many obstacles to overcome, and the road was dauntingly long, but I put blinders on and plowed ahead. I stayed focused on the next small step—the next flight, the next test—and the years passed quickly. One by one I negotiated the hurdles and finally found myself grinning like an idiot amid a tumult of happy voices in the Pensacola auditorium. My winging ceremony was about to begin.

We had just taken our seats when the lights dimmed and a movie began on the large screen in front of us, an attention-getter designed to encourage everyone to sit down and stop talking. For twenty minutes scene after scene of Navy, Coast Guard and Marine Corps helicopters flashed across the screen in a parade of helicopter pornography showcasing the excitement of flying loud, leaky machines in all sorts of cool places.

Nanny, my dad's mom, sat next to me in the darkened auditorium with her hand resting on top of my forearm. Nanny is an adventurous soul and the undeniable matriarch of our family.

Outspoken and confident, she bucked the traditions of her day and joined the Navy as a member of the WAVES, Women Accepted for Volunteer Emergency Service, during World War II. While on official business she met a handsome young ensign and the partnership that would create our family began.

She learned a lot about airplanes from my grandfather, as Poppy spent his entire career flying either a military or civilian aircraft, but helicopters were an enigma to her. My grandfather, father and uncle had all flown airplanes and generally considered helicopters as things to be avoided—my dad maintains to this day that the worst part of crashing his T-28 was the helicopter ride home. I knew that Nanny had no idea what I was talking about when I told her I was going to fly Snakes. She squeezed my arm gently to get my attention and spoke quietly into my ear, her voice just audible over the loud music.

"Tell me Danny, which one of those are you going to fly?"

Her voice carried the slightest hint of innocent condescension. Instantly we were standing in front of a wall of paintings in my first grade classroom and she was asking which drippy hand turkey was mine.

"I will Nanny. It hasn't popped up on screen yet, but when it does I'll let you know."

The fact that I was a Marine officer and not a little boy didn't appear to register with her. I wondered if it ever would.

More footage of helicopters carrying heavy loads, dropping off troops, slinging artillery cannons beneath them on long ropes and other routine missions played across the screen. I wondered if they had forgotten about the gunships until the soundtrack made a definite shift toward heavy metal.

On the screen a group of tall trees stood innocently on a hilltop. The tranquility of the scene starkly contrasted with the intensity of the music until a skinny grey helicopter made its presence known. Then it all fit. Uncoiling like its namesake, the Cobra bared its fangs as it cleared the trees, exposing rows of missiles and pods of rockets beneath its short wings while the 20mm cannon traversed menacingly from side to side.

My adrenaline coursed and I wanted to shout "Fuck yeah! There it is!" Instead I nudged Nanny softly, "That's a Cobra. That's what I'm going to fly."

She didn't reply. Silently she watched as images flashed across the screen that made my pulse quicken; Cobra helicopters ripping through the air as furious streams of rockets and powerful missiles streaked off their stubby wings. I listened to the deep staccato of the 20mm cannon sending out some love and almost couldn't believe that I'd been selected to fly that incredible machine. I opened and closed my fists to fight off the urge to shout and reveled in the tightness in my forearms. Soon that would be me. Soon.

After the video ended a retired Navy Captain got up to speak. He had been an HH-46 pilot during his career and spoke at length about a mission where he and his crew had saved the lives of several mariners adrift in the sea. He held that mission up as the pinnacle of his career and extolled the virtues of saving lives, speaking directly to the Navy and Coast Guard pilots who would spend their careers flying search and rescue missions. Mentally I rolled my eyes—his message had nothing to do with me. Mine was not going to be a career of saving lives, of plucking unfortunate souls out of harm's way and whisking them to safety. No. If I was lucky, extremely lucky, I would unleash that knife-thin gunship in combat one day. The scenario I longed for involved rather the opposite of everything the retired Captain was talking about. I was relieved when he finally sat down.

Nanny leaned in against my shoulder again and asked me a question in a quiet voice. Her tone was different. She wasn't speaking to her little grandson anymore, a change I noted with some satisfaction. Her question was simple, yet the issues it contained were complex beyond my comprehension.

I answered the surface question with all the untested bravado I could muster. Mildly insolent, I parroted a phrase that, when I recalled it years later, would make me cringe in embarrassment.

Fifteen minutes later the Commodore called my name to come up on the stage. After years of fearing it never would, my moment had finally come. After the handshake and obligatory smiling picture with the Commodore, I turned around to face the auditorium as my family gathered around to pin the wings on my chest.

The gold wings that I had earned embodied the spirit of naval aviation, and the men and women authorized to wear them are universally recognized as some of the best pilots in the world. Far more than a simple adornment on a uniform, they identify the wearer as capable of handling any emergency or dire situation, a calm decider of life and death for themselves, their crews, and in some cases, the enemy.

On a more personal level they transferred my family's mantle of service to me, a weight I ardently desired. I was about to assume the position of my father and his father before him and the intoxicating feeling of being *just like them* threatened to overwhelm me.

My father walked toward me on the stage and my heart pounded with excitement as his hand reached into his pocket. The moment had come.

My heart threatened to jump out of my chest when I saw a faded pink box in his hand.

Holy shit. It couldn't be.

I'd only seen them once, a long time ago, but my grandfather's gold wings were unmistakable. Opening the box, Dad pressed them into my hand. I was surprised by their substantial weight and flipped them over in my sweaty palm. Dulled by the passage of time, the proud family heirloom bore three sets of initials and dates engraved on the back: DBS 8/43, DBS Jr 10/68 and now DBS III 12/98. The numbers swam a little as I blinked back tears of pride. Silently I handed the wings back to my dad.

They'd still been shiny in the picture on the wall at Nanny's house. The bright gold stood out crisply against Poppy's dress white uniform as they cut their wedding cake with his sword, their smiling faces familiar yet untouched by time. Nanny had pinned those same wings onto my father's uniform when his turn came and I felt the gravity of tradition shift to me as Dad pinned them to mine.

I looked up from the tarnished gold treasure that adorned my chest and caught my father's eye as he stepped in to give me a hug. He didn't say a word but the crow's feet at the corners of his warm eyes spoke to me of the challenges he'd faced while wearing these same wings, challenges he knew I eagerly sought. His smile bore the marks of what I would later recognize as the peculiar curse of fatherhood—simultaneous fear and pride. At the time I'd thought he was reflecting on how he was standing in his father's shoes. Maybe it was both.

Some events of that day have grown fuzzy in my memory—but one thing remains vibrant and clear: Nanny's question. At strange times since, I've heard her voice as it quietly penetrated the din of the celebration that filled the auditorium that sunny December morning.

"Your helicopter doesn't save lives, does it?"

She hadn't meant it as a question really, more a statement of fact. Missing the rhetorical nature of it I had answered, my purposefully blunt response designed to shock her into seeing me as a trained warrior, a protector, a man. What she was really saying flew right over my head—and I didn't even duck.

"No Nanny, we just kill people."

She'd just nodded and sat back without another word. I think she knew the futility of driving her point home. Some lessons can't be taught, only experienced. What I said was true—I just didn't have a clue what it really meant.

I'd been exposed to years of training designed to make me an efficient killing machine with whatever was available; my hands, E-tool, boot heel, rifle, knife—the means were unimportant, only the end result mattered. I'd absorbed those lessons well and was eager to apply them to my new weapon. The mission of the Cobra is clear: Kill the enemy and blow up his stuff. It doesn't carry troops around, drop off humanitarian supplies, or rescue lost puppy dogs. It all seemed so simple to me.

Later I would realize she knew it wasn't simple at all.

After receiving my wings, my training ground moved to California and was solidly focused on one thing: the mechanics of killing with a helicopter. There had been something academic about the methods of killing I'd learned before—the chances of me ever getting into a bayonet fight were pretty slim. This wasn't academic, it wasn't a training session designed to teach me some intangible leadership trait. This was real—there was every chance that what I was learning in the calm air above Camp Pendleton would pay dividends when lives were at stake.

Everything I learned about the Cobra was tied to keeping me alive and making my enemy dead.

My world became black or white—enemy or friendly. Enemy troops were to be killed immediately by any means available, and friendly troops were to be protected by killing the enemy. Thought and comprehension were removed from the equation, replaced by rote memorization and unhesitating responses. If the ones and zeros lined up correctly, I fired. If not, I didn't.

I'll be the first one to trumpet the efficiency of the training I went through. In a short period of time I went from barely able to start the Cobra to being fully confident I could employ it in combat and win. That confidence is absolutely essential and can only be fostered by realistic training.

But there's a limit to how realistic training can be. Maybe I should have known it, but for some reason I didn't consider that things get different when there are real people, real lives on the line. Sure, the 'fog of war' had been talked about, but that was somebody else's war, somebody else's conundrum to deal with.

If it hadn't been for a near disaster on my first deployment I might have gone to Iraq ignorant of just how confusing—and deadly—the fog could be. The lesson I learned from that incident would serve me well in combat. It was only afterward that it would become a liability.

CHAPTER 3

A MONTH AFTER leaving San Diego, the USS Tarawa arrived off the coast of East Timor. I stood on the flight deck of the helicopter carrier in a foul mood as the night sky melted into shades of blue. The high mountains of the tiny nation stepped forward out of the blackness and the scene would have ranked as the most beautiful sunrise I'd ever seen—if I'd been paying attention.

The 13th Marine Expeditionary Unit (Special Operations Capable) [MEU (SOC)] had orders to provide humanitarian assistance to the United Nations force struggling to stabilize and rebuild the small country. After choosing independence from Indonesia, deadly riots had destroyed much of East Timor's infrastructure and killed over a thousand of its citizens. The UN troops were dealing with a shadowy guerilla presence bent on punishing those who had the temerity to desire freedom and they lacked helicopter support. That's where we came in.

The plan was relatively straightforward; our medium- and heavy-lift helicopters would sling-load tons of construction materials and deliver them to remote mountainside landing zones near the villages that needed them. Three days of flying, then we would leave. On the surface it sounded simple.

What made it a little more interesting were the violent pro-Indonesian militias operating in the thick forests that blanketed the mountainous country. They were the ones who had killed over 1400 people and they would take a dim view of us trying to ρ the survivors.

Therein lay the cause of my distraction that September morning in 2000.

To protect our transport helicopters from ground fire, we would escort them into and out of the zones with our four Cobras and two working Hueys. With full cans of 20mm in the nose and 14 high-explosive rockets under our wings, we were well-prepared to deal with the possible threat.

I'd slept like crap the night before, scarcely able to believe my good luck. Less than a month into my first float and I was about to fly a fully armed gunship around a sovereign nation trolling for a fight?

Are you fucking kidding me? Hell yeah!

Despite tossing and turning all night I'd leapt out of bed that morning like a 10-year-old on Christmas—only to find that Santa had dropped a turd in my stocking. The line-up had changed.

Instead of flying I'd be on standby, relegated to sitting on the bench while other pilots crossed into the unknown. It made sense to keep a section of gunships in reserve in case they were needed to respond to a crisis, but not mine!

Fuck!

Awake and fully pissed I went up to the flight deck—I had to escape the excited chatter of my squadron mates as they prepared to launch. I walked over to the Cobra parked on spot four, thankful it was dark enough that nobody could see me pouting as I caressed the dew-covered rocket pod underneath the bird's wing and engaged in gratuitous self-pity.

The scuff of a boot against the flight deck alerted me to the attack, but not in time. Massive ape arms crushed the breath from my lungs and lifted me off my feet. Freshly released anger drove a couple of quick elbows backward at my assailant's exposed ribs and I was rewarded with a surprised grunt when they landed. The grip loosened completely and I dropped to the rough metal deck and moved away.

"Dammit, Teddy. Y'almost made me swallow my dip!" I complained, spinning to face my friend. I was not surprised to find him grinning from ear to ear in the early light.

A good friend of mine for years, Ted Treadwell was a UH-1N Huey pilot in the squadron and also my roommate on the ship.

"Guess you shouldn't a' been daydreaming, sucka!" he answered, sounding more like Shaft than a white boy from Phoenix—and not at all apologetic. Our friendship was based largely on delivering and receiving physical punishment in various forms regardless of the company we found ourselves in. We provided a never-ending source of amusement for the rest of the squadron.

"You flying with Kid today?" he asked, the ritual beating and insults over with for the time being. Kid was my boss and combat crew. Any time we flew into situations that might involve shooting we flew with our combat crew—the same pilots were always paired together for familiarity and efficiency.

"Naw, we're on standby. Just have to hope for some shit to go down," I replied, trying to hide my disappointment but failing.

Teddy gave an exaggerated *"Ha-ha!"*—mimicking Nelson's annoying laugh from *The Simpsons*. I was already reeling from being bumped off the schedule and the same thing from any less of a friend would have really pissed me off. But coming from Teddy all I could do was smirk. To get mad at him would only show weakness that he'd exploit mercilessly and besides, I knew I was acting like a baby.

I flipped him the bird as he turned and walked to his Huey.

"Try not to fuck anything up today," I called after him.

"Oh I got dis," he replied easily, returning my salute over his shoulder.

Lucky fucker. I hope he doesn't get to do some shooting—I'll never hear the end of it.

My prayers were answered and the day passed without incident. No militiamen were spotted and, with the exception of a load of loose roofing materials that got blown off the side of a mountain by a 46's downwash, everything went pretty smoothly. To my eager imagination the absence of any violence today increased the chances that it would happen tomorrow— the militia would be expecting us. Again I tossed and turned in my coffin-like bed and willed the night to pass quickly.

I got up on the flight deck before dawn. This time I had drawn my 9mm pistol, M-16 rifle and ammunition and was in a much better mood. I put my kneeboard and maps into the front seat and preflighted the aircraft in the predawn darkness.

"Hey Shoe, how's the bird look?" Kid joined me at the nose of our aircraft as I lay underneath the 20mm cannon, inspecting the cable attachments.

"Good, Sir. Nothing big," I answered, letting him know

that I had conducted the preflight inspection and found nothing important amiss. There was always leaking fluid and minor gripes but the main pieces were all there. It takes a lot of trust for one pilot to take another's word for the airworthiness of his aircraft, but that was the point of the combat crew configuration. Kid and I had built that trust over time.

"A'ight den, less do dis," he responded as he climbed into the rear seat and started to strap in, his fake ghetto accent relieving some of the morning's stress.

Smiling, I took a final walk around the aircraft to ensure all the panels were tightly secured, put on my body armor and flight vest and hopped into the front cockpit. Even with my combat gear on I was perfectly sized for the seat at 150 pounds, 5'7". I wondered how the bigger guys did it. Perfectly sized or not, pilot comfort was not a strong consideration of the Cobra's designers.

When we returned from the mission eight hours later I was thankful it was over. My back screamed in protest when I climbed stiffly out of the cockpit. The whole day had been a non-event.

We'd found nothing threatening but not for lack of looking. I spent 90% of the day with my face down in the targeting bucket, slewing the magnified optics along our route and into the various landing zones in the hope that I would spot someone with a weapon in the thick underbrush.

That night as I lay in my bunk, images of the day's flight replayed against the back of my eyelids—an ocean of jungle tilting and vibrating as I probed lush foliage ineffectively with the optics. I'd been looking through a soda straw at a landscape that held thousands of possible hiding places. With a start I realized that dumb luck, not my years of training and preparation, would determine if I would see a threat in time to do anything about it.

There's almost no chance of me spotting someone before they shoot at us.

Hmm. Hadn't thought about that before. Training targets had always stood out clearly against the background.

The sun was just above the horizon as we started the third and final day of operations in East Timor. The heat felt all the more oppressive because of the thick humidity and my face itched where sweat found the small cuts from my hasty shave. This would be our last day to search for a very elusive foe lurking in the thick forests of the picturesque island. I really hoped we would find them.

Given the stories about the brutality of the pro-Indonesian militias that had beaten and murdered defenseless civilians, the thought of administering some high explosive spankings was very attractive—although after the anticlimactic non-events of yesterday I tried not to get too excited.

It was hard to imagine that such a beautiful place had been the scene of violent and deadly riots just a short time ago, but I knew it had.

Lena—then a squadron mate and not yet a love interest—had spent the day before in the capital, Dili. She brought back a horrifying tale from another squadron mate who was serving as liaison with the East Timorese air traffic controllers at the airport. When she told the story to a group of us over dinner, her sunburned face unconsciously betrayed emotions that she'd scrubbed from her voice.

"...the villagers had taken refuge in their church, I dunno,

I guess hoping that God would protect them when the militia attacked. When they came they forced their way in, hacking and cutting the people with machetes before mounting the bell tower and tossing children from the top, like some kind of sick game. Then they left and disappeared into the trees, but not before setting fire to the place."

She paused and drank half a glass of tea in one gulp.

The rest of us listened and fiddled with our food uncomfortably. We had all spent years training to kill but not like that—what she described was pure sadistic murder.

"When Drifty walked through the rubble two days ago there were still teeth and bones lying in the ashes." Lena looked down at her plate without seeing it, adding quietly "I wonder if they're ever going to pick them up?"

I had no answer for my friend. None of us did.

The story, and her obvious discomfort at what she'd seen and heard ashore, infuriated me. I wanted to exact some sort of revenge for what had taken place here. I saw a chance to right an obvious wrong, and now I really, *really* wanted someone to pick a fight with me on today's flight.

Once safely airborne and flying away from the ship, Kid passed me the controls in the front seat. Knowing that I would not fly at all once we got over land, I eagerly took the controls, listening to the sharp sound of Kid rapping his hands against the rear canopy to verify he had relinquished them. Small inputs urged the agile helicopter to maneuver easily behind Knuckles and Lucius, the pilots in the lead aircraft 500 feet in front of us.

I drank in the striking scenery as we closed with the island at 120 knots, the deep blue of the ocean blurry beneath us but stationary as it spread toward the green of the forests ahead. The large mountains, some almost 10,000 feet high, gained detail as we got closer. The cracks and crevasses in the massive rock faces that exploded out of the low-lying hills and valleys were impressive and showcased the ruggedness that explained why our helicopters were needed to move supplies. There was simply no way to drive large trucks around the narrow ribbons of unimproved roads. If we didn't airlift the supplies they'd never leave the port.

Abeam the outstretched arms of a large statue of Jesus I passed the controls back to Kid, smacking my hands on the canopy to punctuate the transfer. I lowered my head to look through the telescopic sight unit in front of me as things became serious in our cockpit.

Our conversation had been a lively discussion of the pros and cons of the various girlfriends I'd had in San Diego—although happily married Kid lived vicariously through my single-guy adventures—but a noticeable shift took place as we got within small arms' range of the deceptively peaceful hillsides.

Without saying a word, both of us assumed a sterile cockpit where only mission-related communications were voiced. I pushed extraneous thoughts aside with practiced ease as my world shrank to the small scene visible through my magnified sights. Everything external to those crosshairs fell away. Last day, last chance to get some payback.

Come on out dickheads...

We spent the morning conducting reconnaissance runs on the landing zones that would be used that day—probing the dense forests for signs of ambush preparations or other nasty surprises lying in wait for our transport helos. Each search turned up nothing of interest.

We saw a UN food truck getting mobbed as the blue-helmeted troops delivered food supplies to a refugee camp, but other than that the morning was pretty boring. After getting gas at a forward arming and refueling point (FARP) at Comodo airfield near Dili, we headed back out for what we knew would be our last flight over the island. The transport helicopters were almost finished with their runs and soon we would all return to the ship, which by this time was already starting to move toward our next stop, Singapore.

A sinking feeling of disappointment grabbed hold of me as we took off from the FARP. I had a nagging suspicion that the best opportunity of this deployment to get into a fight would come to nothing. The thought of the endless training exercises that would occupy the next five months did nothing to improve my mood. I hadn't come around the world just to train and hung all my hopes on this last mission.

After another hour of scanning the vegetation for some tiny glint of a weapon, my disappointment was approaching despair. Kid and I acknowledged that we should just head back to the ship and be done with it. Our asses hurt from the hard armor plates barely concealed by our seat cushions—we were ready to call it a day.

Knuckles, in the lead aircraft, decided to make one final run across to the northern landing zone before heading back to the ship. I felt I'd spent enough time staring fruitlessly through the magnified optics so I took a break.

Flight's pretty much over anyhow—two days to Singapore. And beer!

I sat back against my seat, taking my head out of the foam eyepieces and reveling in the cool feeling as the sweat evaporated from around my eyes. The tightness in my lower back released as

I relaxed. The valley floor beneath us was a patchwork of planted fields separated by wide, rocky riverbeds. It was mesmerizing from our altitude of 2000 feet and I was enjoying the view.

"Clear of terrain." Kid quietly let me know he wasn't going to crash into the huge ridgeline looming in front of us.

"Roger," I replied, bored and tired.

As we flashed across the dirt road that ran along the crest of the ridge I scanned it reflexively, noticing a small cluster of buildings about a mile to our right almost hidden in the trees.

It took a second for what I saw to register in my mind.

Something moving on the road. Two men? Was one of them holding something, a weapon?

I craned my neck for a second look—my despair instantly replaced by excited disbelief. I tried to verify what I thought I'd seen but the jungle had swallowed them up again.

"What's up, Shoe?" Kid had seen my contortions in the front seat as I tried to look behind us.

"Not sure," I grunted, the effort of holding my twisted position making speech difficult. "I got two probables on the road back there—two guys in the street, one with something over his shoulder."

As soon as the words left my mouth Kid ripped our aircraft over on its side. Pulling hard he crossed behind Knuckles and called out over our inter-flight frequency.

"Kid's got tac lead, possible troops on the road at our six o'clock on top of the ridge."

"Two," came in response as Knuckles and Lucius acknowledged the alert. Seamlessly they assumed the position of wingman and turned hard to stay with us.

I was almost quivering with excitement. The ones and zeros were lining up—

These guys must be enemy!

Our transport helicopters had been over-flying this ridgeline for several days and would continue to do so until the end of the operation. They had unintentionally set up a predictable pattern that two men with weapons could easily exploit. Even a half-assed ambush with only one weapon could take down an aircraft and the threat posed by two men demanded a response.

"I'll give you a good long run down the road to look for these guys. If you can determine they're hostile then lead with the 20, I'll put rockets on top of your impacts." Kid finalized our attack plans over the ICS.

"Roger," I replied.

I sure as hell wasn't bored now. My mouth went dry as I realized that we were seconds from getting into a fight but pushed thoughts of the unknown away.

Just do your job.

I chided myself for the brief loss of focus then glanced down to verify the switches were set to fire the 20mm cannon.

We were coming back around to the ridgeline about 3 miles from where the men were walking. Kid picked up the dirt road and followed it toward them 100 feet above the treetops while calling the attack formation over the radio.

None of us had ever fired a shot in anger and the excitement was growing quickly. I smashed my face against the foam eye-cups of the targeting bucket as we rolled out, my right hand rapidly slewing the daytime optics ahead to where I thought the men would be. I was worried that they would have taken cover and disappeared from view—that's what I would have done. Then what?

My concern abated when I spotted the two figures high-lighted against the yellow dirt road. A reflexive flip of my left thumb selected high magnification and their tiny images grew substantially underneath the targeting reticle in my sights.

"I got 'em.... Searching for weapons," I called out.

The two figures shimmered like mirages as the bouncing of the helicopter made the sights shake and jump crazily.

The guy on the left has something slung across his back – but what the hell is it?

I couldn't make it out. My eyes felt like they were stretching as I sought a millisecond of clarity. I could definitely see the object, sticking out at an angle behind the man's head, but couldn't determine what it was.

My mind raced. The size and shape seemed to indicate a rocket-propelled grenade, but I needed to be sure. I felt myself squeeze the left-hand grip hard. We were closing in rapidly and were uncomfortably close when the guy reached up over his shoulder to grab the object. His motions perfectly matched my perception of a fighter readying his RPG.

"I got weapons!" I blurted out over the ICS.

"Roger, Master Arm is Armed," Kid replied as he threw the switch from STBY to ARM in the rear cockpit. Flipping that switch gave me the ability to engage the two men in our sights with just a squeeze of the trigger.

We were within a mile now and their actions told me that they could see and hear us clearly. I was worried they would seize the chance to shoot first but held my fire—my sights were too blurry. I just couldn't be certain that they were hostile and damned the rough mountain air that bumped and jostled the helicopter erratically. In seconds we would be upon them. The urge to open fire was becoming irresistible.

My pulse was already racing at the thought that we were the target of an RPG. Now it went into overdrive as the man on the right brought the object from across his back down into both hands across his chest. His friend dropped to one knee in the middle of the dusty yellow road and raised an object up to his eyes.

I couldn't see what it was but it didn't matter—he was pointing it at me.

Here we go...

My reaction to the threatening motions of the men was ingrained by training and occurred without thought. A large part of my brain assumed the role of bystander as I made yes/no decisions at blinding speed and prepared to fire.

Instantly I was on the brink; my left hand had mashed the action bar to align the powerful cannon with my sights and my index finger rested tightly against the hot trigger, already drawing up slack.

A bright flash erupted from the face of the kneeling man.

Firing?

I began to tighten my finger in response...but something made me hesitate. I knew I'd seen a flash but something didn't fit. The flash was white and quick, something I'd seen before— but not a weapon being fired.

What the fuck is that?

The feeling that something wasn't right exploded in my head, forcing me to hold my fire even though we were right on top of them.

The sights steadied up for just a second as the two figures filled my viewfinder. The sudden clarity chilled me to the bone.

"Abort Abort Abort!" I shouted.

Kid repeated the command over the radio, informing Knuckles and Lucius to hold their fire.

As I sat up the Master Arm indicator in the front cockpit

switched from "ARMED" to "STBY". I noted with relief that Kid had de-activated the firing circuits for all our weapon systems. Nothing was in danger of coming off our aircraft.

Surprised to find I was holding my breath I exhaled as we flew past the two men on the dusty road. Their actions and equipment were now clearly visible to my naked eye and obviously devoid of any hostile intentions.

The small white flashes were separated by several seconds—enough time for the kneeling man's large camera to recharge its flash. The photographer's buddy, the man I'd thought was readying an RPG, was happily strumming his guitar with his head tilted back as he belted out a tune. They had no clue how close they'd come to getting blown to kingdom come.

But I did.

"Holy shit, we almost whacked Johnny Cash!" Kid exclaimed incredulously.

I smiled weakly in response.

"Yeah, that would'a been tough to explain away," I quipped. I kept my tone light in an attempt to hide the fact that I was a bit shaken.

Only later would this occur to me: I had never really considered the thought process by which I would *decide* to open fire or not. All my training had been devoid of that decision—it had always been made before we took off. This was a new development—and unwelcome.

It wasn't just the introduction of a difficult question that had my head spinning—I had also come within a hair's breadth of *totally fucking it up*. My selection of the correct option—*not* to shoot to kill—was from fortuitous hesitation rather than skills I could rely on in the future. That disturbing realization did not sit well with me.

At that moment, however, I stuffed the unease away as tactical lead passed back to Knuckles and we resumed our mission. Nobody mentioned the close call as we searched for other targets for another hour before returning to the ship. When we landed I didn't feel disappointed anymore over missing a fight. Instead I felt relief. At least I *hadn't* fucked up.

Back in San Diego five months later, my life reverted to training flights, trying to run Teddy over with my kayak while he surfed, and generally enjoying the bounty offered by southern California. While the parties and shenanigans that had taken place during the deployment faded in my memory, those few seconds when we were bearing down on the two men in the street retained their razor-sharp focus.

At first it seemed like just a good story to tell around the bar—the time we almost took out the East Timorese Johnny Cash—but the severity of the incident lingered in my thoughts. For the first time in my four years as a Marine I got a hint of the enormous responsibility I'd nonchalantly assumed by becoming a Cobra pilot.

Ever since I decided to serve I assumed that someday I would be called to kill. I was ready for it—as ready as anybody could be. The training seemed so clear-cut—you kill enemy combatants, you don't kill civilians. I'd come uncomfortably close to making a mistake that would have not only killed two innocent men but also ruined me. I was trained to kill, not murder. Every time I thought about how close I'd come to crossing that line my blood ran cold.

That thought was in my head several years later, on the eve of the invasion of Iraq. The lesson I'd learned in East Timor had hardened into an impenetrable mental wall, forming the foundation of my personal preparation for the coming fight.

That lesson was: The only thing I needed to worry about was being *sure* I only killed enemy combatants.

As long as I did that everything would turn out just fine.

CHAPTER 4

AFTER MY FIRST six-month float came a second, and when that finally ended I never wanted to see another Navy ship in my life. Then things started to get interesting in Iraq. The heated rhetoric and bellicose political speeches on both sides hinted that something big was happening. Whatever it was, I wanted to be a part of it.

After three short weeks on dry land my fervent desire never to get on another Navy ship had morphed into a mortal fear of the same. The entire Marine Corps was afire with talk of war and I dreaded that I might miss it. With immense relief, I found myself on the deck of the USS Dubuque as she slowly eased out of San Diego harbor.

The bright, still morning had a timeless feel. If you ignored the modern aircraft on their decks and radar antenna on their superstructures, the ships could be heading to Guadalcanal, Saipan, Iwo Jima, or any number of hallowed battlegrounds of the past. Marines embarked on Navy ships...steaming resolutely toward an uncertain future—although I tried to act nonchalant, the momentousness of the occasion threatened to overwhelm me. This was the beginning of our moment in history, the first movements of our invasion force as it set out to destroy a deserving foe.

I glanced around the ship and almost felt sorry for anyone who might stand against us. Groups of eager Marines nearly quivered with excitement in the cool morning air and the Cobra gunships strapped to the deck oozed confidence and lethality. We were the hounds of war. All we needed was to be released.

My two previous deployments taught me that leaving is bittersweet—that the excitement of what's to come doesn't fully balance the pain of what's being left behind—but I assumed that this one would be different. Confident that I was focused solidly on the challenges ahead I let my mind wander. It was a mistake. Instead of thoughts of future adventures my untethered mind slunk back into the last twenty-four hours, dredging up emotions better left buried.

Yesterday's gentle swell had provided clean, glassy faces for Lena and me to surf at 11th Street in Del Mar. We hadn't talked much, just sat on our surfboards between sets and tossed floating kelp strands at each other, smiling and enjoying the simple pleasure of being on the water. She was home on leave from Okinawa to see me off and we both tried to keep our conversations light, refusing to mention the huge elephant with us.

She knew the dangers of my job as well as I did. Even though we'd both buried friends, Lena knew I accepted, and even desired the risks of flying for the exhilaration they provided.

Neither of us had become Marine helicopter pilots because we wanted to do something safe. She also knew that, although I was good at my job, skills alone do not guarantee survival. The level playing field between us meant that she didn't demand any guarantees that I'd be safe, and I didn't lie to her and say I'd be careful. We just left it alone.

I had been pleasantly surprised when our budding relationship survived that second deployment and even more so when it didn't seem to be slowing down any. Now, 14 months into it, we had reached the point where we shared our ideas and dreams about the future. We were engaged in the thrilling dance to determine if the other was "the one"—although neither of us would admit it. Our intimate discussions hadn't run into the smallest conflict and the harmony of our dreams was almost scary.

And now...this.

The vibrations of the ship beneath my boots brought me to the present and the warmth of my reverie turned cold. The realization that our dreams might never have a chance bloomed in my mind and poisoned my thoughts of home. I shoved the concerns aside as overly dramatic bullshit—but the damage was done.

Now each familiar landmark the ship passed ignited sparks of regret that I might never see them and, by extension, my loved ones again. My eagerness and excitement evaporated and I damned the presence of the San Diego skyline for the unwanted reminders of what I was leaving behind, damned the ship for its snail's pace, and damned myself for getting emotional.

As quickly as they arose I pushed the maudlin thoughts aside and chided myself for being a puss. I couldn't shame my brain into submission though and the thoughts were maddeningly persistent in their ability to return.

Longingly, I eyed the closed watertight door that led toward my room. The gray interior of the ship offered isolation that would end my annoying sentimental fluttering, if only I would go inside.

I couldn't escape yet though. There was one last thing I needed to do before I could go—a final goodbye I couldn't neglect.

Fort Rosecrans National Cemetery stood high on the ridgeline of Point Loma. Teddy Treadwell was buried there, on the beautiful, east-facing slope overlooking the procession of ships as we left the harbor. The geometric arrangement of the grave markers allowed flashes of green to escape as our slow passage brought them into and out of alignment on the hillside.

After the sneaky way the city skyline reminded me I might die, the sight of actual graves felt honest and true. Instead of shoving thoughts of my dead friend aside I embraced them. It felt good to let them run their course. I don't know why, it just—it just fit.

A quiet fell over the four Marines standing beside me—my friends. If he'd been alive, Teddy would have been right there with us. His sudden death had ripped him from all of our lives and our close-knit group was still trying to make sense of the loss.

Just before midnight on Valentine's Day 2002, Teddy was flying back from a training mission when a large part of his Huey's tail fell off in mid-air. The g-forces of the spinning helicopter ripped the night vision goggles from his face and blinded him instantly. Even blind and disoriented, Teddy had managed to guide the crippled hulk as it spiraled down several thousand feet through the blackness. His copilot said if it hadn't been for an unseen hill, they might have all walked away.

As it turned out though, Teddy and one of the crew chiefs, SSgt Rod Nesmith, were killed in the crash.

That anyone survived is a testament to Teddy's piloting skills. None of the test pilots who tried to fly a similarly stricken aircraft in the simulator had been able to reproduce his feat of almost landing it. Only something as unpredictable and catastrophic as the aircraft falling apart in mid-air could have overcome Teddy's abilities, and even then he had almost pulled it off.

I had been flying that night as well and, once we knew Teddy was dead, I accompanied the notification team to his house. His wife Jaymie[1] (a Navy helicopter pilot) had been my friend since flight school. During the thirty-minute drive from Miramar to Oceanside I struggled against my grief. To steel myself against the pain that was to come I chose a CD I never wanted to listen to again and cranked the volume knob, as if it were to blame. The physical pain in my ears was a welcome diversion from the gut-wrenching anticipation of what I was about to do. Tears blurred the highway.

I made it to Jaymie's house and, like a guy in a trance, found myself ringing her doorbell in the darkness.

The porch light flipped on.

The Commanding Officer (CO), Executive Officer (XO) and chaplain stood behind me. But I had never felt so alone. I had no idea what I was going to say. Somehow I didn't think it mattered.

The deadbolt slid back with a solid click and she opened the door. A momentary flash of surprise at seeing me crossed her face...before the awful truth hit her like a truck.

She knew. Before I could croak out—"He's dead"—she knew.

---

[1]Not her real name.

Her pretty face contorted in terrible recognition and I moved forward dumbly to grab her. She sagged in my arms and seemed to shrink. I could almost see hopes, dreams and happiness rush out of her in an impossibly long exhalation. She made no audible sound. But her anguish was deafening.

It was all I could hear for a long time to come.

The weeks that followed became a blur. I stayed close by Jaymie and tried to help in any way possible. I put up a good front and tried to remain respectfully cheerful around her and her family while assisting with the myriad details required to close out a life. All day long I suppressed my grief out of respect for the depth of hers.

Once I got home though, the first touch of Lena's comforting embrace brushed aside my stoic front and I'd weep, sobbing silently into the soft crook of her neck.

I got a lot of support from my family as well. Phone calls to my parents became more than just obligatory communications as I angrily vented my grief in their understanding ears. A discreet period after Teddy's burial, my dad shared a similar experience from his time in the Navy.

Jim had been one of my father's squadron mates in Vietnam. After their tours were up they got orders to the same squadron in Naples, Italy. It was there that my mom and Jim's wife became friends as well.

Then, one day, Jim's aircraft disappeared. The cold calculus of fuel onboard vs. time elapsed made the official status of "Missing" painfully incomplete. My mom and dad stayed with Jim's wife and their two kids during the gut-wrenching week before the status was changed to "Presumed Dead." Jim's plane wasn't found until the snow melted on top of Mt Etna—six months after the crash.

I had known that my father had lost friends, but now I understood what that meant. Teddy's death came to signify a rite of passage for me and I almost welcomed the searing pain of his loss. It became a tangible reminder that I was becoming a man like my father. I was weathering the same storms.

I'd been aware that aviation was a dangerous business—that death comes quickly and without warning. Now I *knew* it.

In my mind Teddy's death also became an inoculation against future loss. I had to assume he wouldn't be the last friend I'd bury and I didn't want to feel this pain again. Very few people were as close to me as Teddy had been and I came to see that closeness as a liability.

Once bitten, twice shy. I kept new friends on the periphery. They would never be let inside. I convinced myself that unless someone closer to me than Teddy got killed then I'd be okay. It was up to me to keep the number of people who made it into that category small.

Coming to grips with Teddy's loss was one thing. Getting back in the cockpit was something else. The capricious workings of fate that conspired to kill Teddy and Nes had damaged my confidence. Until now I had assumed it was within my power to return safely from each flight.

Teddy's bloodstained helmet, cracked and broken where the main rotor blade crushed it, had driven home the uncomfortable truth of my own mortality. I had always been able to convince myself it couldn't happen to me. I was too good, too smart, too prepared for anything to kill me. It was all under my control. Bullshit.

My illusion of control was utterly smashed.

The only way to avoid random, violent death was to quit, to turn in my wings. That option was laughably absurd. I had to do something to get my confidence back because one thing was certain: I was going to keep flying.

To protect myself, I generated a new concept of Teddy in my head. I didn't imagine him as a particularly benevolent guardian angel. Rather, I saw him as a presence that could transcend the confines of death to reach out and smack the shit out of me when I was about to do something stupid. I regained my confidence by resolving to do everything I could not to screw up while trusting that Teddy would take care of things beyond my control.

Some people cling to an all-powerful, all-seeing deity to keep them safe. I preferred to think of my friend—the man who used to smash beer cans against my chest when I wasn't looking—as a more appropriate protector.

A cool breeze ruffled the ship's flags and I glanced at Gash, Weasel, BT and IKE—the guys whose deaths would really screw me up if they went first—standing beside me on the flight deck. We shared the feeling that Teddy was watching over us. We'd survived too many close calls during the last deployment for it to have been just luck.

As we passed by his grave I doubt that I was the only one who silently reminded him of his duties.

Hope you're ready for this one, Teddy. We're gonna need you.

I left my buddies and went below deck. There was nothing to be gained by watching the shoreline recede in slow motion and I was tired of uncomfortable emotions. The solid thud of the heavy steel door closing behind me punctuated my departure. The steel skin of the ship reinforced my tenuous mental separation from home with a welcome physical one.

Finally, fuck. It's over.

If I'd been a philosopher I might have thought about the timeless link between my feelings and those of warriors throughout history. Did ancient Romans feel this way as they stepped off? Did the doughboys of WWI struggle to cut off thoughts of home as their troopships pulled out? Was I feeling the same tumult inside me that "The Greatest Generation" experienced when they left to stomp Hitler? Now I'm willing to assume they did, but at the time I cared nothing for the universality of my feelings among warriors of old.

All I wanted to do was my job—simple as that. I just wanted to go to combat, win, and come home. The price of the coming adventure was the possibility of getting really screwed up or killed. Those were prices I was willing to pay. It was all or nothing to me—with my shield or on it, dead or happily victorious.

In my head those were the only options. There was no middle ground.

The next forty days killed any desire to ever watch the movie "Groundhog Day" again—re-living one particular day is nowhere near as funny as Bill Murray makes it out to be. Boring repetition defined our transit to Kuwait.

We filled our time as embarked Marines have for over two hundred years: working out, bitching about the Navy and spitting tobacco juice into the wake. As much as the monotony of the unchanging routine wore on me, I lived in fear that I'd feel the ship heel over on one side and turn hard to reverse course, signaling that negotiations had succeeded in Iraq. I awoke each morning afraid that we'd turned around while I was asleep and it wasn't until I saw the sun rising over the stern that I could relax and get breakfast.

With miles of empty blue sea in every direction, lingering thoughts of home sometimes intruded, but they were short-lived. Knowing that every turn of the ship's big propellers brought me closer to battle made shoving those thoughts aside easy. I only had to remind myself where we were going and incredible energy would flood my body.

It was dangerously intense energy, the kind that makes football players head-butt lockers, gorillas rip trees out of the ground and soccer hooligans explode in apoplectic ecstasy. I had to do something to dissipate it but the Navy takes a dim view of its passengers fighting, smashing things or screaming at the top of their lungs. Those outlets weren't available so I worked out—a lot.

I struggled to keep my excitement under control while my gray prison plodded along. We weren't going to another scrimmage; there was no training exercise waiting after landfall. This was the real thing. At odd times a low drumbeat would burst forth into my consciousness: *You're going to war. You're going to war. Holy shit, you're going to war!*

Adding to the sense of adventure was the fact that I wasn't alone. Not only was I going to war with the best Cobra pilots on earth—they were also my best friends.

Weasel[2] and BT (Belligerent Todd) were the 'Jedi knights' of our division—they held every qualification the Marine Corps had created for gunship pilots. They'd devoted years of their lives to attain the ultimate designation of Weapons and Tactics Instructor (WTI) and had reached a professional pinnacle

---

[2]All Marine pilots have callsigns. They are individually assigned and generally make fun of personality traits and personal shortcomings, real and imagined. To avoid confusion, I have chosen to identify my squadron mates by callsign only.

enjoyed by a select few.

WTIs are recognized by the Marine Corps as experts in their field. It uses them as a whetstone to sharpen other Marines to a razor's edge. Flight school makes new pilots, WTIs make them lethal.

Even among WTIs, BT and Weasel stood out. Known for their tactical acumen, encyclopedic knowledge and peerless flying skills these two men embodied the cliché phrase "the best of the best." They were it.

No less skilled were Gash (named for a six-inch scar on his butt) and IKE (I Know Everything)—although they were not WTIs. What these two brought to the fight was a mixture of bravado and audaciousness backed up by proven skills and unstoppable determination. These characteristics have defined Marine heroes since 1775 and Gash and IKE had them in spades.

They were kindred souls with Pappy Boyington's tenacious Blacksheep, and with the grunts who stood against impossible odds on Wake Island, cocksure in the face of death. They never missed a chance to pull a prank and loved a good laugh, but if anything threatened one of their friends they got ugly—quick.

My four closest friends are men who will never falter, who will never leave a comrade behind. They're not angels—far from it—and they are exactly the kind of men you want to go into battle with.

We knew each other better than most married couples. Our friendships went back years and we had trained, flown and lived together for most of the last thirteen months.

We'd shared the grief of Teddy's death, the white-knuckle terror of flying in sandstorms in Djibouti and drunken escapades in liberty ports around the Pacific. Those and many other intense experiences cemented routine bonds of friendship into something more. We finished each other's sentences, argued without anger and would stand back to back against the world. In short, we were brothers.

Alone we were formidable. Together? Stand the fuck by.

It was late February 2003 when we flew off the ship and landed 40 miles from the Iraq border. Still bearing the bullet holes and bomb craters of the first Gulf War, Ali Al Salem airbase was our new home in Kuwait. I had spent a month there in 2000 but the base had changed so much I barely recognized it. A massive influx of troops and aircraft had swelled the base monstrously and pushed property values to a premium.

The Marine Corps never pays premium.

The naval construction battalions built a tent city for us on what had been empty desert just days before our arrival. At first I thought the accommodations were pretty nice—at least we had framed tents to sleep in and store our gear.

Then the smell hit me.

It started sickly-sweet but quickly turned rank, like someone had shit in a cotton candy machine. The light of the morning revealed a steady stream of 'honey wagons' dumping thousands of gallons of porta potty juices into foul ponds a stone's throw from our tents. It being an Air Force base, we were unsurprised that they kept the choice accommodations for themselves and graciously allowed us to live in Shitville. That's just the way it goes.

That was the least of my worries. Kuwait was simply an intermediate stop. Now that we were here all I cared about was when we were leaving—for war.

In the days that followed our arrival the squadron worked at a breakneck pace. Nobody knew how much time we had before the fighting started and there was a lot to accomplish. Years of training exercises in desert shitholes around the world paid off and within a day or two the squadron was fully operational.

We flew our aircraft several times a week to keep them fresh. If left to sit for too long the birds would develop leaks in weird places, sand would wreak havoc on seals and sensitive electronics would mysteriously stop working. They broke while we flew them as well but that was better. At least then we knew they were broken and could get new parts.

Most of our flights consisted of tooling around the desert and marveling at the massive amount of troops and equipment accumulating in northern Kuwait. The energy of the troop build-up was incredible. Vast encampments erupted from the shifting sands and long convoys of every type of military vehicle known to man emptied into them after driving from the port in Kuwait City. From a couple hundred feet above the ground, the brown wasteland resembled something out of "Mad Max." Speeding tanks and armored vehicles threw up rooster-tails of sand during daylight maneuvers and firing ranges sparkled brightly at night. Every unit seemed to be training intensely in preparation for the big event. We were no different.

Gash and I spent several flights running simulated attacks on the armored vehicles that sprouted like mushrooms on the desert floor. We had already flown together for hundreds of hours and knew each other's strengths and weaknesses intimately. We didn't focus on switchology drills or general flying skills, those we had. What we did need to do was burn the images of the friendly vehicles into our brains.

I'd studied pictures of armored vehicles for years but no 8x10 glossy could replicate the fuzzy blobs that skittered like glowing beetles on the FLIR screen before me. I knew that soon I would have to distinguish between friend and foe amid the confusion and adrenaline of combat and was terrified of making a mistake.

Years ago I'd seen gun camera footage from an army Apache helicopter during the First Gulf War. Those images haunted me. On the tape the pilots can be heard questioning whether a hot spot in the desert is enemy or friendly and, deciding it is enemy, destroy it with a missile. After gunning down the running soldiers who escaped the flaming vehicle, evidence mounts that they had made a terrible mistake. The agony in their voices was hard to listen to as they realized the horrible truth of their actions. The vehicle had been friendly. They'd killed their brothers.

Watching it, I'd felt sick.

Unlike many other training videos I had no mental defense against this one. I couldn't confidently predict that, if placed in the same situation, I wouldn't have made the same decisions the Apache crew had. I learned little that relieved those fears until East Timor. That experience taught me to trust my instincts— even though I knew luck had played an uncomfortably large role in that positive outcome. But I dreaded making that mistake for real and had no idea how I would deal with it if I did.

Gash and I were combat crew together—we'd fly together until one or both of us got wounded, killed or the war ended. When the time came to decide which cockpit I wanted, my choice was clear. I had to sit in the front where I would decide whom we should kill. I trusted Gash with my life. I knew he was more than capable of making the correct choices in the heat of the moment, but that wasn't enough. I had to see it with my own eyes, and only the front cockpit held magnified sights.

I wasn't so naïve to think that pulling the trigger would

be easy, and on some level understood that there might be a mental price to pay for killing. But I also knew I would bear the responsibility for anyone we killed, regardless of where I sat. At least if I sat in the front I wouldn't have to second-guess my friend if something went wrong.

I really wasn't worried about killing in general—that's kind of what Marines do. When I envisioned killing the enemy I figured that I would feel a sense of accomplishment. After all, the only reason I'd been given the opportunity to fly this magnificent machine was on the condition that I be ready to use it to kill the enemies of my country. I was determined to uphold my end of that bargain.

Like the ancient sailor who knew the world was flat, I knew I could handle killing the right people—there was simply no evidence to the contrary. I only got anxious when I imagined killing the wrong folks by mistake.

After doing what I could to prepare, I pushed those fears away. Now wasn't the time to get all whiny.

After the initial hectic scramble to set up the squadron, fix broken aircraft and make maps, we settled down to wait. The political steps to set the stage for war continued and we watched the Fox News' reports with interest. I had never been in a position where what was being reported on the TV had such a huge, immediate impact on my life and the effect was exhilarating. I truly felt like the eyes of the world were focused on what we were doing and I loved it.

But the shine quickly wore off. As the weeks passed our desert camp turned into purgatory. I felt like a thoroughbred horse nervously pawing the ground before a race. The entire reason for my existence as a Marine was right in front of me but it wasn't within my power to reach it—I needed the politicians to open the gate.

The speeches and posturing seemed to drag on forever and fed my fears that the whole conflict would get negotiated away. Exercise and healthy skepticism provided some relief from the tension but it wasn't always enough. Rumors of orders to attack or return to the States made their rounds several times a day, slamming my mood from excitement to despair. It was emotionally draining to be sitting on the knife-edge, struggling to stay ready while not getting too amped up.

One day I caught Weasel peering intently at a computer screen in the empty planning room tent. He hadn't heard my boots in the soft sand and looked up guiltily when I spoke.

"'Sup Fool?" I looked over his shoulder at the webpage he'd been studying.

"Ahh, nothing"—he tried to close the window but not fast enough. A flash of bare shoulder drew my attention.

"Dude, what the fuck are you looking at?" I couldn't quite keep the laughter out of my voice as I processed what I'd seen—a website for nursing mothers.

"Are you really that hard-up man? Gash has some porn in the hootch—if you like biker chicks." I continued rolling in hot on him.

"Fuck you—he does? No, wait—I mean, well, I uh…"

I was really enjoying his discomfort. I'd never imagined beneath Weasel's squeaky-clean exterior lurked a mother-fetish. This was going to provide hours of entertainment for the rest of the guys—pure gold.

His embarrassment at my suggestion quickly faded, replaced by a look of serene wonder. When he spoke his voice was quiet, almost like he was talking to himself.

"Mae's pregnant." It was a word combination he'd never said before. But it was obvious he'd wanted to.

"Holy shit dude, that's great! Congratulations!"

His eyes focused on me again and he snapped into a big smile. The wonder of the announcement was still plastered all over his face and he launched into his explanation.

"See, there's this website that tells you all the changes that are happening to the mother during pregnancy, broken down by weeks ..."

He kept talking excitedly, obviously enthralled with the concept that he and Mae were starting a family.

"...and see here, right here is where the Boob Fairy comes."

His face fell. Even if the war got cancelled there was no way he'd be home in time.

"Aww, shit. I'm going to miss the Boob Fairy? Shit!"

Laughing at his crestfallen face I clapped him on the shoulder and walked out the tent, leaving him to explore the joys of motherhood unmolested.

I was happy for him, I really was, but I didn't envy him in the least. I'd stuffed thoughts of home so far away that they couldn't intrude in my preparations for what was to come. I knew Weasel had done the same, but now he'd have to start all over again.

Having to contain happy thoughts of the amazing impact this news had for his future was going to be tough, but I knew he'd do it. Weasel is like that, he can flip a switch and go cold. It's a skill I'd seen him use before and the speed with which he could switch between happy-go-lucky and coldly professional was impressive.

Still, I was glad that wasn't on my plate.

Finally the orders came. Our squadron was tasked with removing the Iraqi eyes and ears along a 50-mile stretch of border to clear the way for the ground invasion. While they were only preparatory orders, excitement rippled through the squadron when they were verified. At last we had something concrete to devote attention to and the squadron's plan of attack was quickly ironed out.

The plan was simple and ensured each Iraqi position would be destroyed at precisely the same moment. Five separate divisions of Cobra and Huey helicopters would depart Ali Al Salem, fly along separate routes until they reached their assigned observation posts and then destroy them at a predetermined time.

That's it.

One second they are happily sitting in the desert, the next they are totally gone. No time to raise the warning as our ground forces blast straight through the burning wreckage. The first indication the Iraqi leadership would have of the invasion would be the appearance of America's finest, miles inside their border.

I would fly as part of the fifth division. With Weasel and IKE flying the lead aircraft, Gash and I would fill the -2 position and Willow and Spooner would bring up the rear in their Huey. Our three aircraft were to annihilate a small cluster of buildings known as Observation Post (OP) 11.

The plan called for our two Cobras to initiate the strike from long range with Hellfire missiles, before our presence could be detected. Once the buildings were destroyed we would press in and blanket the area with high-explosive and flechette rockets, then clean it up with cannon fire. The door gunners on the Huey would lay down suppressive fire from their 7.62mm minigun and .50cal machine gun throughout the attack.

One pass, expend all. Fast, savage, overwhelming. Fair

fights are for the movies, we're here to do a job. If there were defenders on the OP they wouldn't stand a chance.

For the next two weeks preparations for the border strike mission dominated our lives. Briefings, walk throughs, more briefings, full mission rehearsals...By the end of the second week of preparations I'd flown the mission so many times in my chair that I could do it in my sleep.

The waiting was the worst part—I just didn't trust that this thing would happen at all. The continued absence of orders to execute reinstated worries that negotiations had gained ground and the whole adventure was slipping away.

We're close, so fucking close. Just open the gates, release the hounds...Fuck man, just let us go!

I didn't really care what might happen afterward, I just wanted this damn thing to start. Forget about the real dangers. The possibility of going home without a fight was the worry that kept me up at night.

On March 18th I listened with excitement as President Bush issued the 48-hour ultimatum. The wheels were turning at last. That night I got my last email from my parents.

Hi Dan,

We've just spent the evening listening to the President and lots of other people. We figure that you may be on the move and it may be a while before you get this. I just want to say that I am thinking about you and praying. I love you.

Many hugs,

Mom

Dear Dan,

We've just finished listening to President Bush's 48-hours to get out of dodge or you'll face "action at a time of our choosing." You're better trained and far more seasoned and qualified than I was when I went to war. Vaya con Dios, Dan. I love you.

Dad

As I read the quick notes from my parents I felt a sense of relief. A sort of release, even.

Their words were more fortifying than they could ever know. It would have been easy for them to rail against the coming danger or beg me to stay safe, but they refrained. I already felt guilty for making them worry about me and would have had a difficult time ignoring blatant pleas. I would have, but it would have been tough.

Instead, they freed me to do what I had to. My dad was right. I had ten times the flight experience he'd had before going to Vietnam and had received the best training in the world. They knew I was as well-prepared as possible and would do my job regardless of what they begged via email. Still, it is to their credit that they didn't shift the burden of their fears to me. I now know it cost them dearly.

Confident in myself, fully supported from home and surrounded by my best friends I was ready to go.

Nobody is without fear on the verge of combat though. Including me. Strangely, I wasn't really worried about dying. Instead, the fear that I would screw up and shoot friendly troops or civilians would leak into my thoughts—although I tried not to think about it.

I didn't want to think about anything anymore. I didn't want to wonder what might happen—I just wanted it to happen. I was going to do everything I could, the enemy was going to do everything he could, and one of us would win. That's it. Simple. I could deal with concrete actions and events, just no more of this damned 'what if' crap.

I chained the fears to something heavy and tossed them away, locking the door to trap them once and for all.

Fuck you. Sit. Stay.

Even then I heard it, a voice faintly taunting me from the darkness.

"Don't screw up. Don't kill the wrong people."

The warning lingered in my head, underlying all my nervous excitement and eagerness to get things started. It wouldn't go away—to be honest I didn't really want it to. The reminder was valuable, if annoying.

As long as I avoided that mistake I figured I could deal with everything else.

CHAPTER 5

AS SCUD AND AL SAMUD MISSILES began to fall on Kuwait, I felt a detached sense of relief. Even as I fumbled to don my chemical suit with hands like clubs, I was almost giddy with excitement. The wait was over. The war was on.

Throughout the morning sirens echoed across the otherwise eerily silent airfield, warning of incoming missiles. Very few of us had ever had to take cover for real before, and at first the bunkers filled up rapidly with wide-eyed Marines. But with each warning that was not followed by a missile landing nearby, our response became slower and slower.

Feigned indifference replaced urgency—like having huge missiles potentially carrying chemical weapons dropping out of the sky around us was but a minor annoyance. Nervous laughter and stress yawns behind gas masks betrayed the truth though—being a target sucks big time.

Mid-afternoon we received orders to execute our strike

mission. The time-on-target (TOT) for our squadron to destroy the five Iraqi border posts was set for 2200 that night.

I was surprisingly calm. Until now my most pressing concern was that the war wouldn't happen at all. Now that it had started my concerns just seemed to disappear. My mind was filled with excitement and eager anticipation for something I'd spent years preparing for and was convinced I understood. I knew what I'd been taught and trusted that it would be enough.

Everything that needed to be done to prepare for the strike mission had already been accomplished—twice. Instead of the normal hustle and bustle the squadron was subdued, like everyone was conserving energy for what was to come. Groups of Marines gathered around the squadron tents, talking in low tones, reading or just trying to look relaxed. Tension permeated the quiet though and showed us all to be liars.

A little before 1700 that afternoon I got up from the sandbag I'd been sitting on and wandered over to the chow hall tent for a cup of coffee. I'd read the same page of my book four times before admitting it was futile. There were over three hours before I needed to be at my aircraft but I just couldn't sit still anymore.

The sound of a racing engine and slipping tires drew everybody's attention. Closely shaved heads turned in unison toward the sound as a tan SUV whipped around the corner and skidded to a stop behind the ready-room tent.

Who's that driving like an asshole? I wondered.

A second later my question was answered as the squadron CO and XO came barreling out of the front seats. Without a word they burst into the ready room.

I had no idea what was going on but knew it was serious. Lieutenant Colonels don't run around like that without good reason. I veered off from the chow hall and headed toward the ready-room tent along with the twenty other Marines who'd been hanging around. Unconsciously, I broke into a run as feigned calmness was brushed aside by a ground swell of excitement.

Could it be? Is it on?

Just then the wailing of a siren announced an inbound attack. I froze like a deer in the headlights, muscles quivering but mind torn.

Shit! Go to the bunker? Find out what's going on?

The choice was made for me as the CO, Lt Col Heywood, and his copilot came running out of the tent.

Forestalling any questions from the Marines converging on him like piranha, the CO yelled, "There is no TOT, *Go Go Go Go!*"

His words and the direction he was headed made it clear that we were launching—the timeline was gone and the race to destroy the observation posts was on. Cups of coffee, half-read letters and tattered paperback books all fell into the sand as the squadron exploded into action.

Training and preparation took over as the pilots, crew chiefs and mechanics dropped whatever they were doing and raced toward the flightline. In a heartbeat the squadron changed from two hundred individuals meandering through the day into a single organism with one purpose in life, one imperative: Destroy the targets.

Nothing else mattered. Thoughts of home, worries about hitting the wrong target and fears of what might happen simply disappeared, buried beneath the claxons and flashing red lights that flooded my head.

I remember nothing of the half-mile sprint to my aircraft. All pretense of calmness was gone. The only thing I could focus on was running, just run, faster and faster, just run.

A dull boom echoed from somewhere out in the desert and underscored the urgency of getting airborne.

Thoughts flashed quickly through my hyperactive brain.

Would we even get off the ground? Were there chem's in that last missile? Are more damn missiles inbound right now? Fuck it. Run, just run.

Our crew chief, LCpl Bottama, had removed the securing gear and had our cockpits open and waiting for us. I reached the bird just steps ahead of Gash and yelled at him through the open canopy.

"What the fuck happened?"

Gash responded between gasps. "Don't know...saw you running...figured I'd go too."

With our helmets, armor and flight vests on in seconds we climbed in our aircraft. My heart was pounding against the inside of my flak jacket with such force I imagined it might break through. I plugged my helmet into the ICS and heard Gash breathing rapidly as he went through the quick-start checklist.

My brain was in overdrive. Thoughts flashed by so fast they barely registered and I was in danger of being overwhelmed. I nervously followed Gash through the checklist just to try and calm down.

Within a minute Gash had the first engine running and I could begin my checklist in the front seat.

There was no pent-up stress in my body—it was being consumed like jet fuel tossed on a fire—and I began to function mechanically. Without thinking I flipped on our two radios and set the frequencies for check-in.

Our 43-mile route to the target was already saved in our navigation system, so all I had to do was align the GPS and activate the route. Gash got the second engine started and as soon as the blades were at 100%, we ran through the arming checklist in record time.

Unable to do anything while the ordnance crew armed our weapons, my mind started to break free again.

What the fuck is going on? Are missiles inbound right now? What if I get shot? What if Gash gets shot? Do I have a fresh canister on my gas mask? Shit! This is for real! What have I forgotten?...

While my frenzied brain spun out of control, the ordnance crew armed all our weapons and raced out of our rotor arc. Out of habit I shifted my eyes to the ordnance team leader in anticipation of his salute. It's always the last action the team leader takes after the aircraft is armed. This time it was anything but a formality.

Standing ramrod straight the Marine slowly raised his right hand, fingers extended and joined, to his cranial. With his fingertips hovering an inch over his right eye, he held stock-still amid the tumult of the flightline, waiting as if he didn't have a care in the world.

His calmness and demeanor brought my screaming mind to heel. Seeing his example reminded me that we do this shit all the time, the only difference is that it's for real. That's not as big a difference as I was making it out to be.

Calm descended over me as Gash and I returned his salute.

Chill fuckhead, you know what you're doing.

My internal pep talks were always profane.

The Marine's right arm came down faster than I thought possible and in the blink of an eye he was gone, running to the next aircraft. That was all it took. One time-honored gesture of respect between warriors and all the extraneous bullshit whirling around my head evaporated.

You're a goddamn Marine Cobra pilot, quit fucking around and do your job.

The white-hot energy that fueled my mindless sprint still raged within but that one thought gave me control. Like a steam engine I harnessed the fire and made it work for me. Now I owned it.

I took a deep breath to calm myself. Then I went methodically through the after-arming checklist with Gash. The comfortable cadence of the challenge/response was reassuring and soon we were ready to go.

Weasel was our division leader for the strike. His calm voice initiated the radio check-in and brought us up to speed over the inter-flight frequency.

"I don't know the reason, but the TOT is gone; it's each division for itself. We destroy the OP and then recover at Astrodome FARP to await tasking." If he was suppressing any thoughts of his pregnant wife at home it didn't show—Weasel definitely had his shit together.

I rogered up, followed a second later by Willow in the Huey.

Like most Cobra pilots who'd never been in combat, I usually made fun of the Hueys in our squadron—they were slow, overweight and lacked long-range weapons. Not this time though. Now that it was for real I was happy to have the fat kid tagging along. With its door guns manned by aggressive and accurate Marines, any threats that popped up close to us would immediately get cut down. The Cobras could take care of the long-distance stuff but there was nothing better than a Huey with door gunners for close-in work.

Nothing else needed to be said. We all knew the plan and the desired end state; now it was just a matter of execution. We took off a second apart and stayed below 50 feet for our join-up. Once we were all together, Weasel turned to the north-east and our three ships headed toward the Iraqi border, low and fast into the darkening sky.

The pressure in my boiler was running high but still contain-able. I settled into a tenuous balance between hyper-alert and calmly efficient. Like riding a bike, it was a balance that would become second nature.

It wasn't a long flight to the border and Gash and I quickly readied our aircraft to fight. Although we could do it by memory, this wasn't the time to risk missing something. As we went step-by-step through the checklists, the worn and soiled pages on my kneeboard reminded me of the hundreds of times I'd done these exact same actions in training. The familiarity kept my mind focused and reassured me that I hadn't skipped something important. I was right where I needed to be.

Peering through the sights I looked for something to focus my sensors on. There was nothing but brown sand. Surprised, I looked up. As far as I could see the entire desert was empty, devoid of anything man-made. A couple of days ago this area was a seething anthill of men and vehicles. The hundreds of thousands of coalition troops and tons of equipment had simply disappeared. I wondered, somewhat foolishly, where they had gone before snapping my mental blinders back on.

Doesn't matter. Get your head in the game. Nothing else matters.

Picking an empty patch of sand I shot the laser and got a good return that verified it was working. Next came the 20mm cannon. The long barrels underneath my feet slewed left and right and up and down but when I pulled the trigger, nothing. I could hear the barrels spinning but the gun wouldn't fire. Gash verified that all the circuit breakers were in and then pulled up next to Weasel so he could check us out. I tried to fire it again and IKE reported that we were dropping rounds out of the bottom. The gun was mechanically fine but no firing voltage was reaching it.

Fuck!

First time into combat and my gun doesn't work?

Fuck me.

We still had missiles and rockets—but I really wanted the cannon. This was not an auspicious start but there was nothing I could do. We couldn't fix it from the cockpit and there was no time to go home to get it fixed. We'd just have to make do without.

We were still miles from the border when we completed all our checklists. With nothing to do, my mind started to chafe at the inactivity. Several times my imagination broke free and assumed the random trajectory of a pinball. Horrible scenarios of what might happen lit up brightly as my thoughts careened off bumpers of imagined dangers and got slammed by flippers of fear. With practiced effort I forced myself to remain in the moment. I couldn't risk thinking about the entirety of what we were doing. I just needed to stay focused on the next little step and not jump ahead.

Step-by-step, one foot in front of the other. Keep going.

The calmness came back; this time for good. We were at our initial point.

Weasel turned toward the target and slowed to 30 knots as Gash and Willow maneuvered into an echelon right. I knew the observation post was 6300 meters off our nose and I buried my head in the targeting bucket to acquire it.

Cold now, step-by-step, no thinking.

"With positive ID, flight is cleared hot." Over the radio, Weasel cleared us to fire. The only thing left to do was positively identify the target buildings. There were Kuwaiti and UN compounds nearby that we really didn't want to hit.

"Two."

"Three." Gash and then Willow answered a half a second apart.

I tried to use the daytime optics but the picture wasn't worth a shit. Everything was hazy and grey in my sights like I was looking at the inside of a ping-pong ball. Switching to the FLIR with a flick of my thumb I searched out in front of our aircraft, eager to be the first member of the division to acquire the small cluster of buildings.

6000 meters in front of us, along a heading of 325 was our target—I should have been able to see it already through the FLIR. To my surprise there was nothing but empty desert that morphed into sky with no visible horizon. On the fuzzy screen I couldn't discern where the sand ended and sky began. I moved the sensor 5-10 degrees either side of where the target should be to be sure I wasn't off a little on heading.

Why can't I see anything?

5000 meters away, still nothing. I started to get antsy. Per the plan I should have already acquired the buildings and been firing a Hellfire missile at this point. Gash could see the distance-to-target ticking down on his HUD and knew the plan as well as I.

"Got anything yet?" His interest was not academic. The closer we got to the Iraqi positions without firing the greater the danger that the Iraqis would shoot us first.

"Searching," I replied tersely.

I can't shoot it if I can't see it, I thought. *Now where the fuck are the damn buildings?*

3500 meters. I should have been firing a TOW missile into the flaming remnants of the Iraqi observation post but I still couldn't see a damn thing. A sick feeling began to grow in my stomach.

Something caught my eye. A hint of a wavy line on my FLIR screen, a slightly brighter ribbon of green against the otherwise uniform pale background.

Is that the road?

I scanned up and down the ribbon. The fact it remained stationary proved it wasn't a weird pixilation and gave me the first good news of the day. My spirits rose as I identified the Kuwaiti border post, then the UN post, and then spotted the faint outline of several small buildings further north. Their arrangement matched the satellite photos I'd spent hours studying. It was OP 11.

Finally, damn.

"Got it."

"Roger," Gash replied. There was no question what 'it' was.

I set the FLIR to autotrack on the largest building and gingerly checked to see if it would hold. To my relief the four little dots on the screen remained firmly attached to the building. Certain of the target I fired my laser.

2100 meters, the Hellfire symbol switched from 'Ready' to 'Tracking.' I lifted the final interlock and depressed the launch button with my left thumb.

"Firing."

"Roger."

Going through the rehearsed, sequential motions I felt detached, like I was watching someone else do them. There was no musing over existential questions of life and death, nothing special to separate this missile launch from all the ones I'd fired before. Mechanical steps. Just execute.

The calmness was almost unnerving.

Less than a second later the 100-lb missile roared off of our right wing. Climbing along its predetermined trajectory, the missile disappeared into the haze. I didn't look at it though, my existence revolved around making sure the autotrack stayed locked on the building.

Seven seconds. Seven seconds to target. Fuck, uh 2...3...4...

I knew the missile should reach the target in about seven seconds but I screwed up the count. Didn't matter, there was an automatic timer. With the crosshairs firmly parked on top of the largest building I continued to squeeze the laser designator as if the pressure I exerted would make a difference. Unconsciously I held my breath and waited for the explosion.

Come on, come on...

At 2000 meters the aircraft's nose dipped forward and the vibrations increased—Gash was accelerating into the final attack. At this range, any Iraqis on the observation post could hear our aircraft and would be trying to engage us with whatever they had. Speed became our only defense. The OP should have been a flaming mess already but the dust and smoke had really screwed up our plan. Now we were well within range of their weapons and we hadn't hit them with anything yet.

Gash couldn't stand it anymore.

"Is it going where it should?"

The eighth second ticked by on the timer with no explosion.

"Nope," I replied, much more calmly than I felt.

I had no idea where the missile went but it obviously hadn't hit the building. Ignoring the fact that my Hellfire was streaking off somewhere into a sovereign nation, I switched to select a TOW missile.

"Switching to TOW."

"Roger."

1500 meters away from the OP I could see the two buildings and a flagpole quite clearly in the FLIR. Gash was just able to see the compound with his naked eye from the back seat.

Fuck we're close.

Mashing the action bar with my left hand I got solid ATK and READY flags and pulled the trigger. The second and a half delay between trigger pull and missile launch seemed to stretch to eternity.

Time froze as several small explosions flashed on my FLIR screen—impacts from Weasel's 20mm cannon.

Fucking launch already! The wait was excruciating.

With a roar and flash the TOW missile ignited on our left wing. Like a pitcher's curve ball its hot motor looped into my line of sight from the left. It corrected to align momentarily with the crosshairs in the FLIR and then slammed into the lower left corner of the largest building. The screen flashed white as the blast of my missile and multiple rocket explosions from Weasel and IKE rendered the heat sensors in my FLIR useless. I looked up for the first time in what felt like hours.

The only thing I could see was an angry fireball of orange flames, black smoke and pieces of debris reaching up toward us. Before I could shout a warning Gash opened fire with rockets and pulled hard to avoid flying into the flames. His seven flechette rockets blanketed the compound with thousands of steel nails that sliced through buildings, vehicles and flesh as if they were butter.

Gash continued pulling hard left and I lost sight of the

burning compound for several seconds. With relief I saw Weasel and IKE rolling back inbound to cover us. Anyone still alive down there wouldn't have a clean shot at our backs.

A couple seconds later Gash returned the favor as Weasel pulled off target. With no 20mm I watched powerlessly as Gash covered his back. It felt like I was on a carnival ride as Gash whipped us through impossibly tight turns and stomach-dropping dives, all the while decimating the compound with accurate rocket fire.

Setting up for another attack Gash bled some of our energy off in a climb to 300 feet. IKE and Weasel stayed at 50 feet so one burst couldn't take us all out. Any enemy gunner would have to target one of us and in doing so, expose himself to the other.

It's not supposed to be fair.

Willow's door gunner peppered the compound with .50-caliber rounds to cover all of us as we dove in for another attack. A stream of bright streaks rippled off Weasel's bird as IKE fired his rockets and pulled off left. Their cannon puffed angrily as Weasel hammered the compound with the 20mm.

As soon as they were clear I fired our second TOW. The extreme short range allowed the missile only one correction and for a second I thought it was going to miss. Still turning hard to align with my crosshairs the missile slammed into the burning building and blew it flat. Gash followed it with several high explosive rockets for good measure before ripping us away from the clawing explosions.

Gash jinked unpredictably behind Weasel as we raced toward the safety of Kuwait. The strike was over—now we just had to get away. Although I hadn't seen anyone on the OP, I imagined hundreds of weapons were opening up on our exposed backsides.

Self-consciously I tucked my right elbow back behind the seat armor and tried to make myself as small as possible. I needn't have worried. Almost all the way to Kuwait Willow's crew chief hosed the burning compound with a stream of red-orange tracers at 6000 rounds per minute.

Nobody back there had a chance.

Before I recognized what it was, the berm separating Kuwait and Iraq passed just beneath our skids—Gash had to pop up a little to keep from hitting it. Good thing he did because just behind the wall a light armored vehicle was moving into position at the head of the invasion force. One second there was nothing in front of me, the next I was eye-to-eye with the commander of an LAV-25. The sudden appearance of the grunts told me we were back in Kuwait. Safe.

Holy fucking shit we did it!

The release was incredible. Elation at having survived my first combat mission flooded my brain. I felt like I had just stormed the beach on Guadalcanal, turned back the Chinese at Chosin and taken back Hue City. Finally I'd been in combat, seen the elephant and faced the ultimate test. And totally fucking destroyed the target! Years of having the holy grail of 'combat' held over my head by trainers who'd never experienced it made my accomplishment all the sweeter. Nobody could ever say "you'll need to know this if you ever get to combat" to me again.

That's right fuckers! I've been there! You can't tell me shit!

I didn't even consider that the mission had not gone as planned, that I'd almost had to stumble on the target to see it and that my first shot of the war might still be traveling north. It didn't register that the entire strike had been easier than most of my training missions and I certainly didn't think about who might have been inside the buildings.

Instead I just felt good. Like I'm finally a *real* Marine.

The thrill stayed with me as we completed the flight. Once we were well inside Kuwait we climbed to 300 feet and checked each other for battle damage. Finding none we headed to Astrodome FARP for gas and ordnance. We could have made it back to Ali Al Salem with the gas we had, but the plan was for all sixteen aircraft from the strike mission to recover at Astrodome and wait for further tasking. Being at the FARP would protect us from retaliatory missile strikes against Ali Al Salem as well as allow us to respond quickly to the invasion force when they needed air support.

Nobody answered Weasel's radio calls on the FARP frequency so we cleared ourselves in. Knowing that thirteen other aircraft were converging on the same narrow strip of blacktop in the darkening haze we came in slowly with a minimum of maneuvering. We got on the deck quickly—lucky for me because in all the excitement of the launch I forgot to bring my night vision goggles into the cockpit. They are quite useless when stuffed in the tailboom.

Still riding the high of success and survival, Gash and I secured our aircraft, joking and yelling at Weasel and IKE as we tied down our main and tail rotor blades. I heard the clattering of another division nearby and, somewhat belatedly, wondered how the other strikes had gone. I'd been so caught up in my own little victory dance that I hadn't even considered that some of my friends were still in danger.

Over the next forty minutes the FARP became a beehive of activity as the rest of the birds dropped out of the darkness to land. A thick layer of black smoke made it seem like it was later than it was and I was glad we'd gotten down first. The visibility was really getting bad.

Now that the strike was over we reverted to our normal combat division of four Cobras with BT as our lead. Leaving our aircraft, Weasel, IKE, Gash and I walked up the narrow road to find him. Realizing that I'd forgotten my kneeboard in the cockpit I ran back to get it as they continued on. I was still riding high on adrenaline and couldn't imagine a better feeling in the whole world. I don't think my feet hit the ground as I grabbed my kneeboard and hurried to catch up.

The sound of the Cobra's engines barely registered amid the celebration in my head—just another bird coming in to land.

Ahead of me I saw the faintest outline of a Cobra parked on the road, its grey paint scheme making it barely lighter than the surrounding blackness. Off to my right I could hear the inbound bird's engines spooling up as the pilot began his descent.

He must be landing on the other side of this one, I thought.

The elevated road was only 10 feet wide, with soft sand all around it. Birds had to land next to each other.

Something felt weird but I ignored it—*don't bother me with piddly shit—I just started a war!*

I hurried past the first parked aircraft—I didn't feel like waiting for the landing bird to set down before catching up to the guys. Coming around its nose I was surprised to see another bird parked very close by. The weird feeling came back—stronger now.

Where's this dude trying to land?

From where I stood, the entire stretch of road was full of helicopters. There was no room for another to land between them. My confusion deepened as the whine of the engines and percussive beat of the main rotor blades grew in intensity.

Something was wrong, very wrong.

The impossibility of what was happening took a second to register. Then it hit with a flash—they were setting up to land on top of a parked bird!

"NO!" I shouted with predictable results. The bird kept coming.

Fight-or-flight considerations took control and I tensed in anticipation. To stay put meant I would die. I had to move, but where?

Dive for cover...or try to do something?

Diving for cover wasn't really an option. Even if I escaped the impact I would get caught in the fireball. Might as well try something.

Pulling a flashlight out of my pocket I ran toward the noise.

Oh shitohshitohshitohshit!

Slamming against the side of the parked aircraft my heart was pounding out of control. I mashed the switch and pointed the dull beam of light down the length of the bird, trying to make it visible to the guys about to land on it.

Here it is fuckers! Look at it!

Waving my flashlight underneath the descending helicopter I had a brief realization that this would be a really stupid way to die.

I flinched. Cringing like it would deflect the thousands of

metal shards about to come shrieking out of the darkness I ducked. The noise was relentless, overpowering. Here it comes...

This really sucks. Fuck fuck fuck.

The tone of the engines changed abruptly—the screaming turbines told me I might yet live.

They'd seen it!

As the pilots waved off my fear turned to anger.

Dipshits! Get your heads out of your asses!

I kept shining my little light as the pilots reacted to the danger and moved away. It wasn't needed anymore but my brain just wasn't thinking that way. After the noise of the helicopter shifted from intense to ambient I gathered myself and walked away like nothing had happened. If Marines whistled I would have tried to force a tune.

Just another day at the office ...

Bullshit.

Fuck me, I thought as the adrenaline wore off. *What's next?*

The dull circle of light underneath my right hand reminded me that the light was on. I had to try three times to turn it off, the shaking of my hands making fine motor skills impossible.

What the fuck is this?

I'd gone through a full strike mission without the slightest tremble, but now I shake like a leaf? That just didn't make sense—but neither did almost getting killed in the FARP. I didn't want to go there.

It's over. Forget it.

After jumping up and down a few times to dissipate the energy I was back to level. Shaking my head at the weirdness of it all I ran to catch up to the rest of the guys.

No sooner did I find them at BT's aircraft then LtCol Heywood called all the aircrews together. The debrief took on the feeling of a long-lost reunion with everybody laughing and joking as we gathered around the CO's bird. Missile shots and secondary explosions were re-enacted with comic book sounds and expansive hand motions, while backslaps and hearty handshakes were freely given and received—even between guys who didn't really like each other.

LtCol Heywood's voice rose over the din.

"Shut the fuck up!"

The noise died down a little and he continued.

"Division leads gimme your ordnance expended, BDA and any damage. Grimace, you first!"

The CO wasn't one for loud yelling and the change caught our attention. Usually he mumbled under his breath. Not now though. His message came through loud and clear: Can the bullshitting and get your heads in the game, this shit is just starting.

The mood remained elevated as each division leader reported the results of their strikes, but nobody interrupted again.

Every target had been destroyed and none of our aircraft received any battle damage. I didn't hear anybody mention if they had seen anyone on their target but it didn't matter. Our mission had been to wipe the observation posts off the map and we'd been successful.

If it keeps up like this it'll be a walk in the park.

My gloating might have been a little premature but the success of the strike mission seemed like a good start to our war.

After the debrief, LtCol Heywood sent us back to our birds with orders to try and get some rest. From here on out we were on standby—as soon as the grunts ran into trouble we'd launch. Could be five minutes from now, could be in the morning. Better get some rest while we can.

After making sure our bird was refueled and re-armed Gash and I asked the ordnance crew to take a look at our cannon. They found a loose plug on the back of the turret and tightened it up. I sure hoped that fixed it because not having the cannon made me feel very vulnerable. I'd felt naked without it.

The evening passed in a blink of an eye and it was almost one in the morning before I got my head down. Lying next to an aircraft, the thin fabric of my sleeping bag provided little protection from the asphalt but it didn't matter. I was so tired it felt like a featherbed. Fatigue pinned my arms and legs to the ground but my mind remained amped up. I lay awake, listening to the whine of cruise missiles passing overhead and rumbling explosions in the distance and wondering if sleep would ever come.

Starting with the Iraqi missile attacks, the events of the last twelve hours had been unreal. I couldn't have imagined a more exciting way to start the war. Manning my aircraft amidst wailing sirens and inbound missiles had seemed like a dream come true, a replay of Midway or the Battle of Britain.

Although I'd felt an undercurrent of fear, it had been the good kind, the kind that provides fuel—formidable, addictive fuel that even hours later made my fingertips tingle and leg muscles tense. Nothing in my life had prepared me for the tunnel vision, pounding heart and sheer excitement of the scramble—or maybe everything had.

I took pride in the fact that it had *almost* overwhelmed me. Almost, but not quite. I'd harnessed the fuel and made it work for me, riding it like a wild bull until it stood quietly under my weight. The rush made me feel alive in a way I never knew existed and now that I'd tasted it one thing was certain: I wanted more.

After the madness of the scramble, destroying the buildings on the OP had been startlingly easy. So easy, in fact, that the shooting had felt routine—like training. Every time my brain had been in danger of getting overwhelmed by reality I'd wrestled it back. Each time I stuffed the fears away my confidence grew. Lessons learned through years of training reduced my mental gyrations to manageable levels and now, lying in my sleeping bag, the truth dawned on me: Just do what you've been taught and you'll be fine.

I didn't have to worry about what-if's, or entertain niggling self-doubts about how I might react to combat. After today I knew. All I had to do was rely on my training and do my job. That's it. Do your job and live, don't do it and die. The beautiful simplicity of what my life had become was a tremendous relief. There was no past to worry about, no concerns for the future. The only thing that mattered was the present. As long as I kept my mind there and did my job then this whole combat thing would work out just fine. I could worry about the other stuff later.

With my mind anchored firmly in the here and now, I drifted off to sleep.

CHAPTER 6

I DON'T KNOW what woke me first, the low moan of a Cobra starter engaging next to me or the distant yelling, but before I knew it I was scrambling out of my sleeping bag and running for my bird.

It had not been a restful night. Several false alarms of chemical attacks had done little to enhance my slumber and my brain remained fuzzy even as my body exploded into motion. Jamming our sleeping bags into stuff sacks Gash and I raced for our aircraft, 500 meters away.

Shit, shoulda slept closer to the bird.

The urgency to get airborne grew as the sand slipped beneath my boots. Lungs screaming, legs pumping, arms full of rifle, ammo, gas mask...I could do ten miles without blinking an eye but this sprint was kicking my ass. Around us the stillness of the morning air was ripped apart by the guttural *thwop* of massive spinning blades and the whine of turbine engines—a suitable soundtrack for the first full day of a war.

Fifteen minutes from a dead sleep we were airborne and heading toward the border. We'd had no time to brief and no idea what we were heading into, but it really didn't matter. Most of us had flown together for years and were well prepared for this sort of scramble. We'd divided up the flight-member responsibilities long ago—everybody knew their job.

BT was the division leader—he called the shots for our four aircraft. During most engagements he would be the only one talking to the ground unit. The rest of us would listen in and take our cues from the discussion. Fuse, an augment pilot from MAWTS-1, was BT's copilot. Working seamlessly as the brain of our division, Fuse would fly and fight their aircraft while BT coordinated our attacks with the ground unit and orchestrated the movements of the division as a whole.

Spock and Count were flying the –2 bird. As the senior officer, Spock sometimes chafed at not being picked to lead the division. I think he recognized the tactical superiority of BT and Fuse but it was still a bitter pill to swallow. Count, an easygoing polyglot none of us could understand, was his front seater. He got his callsign from Sesame Street's Count Von Count because their accents were indistinguishable.

Weasel's bird cut hard in front of us. Gash moved a split second later, crossing behind the three other aircraft until we were on the far left side of the division. Nothing needed to be said—our four aircraft moved as if controlled by a single mind.

Our second section consisted of Weasel and IKE in –3, and Gash and me in –4. Although we were all well-trained and serious about what we were doing, we were also best friends. There was no parental supervision in our section and I often felt like we were sitting at the children's table at Thanksgiving. While the grown-ups sipped wine and sat with folded napkins, we were busy making milk squirt out of each other's noses. More than once BT and Spock would be arguing about something over the radio while behind them we pantomimed whacking-off between our aircraft.

We weren't screwing around this morning though. We were all business as the border flashed beneath us—it was game time.

It was a bright sunny morning, the horizon a bit hazy but still visible. The wind must have picked up and blown some of the oil-fire smoke away. The black layer that had been so sinister last night at the FARP was now thin and unimpressive in the sunlight. Stretching out in front of me as far as the eye could see was desert wasteland, the vast sandy expanse speckled with thick black columns of smoke that rose vertically for a brief time before the winds decapitated them.

I imagined hundreds of Iraqi tanks lying in wait out there, their turrets just barely visible above the top of their fighting positions as they watched our small helicopters grow larger on the horizon. I conjured up images of mustachioed Saddam look-alikes passing out ammunition and barking orders to their minions—Kill the infidels!

Bring it fuckers, you have no idea what's coming your way…

Scenes of Hollywood battles flashed through my mind and my heart pounded in anticipation. I listened intently as BT contacted the FAC, Grizzly. The sound of his voice would tell me if we were rolling into a big fight—I really hoped he would sound strained.

No response from the first call. BT tried again, his words clipped and clear. My hopes for a fight grew stronger as I imagined maybe Grizzly was too busy to talk. Then the radio crackled in response.

Here it is, big fight, cavalry time, swoop in and save the day...

Grizzly's bored voice came across the airwaves strong and clear and took a big fat dump on my little fantasy. He reported no contact and asked us to take a look at a gas/oil separation plant that they were about to move on, tasking us with reconnaissance instead of immediate requests for close air support. If BT felt the same disappointment I did he didn't show it. His tone remained cool and professional as he rogered up and passed our time-on-station and ordnance load to Grizzly in response.

Shit. We scrambled for this?

"Well that's bullshit," Gash drawled, his Tennessee accent stretching the last word over several extra syllables. The tension left my arms and I slumped a little in my seat, annoyed. All that adrenaline and excitement for what? To do recon?

Crap.

I was slipping toward a full-blown righteous sulk—then I saw them.

Dark shapes appeared in the distance—greenish blobs against the monochrome brown background—and they were moving.

What's that?

My heart rate surged. Excitement swept aside my annoyance. A moment ago I'd been sagging in my seat—now I quivered like a hunting dog picking up the scent. BT called them out to the flight and we moved in concert to engage the threat. Our cockpit fell silent as I jammed my face into the foam eye-cups of the targeting bucket and slewed it toward the shapes.

Men in uniform...Soldiers...Iraqi soldiers.

I saw their green uniforms as brightly as if they were orange hunter's vests. From this distance that was all that mattered— enemy. I realized I was now gripping the sight hand control so tightly I thought it might snap off. I'd been here before—in East Timor—but now there was no question, no "if."

Oh boy. Here we go.

I had a missile ready to fire—the quick fix on our cannon hadn't worked and it was again dead weight. Gash dipped the nose toward the group and prepared to cut them down with rockets. Then...something about the men on the ground made me balk.

Hang on a sec—they're walking upright and out in the open, shouldn't they be taking cover? And where are their weapons?

Something wasn't right.

The white flags and big smiles on their faces registered at the same time.

"EPWs"[3] I told Gash over the ICS as BT called off the attack over the radio.

"Roger." Gash's response was cool, emotionless, like their decision to surrender didn't affect him in the least. Now that I think about it, I felt that way too. We had no hatred for them but if they had chosen to fight they would have died. They chose to surrender so they lived.

---

[3]Enemy Prisoner of War

It was black and white, easy. I'd given more consideration to answering the question, "Do you want fries with that?"

My predator's alertness shifted to curiosity. As we drew closer their features became clear. Big smiles split their dirty, bearded faces and gave some indication that they were eager to be taken prisoner. I couldn't imagine a scenario where I'd be happy to get taken prisoner, but these guys obviously could. I wondered what sort of hell they'd been living through.

BT reported the position of the group, which numbered around twenty men, to the Direct Air Support Center (DASC)[4] as we continued on our mission. Although it looked like they were genuinely surrendering they had not been searched. The possibility that at least one of them retained a weapon was impossible to ignore. From our low altitude even a handgun could screw us up so we gave them a wide berth.

They were somebody else's problem now.

Other groups became visible on the horizon, all clearly surrendering and walking south toward Kuwait—just like the pre-war psy-ops leaflets told them to. Our track over the ground zigged and zagged as each new group of surrendering Iraqi soldiers forced us to turn a bit to avoid overflying them. BT reported their positions for a while then stopped, the bored response from the DASC indicating that they didn't care about these guys either. As soon as the white flags came out it was like they ceased to exist.

Their continued presence on the battlefield became annoying—like extras on a dodgeball court. I wished they would just

---

[4]The DASC is an aviation coordination agency. We received mission tasking from the DASC and reported pertinent tactical information back to them.

go away. They made it harder to spot the guys who hadn't sur-rendered—if there were any.

For the next hour and a half all we saw were groups of surrendering Iraqi soldiers. From what I could see they were all empty-handed except for the tattered white cloths they waved enthusiastically any time we were nearby.

This sucks. What if nobody wants to fight?

My cheeks flushed with embarrassment as I recalled all my excited fantasies of shooting down Iraqi helicopters and whack-ing a bunch of tanks. Where was the evil foe so I could open up the can of whup-ass I'd been carrying for seven years? Right then, I'd have settled for one dude in a pickup truck with an AK. Something, anything. I really didn't want my war to go like this—I wanted to fight.

After refueling at Astrodome we crossed back into Iraq. Gash and I went through the standard preparations to fight but our eagerness and excitement were muted. Instead of main battle tanks and fat, lumbering helicopters, we were expecting more surrendering troops. It was hard to get jazzed up over that.

What I saw when we crossed the border got the juices flowing again. The groups of smiling Iraqi soldiers walking south were noticeably absent. While we'd refueled, the deso-late landscape had assumed the sinister emptiness of 'no man's land.' Something had changed.

Our tasking was to conduct reconnaissance for a ground unit as they approached a power station. Their FAC, Cooter, sent us out to discover what surprises might lie in wait behind the high walls of the compound.

I kept my face in the targeting bucket as we flew toward

the grid, anxiously scanning the desert floor in front of us in an attempt to spot hidden enemy troops before they had a chance to engage us.

It felt futile. So much crap was strewn about the desert floor—piles of pipes, old wellheads, decrepit vehicles and tons of scrap metal—that a whole battalion of AAA guns could be scattered among them and I'd never know. It was like using a telescope to search a junkyard from the back of a speeding motorcycle—if a crushed Pinto could fire several thousand rounds a minute.

My left thumb was receiving a thorough workout as I switched back and forth between high and low magnification on my sensors. I'd scan in low mag until my crosshairs centered on something suspicious and then flip to high mag to figure out what it was. Gash's high speed maneuvering wasn't helping any. His random turns and unpredictable flight path caused me to lose track of the areas I'd scanned and those I hadn't. More than once I found myself examining the same pile of crap several times. I didn't ask him to slow down or steady up though, his actions were providing more protection from ground fire than my sporadic searching. There just wasn't enough time to scrutinize everything in front of us.

The power station materialized without warning. I tensed up as a fresh dose of adrenaline spiked in my veins.

Where the fuck did that come from?

The dull brown of the building kept it camouflaged until we were uncomfortably close. It made me wonder what else lurked unseen.

My concern about hidden threats suddenly didn't seem so important as my face got pressed hard against the sights. Gash yanked the bird skyward and my stomach dropped into my boots.

What the fuck?

I pulled my head up to bitch at him as Gash rolled left to keep positive G's on the rotor head. Flying over 50 feet was like screaming "Here we are—shoot us!" The angry words died in my throat when the scene that met my wide eyes explained Gash's climb in an instant.

We just barely cleared the first set of huge power lines that emanated outward from the compound in every direction. The towers were over a hundred feet tall and the high voltage lines connecting them formed a spider web just aching to pluck us out of the sky. We might survive a couple of bullet holes, but coming in contact with the wires or towers would be game over.

Do they paint them brown on purpose? I wondered.

I don't know if it was static electricity that caused the dirt to stick to the wires and towers or what, but they were the exact same color as the surrounding desert. No big orange balls or flashing hazard lights here—it's almost like the Iraqis wanted us to fly into them.

That's just rude.

BT split the division as we entered a holding pattern to search the compound. He and Spock stayed on one side of the oval while Weasel and I stayed on the other. The 180-degree difference between our aircraft allowed for continuous coverage of the target area while maintaining the protection afforded by airspeed.

From our elevated position I could see enemy equipment strewn about the power station. There were heavy machine guns, artillery pieces, antiaircraft artillery and obvious fighting positions. But not many troops.

Several positions contained some rather bedraggled-looking soldiers—most of whom were frantically waving white flags toward the sound of our helicopters. Each new group we rolled in on Gash would ask, "Hostile?"

"Negative," I'd reply, the white flags impossible to ignore. No coalition forces had come through this area for these men to surrender to but their intentions seemed clear enough. Over and over again we pulled off sharply without firing, Gash's aggressive maneuvering betraying his mounting frustration.

Weasel spotted another group of men and something about them grabbed his attention. He called them out as a possible target and described their location. On our next orbit I got my sensors in the area and flipped to high mag, TOW selected and ready to fire. Tons of discarded oil field garbage littered the area.

Pile of crap, pile of crap, pile of...There!

Between two large piles of scrap metal I saw movement and shifted the crosshairs to it. Four men became visible in my field of view. They were standing in the corner of a large, square fighting position about chest deep. Their actions gave no indication they were aware of four enemy attack helicopters bearing down on them.

The whole situation seemed weird. I scanned the position with a missile at the ready, trying to figure out what the hell was going on.

In the corner across from the men, a tarp was stretched out flat and formed a roof over part of the hole. I assumed it was there to provide protection from the cold rains that make winter desert camping quite miserable. Small bundles of mats and clothing indicated where individual men stored their gear and it looked like they'd been there a while.

The bearded men wore solid green uniforms—strange camouflage for a desert army I thought—and were huddling together over a small fire. One man with some impressive bedhead tended a pot while the others stood with hands jammed in their coat pockets against the morning chill. Except for the AK-47s slung over their shoulders they could be any group of campers greeting the morning.

I knew well the feeling of the posture they had assumed—shoulders hunched up to include their necks in the warmth of their jackets while waiting for the first cup of caffeine to start the day. I'd spent many mornings like that when I'd worked on a trail crew in New Hampshire, my feet stuffed into cold, stiff boots as I stared at a camp stove and willed the coffee to percolate faster.

It was not a welcome connection.

From the nervous glances they kept stealing in my direction I realized they were aware of our presence—our loud rotors were impossible to miss amid the calm of the desert morning. Their response was perplexing. Instead of unslinging their weapons and diving for cover to engage us, they just stood there, actively trying to appear unconcerned. They didn't wave white flags, or smile broadly in our direction like so many others this morning, but neither did they do anything remotely hostile.

Now what do I do?

I hadn't expected this. We continued to close with the group but I didn't fire—how could I? They weren't *doing* anything. They were just…just there.

"What are they doing?" Gash asked.

"Nuthin, just hanging out," I answered.

"Weapons?"

"Yeah, slung. Can't tell if they want to play or not."

"Hmm." Gash's response pretty much summed up my own confusion.

This hadn't been covered in training. Everything there had been so black and white—find the enemy, kill the enemy. Well, we'd found the enemy, but were they really *enemy*? Or just some unlucky saps in a hole?

Questions I had never expected suddenly assumed critical importance.

Were they waiting for a ground unit to surrender to? Or maybe they were waiting for us to get closer before opening up? Maybe they just didn't know we were at war?

All my bravado about 'it's not supposed to be fair' came echoing back into my head. I was supposed to eliminate these men simply because they wore the wrong uniform—that's it.

Don't think. They meet the criteria, they've been declared hostile, kill them.

I was psyching myself up to throw the first punch—at the weakest kid on the playground as he ate his snack. He might be a dick, but who throws a sucker punch at a weakling? I didn't like this feeling, not one bit.

Come on fuckers, do something!

I think all of us were thinking the same thing. We could kill them easily at any time, but something inside us wanted them to *deserve* it.

The tense standoff stretched for several orbits. On one side a group of shivering soldiers staked it all on a bluff. On the other, eight men with high-tech weapons tracked their every movement—looking for a reason. It couldn't last forever though. Someone had to blink.

A gust of wind flipped up a corner of the tarp in the fighting hole. Spock spotted the unmistakable fluted muzzles of a ZPU-4 hidden underneath.

Oh, that's a no-no.

As soon as Spock called it out, Cooter cleared us hot. The threat posed by the quad-barreled, 14.5mm antiaircraft gun with Iraqi soldiers nearby warranted its immediate destruction.

Weasel turned inbound to engage as BT called *"Firing."*

Flames shot out of one of the missile tubes on BT's aircraft—but it didn't look right. Instead of smooth corrections the TOW missile made a series of abrupt, jerky turns before smashing into the desert—well short of the target.

That's a pretty clear blink, I thought.

The race was on. We'd opened up on them...return fire would come at any second. Could we get another missile into the heavy machine gun before the men were able to bring it to bear against us? BT and Spock were too close for another shot and pulled off target to clear the way for Weasel.

The instant Spock and BT's aircraft moved out of our line of sight Weasel fired. I didn't look up from my sights but heard the launch of his missile from several hundred feet away. It took all my self-control not to slew my sensors onto the target but I knew I shouldn't—Weasel and IKE were dealing with that threat. My eyes were better employed looking for other targets.

Gash kept us in perfect firing position off of Weasel's four o'clock, allowing me to scan underneath and around Weasel as he focused on the men in the hole. Pieces of debris blasted through my line of sight from the impact of Weasel's missile. Then the pull was too strong—I had to look.

Drifting smoke revealed the chassis of the weapon still intact. Weasel hit it again. The second explosion was even more violent than the first as the gun's ammunition was added to the mix. Sleeping mats, cookware and clothing were swept out of the hole and hundreds of spurts of sand marked the impact of shrapnel all around the area.

I'd like to say that I looked for the men, that I cared if they had lived or died, but I didn't. The instant it became clear that they were hiding a big gun they moved out of the grey and labeled themselves combatants.

Were they deviously hiding the gun? Or were they waiting to surrender and just 'forgot' about the AAA gun?

I didn't know, didn't care. Figuring motives and what somebody *might* do in the future belong in fantasy, not war. I tried to steel myself to that reality.

Tough shit, they made their choice.

If the men had stayed in the hole then they had died. I convinced myself the only reason I thought about them at all was totally self-centered—they were no longer a threat.

We headed back to Astrodome FARP for gas and more ordnance. After four hours in the cockpit I was really looking forward to shutting down for a little while—my morning biological needs required attention. But my hopes were dashed when the DASC told us to hot refuel and standby for tasking. They had an immediate request over by Al Basrah. Personal need would have to wait.

After the tension of the first two flights—getting airborne and immediately prepping to fight—this one felt relaxing. Al Basrah was well to the east of Astrodome and we stayed safely inside Kuwaiti airspace for almost the whole transit. The ominous presence of the border was out of sight to the north— out of sight, out of mind.

The bright sunny morning made it easy to avoid the power lines and random towers that dotted the landscape and there was no danger of ground fire. I was alert, but no more so than I would have been flying at home. I slipped into a comfortable calm—Iraq might as well have been a thousand miles away.

Gash maneuvered gently behind Weasel's bird. The smooth motion of our aircraft reminded me of a dolphin playing effortlessly in the wake of a boat as we weaved back and forth. The consternation I had felt during the last on-station time was totally gone. Times like this made flying fun.

Piercing electronic tones shattered the tranquility. Reflexively my hand shot to the ICS box and turned down the volume. In an instant I recognized the sound of an Emergency Locator Transmitter (ELT)—an aircraft had gone down. Knowing that the range of an ELT was not very far I scanned above us, worried that a parachuting pilot might be descending into our flight path. Gash called my attention to a group of vehicles parked together at our one o'clock position. I abandoned my nervous searching above to check them out.

It was a strange mixture of vehicles. There were some civilian SUVs, a couple of HMMWVs and several flat-faced boxy trucks that the British were fond of. Peering through my sights I found a group of soldiers standing about a hundred meters from the vehicles.

My curiosity spiked.

They weren't doing anything, just standing shoulder to shoulder with their backs to us. There was something odd about their stillness though—like they were afraid of stepping on something. The sound of the ELT remained strong in my helmet and I, somewhat belatedly, began to associate the peculiar gathering with the origin of the now annoying tones.

BT put our flight into a holding pattern just south of the group and contacted the DASC to offer assistance. I couldn't tear my eyes away from what I now recognized as a crash site.

I'd seen cracked and broken aircraft before but never the absolute dismantling of men and machine now spread out before me. It was just so *total*. The somber scene entranced me with morbid fascination.

From a particularly disturbed patch of sand the wreckage spread out like a lady's hand fan, the blackened sand beneath the scattered pieces telling the story of the explosion that followed the initial impact.

"Can you tell what it was?" Gash asked, his solemn tone just barely bending the silence that had descended over our cockpit.

I began to answer in the negative—the pieces were just too small—but then something caught my eye.

"Yeah, it's a Phrog," I answered quietly, the characteristic shape of a CH-46 ramp betraying the identity of the crashed aircraft. I couldn't believe that the blackened chunks before me had been an aircraft just a short time ago. The extreme forces in evidence were just unfathomable. Nobody could have survived.

A mental rolodex of CH-46 pilots I knew flashed uninvited in my head, each face recognizable for a moment before being replaced by the next. The Marine Corps helicopter community is small enough that there was little chance I didn't know those who'd died, at least in passing. With effort I stopped the parade of possibly dead friends—now was not the time.

The DASC broke through the electronic tones of the ELT on the radio and directed BT to proceed on mission. There was nothing we could do to help at the crash site. We'd suspected that from the beginning but had to ask, some things you just don't fly past.

The ELT faded quickly as we flew away, taking with it any lingering thoughts about those who had died.

For a fleeting half-second I realized how strangely effortless this had become: My ability to compartmentalize was rock solid. I simply banished any concerns for the dead lest my inattention to the demands right in front of me should cause me to join them.

Minutes later I was literally miles away, scanning for targets in the scrub brush of southeastern Iraq. Thoughts of those killed in the CH-46 were the farthest things from my mind.

For the next hour our division provided flank security for a battalion as it moved through the oilfields on the outskirts of Al Basrah. I thought that it had been difficult to see things amid the debris of the open desert but this was a nightmare. The deep wadis and jumbled tumbleweeds that crisscrossed the terrain in front of us could hide a thousand different threats.

No wonder the grunts wanted us watching this area.

BT and Spock kept their eyes oriented to the north, scanning the area closest to the grunts, while Weasel and I looked to the west and monitored traffic on the paved roads in that direction. It was gearing up to be a boring flight when Weasel called out a speeding truck on the road and pulled our section over to check it out.

Keeping us in a position to put rockets underneath Weasel's aircraft should a threat pop up there, Gash followed him toward a large truck barreling out of the desert wasteland. I got my eyes on it and zoomed in for a closer look—a big yellow tanker truck. Weasel reported it and the FAC wanted us to determine if it was hostile. If it was, we were to take it out.

Weasel called out "45 left." Gash moved off Weasel's right side in preparation for the attack. If the truck broke through and detonated amid the Marine convoy there would be massive casualties. It was still far enough away that we could destroy it safely—but not for long.

This decision would have to be made quickly.

My crosshairs bounced and jerked as I tried to keep them on the cab of the truck, the vibration of the aircraft complicating my job in a familiar manner. With a TOW selected and ready to fire, I flipped up the trigger guard and waited.

What's it gonna be?

As if he could read my thoughts the driver slammed on his brakes. The big truck skidded to a stop miles away from the grunts. The driver and passenger had seen our skinny birds and read our actions correctly—we meant to kill them if they didn't stop.

As soon as the driver jumped out of the truck he ripped his pants off and waved them over his head in an enthusiastic gesture of surrender. The passenger kept his drawers on but his uplifted arms and the absence of any visible weapons indicated he was harmless as well. We pulled off without firing.

While we had been subjected to an impromptu "Chippendales" show, BT and Spock had spotted a technical vehicle with a recoilless rifle mounted on the back. It was parked in the broken terrain to their front but they had seen two men jump out and take cover nearby. Assuming that it was a manned weapon, the FAC gave them authorization to take it out.

Weasel brought us back into our original position and we

quickly located the blue vehicle amid the scrub brush. There didn't seem to be much of a threat so I brought my head out of the sights to watch BT take his shot.

To my surprise—and I'm sure BT's as well—his whole wing seemed to explode. Somehow all four of his TOW missiles fired at once and went spinning crazily through the sky like a fireworks display gone spectacularly wrong.

"What the fu...?" I never even got a chance to finish my question before four explosions went off in quick succession as the missiles exploded close to BT's aircraft. The reports were loud in my cockpit several hundred meters away. They must have been deafening to BT and Fuse.

"Ahh, hey. I just uuhh, I think I just shot all my TOWs." BT's voice came across the back radio with a slightly bemused tone. He quickly turned serious.

"Coming off left, we've got a weird vibe." Helicopter pilots are very attuned to weird vibrations—they are often the only warning given that the bird is about to come apart.

BT and Spock pulled off the firing line to determine how much damage BT's aircraft had sustained and Weasel took out the technical vehicle with a Hellfire. We followed with a couple rockets to frag the guys who'd gotten out, then pulled back to join BT and Spock. No way to know if we got the two guys or not and no reason to find out. Their truck was a flaming mess and they were miles from anywhere.

We checked off-station with the FAC and headed back to Ali Al Salem; the vibrations in BT's aircraft were troubling him enough to call it a day. If there had been any reason to stay out longer we would have, but things were quiet and the DASC cleared us to return to base. Later we discovered BT's aircraft wasn't damaged at all. The guidance wires from his missiles had wrapped around his tail rotor and caused the disconcerting vibration they had felt. Better to be safe than sorry, though. Losing the tail rotor is usually a death sentence for a helicopter pilot.

I awoke before dawn the next morning. I'd gone straight to bed after the debrief yesterday afternoon and felt well-rested despite the early hour. Sleep had taken on the importance of water, fuel and ordnance—a basic requirement that had to be attended to if I was to continue to operate. When we'd landed yesterday I didn't know when we'd launch out again; it could be a couple hours or a couple of days, and gaining a few hours of sleep became of paramount importance. If I had any concerns about the previous missions they didn't register. My mind was preoccupied with preparing for the next mission, not rehashing the last.

In the comfortable cool of the morning I sat outside the ready room. The sandbags holding down the edges of the bottomless tent formed a pleasant spot to sit and have my coffee while I watched the squadron come alive. I thought a little bit about yesterday's missions—they seemed like a pretty good way to start the war.

We'd supported the grunts as they moved into enemy territory, took out some heavy weapons that might have been problematic, and even had a little fun. At one point the FAC, Cooter, had cleared us to shoot some of the abandoned Iraqi equipment that was strewn about the power plant.

It was like plinking beer cans with a BB gun. Okay—the BBs were really expensive and the beer cans potentially lethal—but you get the picture. I'd even had a chance to blow up a tanker truck. I had hoped it was full of fuel and almost giggled in anticipation of the fireball—it was going to look so *cool*! But my missile just poked a hole through the empty tank. I'd felt cheated.

Our division was scheduled to go on alert at 1100 this morning. I had hours to relax and enjoy the simple pleasures of unhurried caffeine and nicotine ingestion before I needed to worry about flying again. All felt right in my world until Gash pulled up a sandbag next to me.

I could tell something was wrong as he sat down—the absence of a rude greeting being the first indication. His mouth was stretched tight in a half grimace and he rubbed his shock of brown hair roughly before beginning to talk. After I had gone to bed yesterday he had stayed up for a bit, talking with some of our squadron mates. I sat silently as he filled me in on what had happened to them.

The operations officer's division had been working in the same area that we'd been in, replacing us on-station when we had run low on fuel and vice versa. I'd known that they were there but didn't know that three of their four aircraft had taken battle damage. Bullets had penetrated their cockpits and tail booms but luckily didn't hit anybody. It turned out that some of the "surrendering" Iraqi soldiers had not quite played by the rules. They'd held up white flags while the aircraft were pointing at them but opened fire when the birds turned away.

While he talked, I remembered multiple groups of Iraqi soldiers from yesterday's flight. My interest in them had bloomed brightly until their white flags rendered them as inconsequential as the sand they walked upon. To my black-and-white mind they were either fighters or not. Once the white flags had come out they incontrovertibly switched out of the fighter category and were of no further interest. I tried to find an alternate explanation but couldn't—my naïve concept of fair play had been exploited. I felt like a sucker.

Some damage to our squadron's aircraft wasn't the worst part. Gash had found out that a 2nd Lieutenant had been killed in fighting near the power plant after we'd left.

Gash didn't say it—he didn't have to. An ugly thought exploded in my head: What if one of the "surrendering" Iraqis had killed him?

Not all the soldiers had been effusively surrendering yesterday, yet I had lumped them in with those who were. I could remember at least two instances in which guys on one end of a trench had waved flags while a group on the other end of the same trench had just stood and watched me.

How many flags did I need to see? One per man? One per fighting hole? My weapons don't allow me the luxury of picking off one or two guys out of a group—if I open fire then everybody dies. I'd exercised my judgment and hadn't called them out as targets.

Now I was left to wonder if I'd screwed up.

Maybe I should have sought clarity about those issues before—but I hadn't even known they existed. Never in my years of training had I envisioned that one day I would have to look upon a group of people and decide "Ho hum, I guess you will die" like some sort of thoughtless or malevolent deity.

I'd wanted to feel threatened by them, to see them acting aggressively toward me in a way that demanded action on my part to avoid being killed. Kill or be killed—I was ready for that. I wasn't ready to be an executioner.

I knew the decision to fire or not rested solely on my shoulders. Gash had no ability to see through the sights from the back seat and had to rely on me to be his eyes. I'd chosen my seat exactly for that reason. My moral compass demanded I be one hundred percent certain before I pulled the trigger. Now I realized that was a pipe dream. There is no such thing as 'one hundred percent certain.'

I would have to choose. I would have to decide life or death and couldn't afford to wait for indisputable evidence to do it for me. My internal dialogue started to mock me.

What did you expect to see? Iraqis bayoneting babies? Saddam's henchmen raping grandmothers?

You dumbass.

Those dudes shivering in the cold while they waited for their tea—that's what they look like. Those are the guys you have to kill.

The asshole in my head was right. The costs of inaction were now clear to me in the form of bullet holes and a dead Marine. I was ashamed that I'd never thought of it like that before.

I mulled over the information about the false surrenders and realized we had taken far too many chances yesterday—that *I* had taken too many chances. Without optics Gash was basically blind, relying on me to decide to shoot or not. He trusted me to bring him home to his wife and daughters safely—and that meant killing anyone who stood in our way. He didn't ask it, but the question was there, poisoning the air between us. Gash had realized that it had been dumb luck that we hadn't gotten shot yesterday. He'd known it since hearing about the fake surrenders, now he needed to know that I knew it too. He needed to know I wouldn't rely on luck, not again.

Over coffee and eggs we resolved to kill any Iraqi soldiers we found. Unless they dropped their weapons, waved a white flag and were walking south toward Kuwait they would die. Simple. That's it. We're not here to consider motives, how crappy their situation might be or if they really wanted to be there. We're here to kill every one of them who doesn't immediately give up.

As we finished breakfast Gash's relief was evident. He'd been in a tough position, believing that we should have shot more yesterday yet trusting me when I'd held fire. In hindsight I can see just how tactfully he brought the issue to my attention, and how relieved he was that it was resolved.

At the time though, I was solidly internal. My self-imposed curtains of humanity opened wide and made available an arsenal of actions I'd refused to employ yesterday. Never again, not if it meant we might not make it home. In my head the tinny voice of misplaced compassion was obliterated by the booming baritone of the asshole.

This is what you've been trained for. Do your fucking job.

CHAPTER 7

THE POSSIBILITY that my inaction the day before had led to a Marine's death didn't sit well with me. It wasn't just too much coffee that was souring my stomach and I needed something to dilute the acid released by my perceived failure. Luckily I didn't have long to wait—we received a mission shortly after Gash and I finished breakfast.

When our four-ship division took off at 1600 I was aching for a fight. I needed some stupid SOB to stand up against me so I could knock him into next week. The stain from the last mission could only be wiped clean by unleashing furious destruction on the first Iraqi combatants I found.

You poor fuckers—you have no idea the hurt that is coming.

I was ready now.

Wouldn't that be great? I'm ready, they're ready, we can meet at the bike rack at 3pm and fight…

Yeah, didn't quite turn out that way. Oh, we fought—just later. Much later.

Our original mission was to escort some CH-46s around the southern Iraqi oil fields—a sightseeing trip for some VIPs. It was hardly the epic battle I was looking for but at least it got us out of Kuwait. Nothing interesting would happen back there.

The escort mission was as annoying as it was uneventful. The VIP aircraft were an hour late to begin with—but hadn't seen fit to let us know. After we flew in circles for an hour at the rendezvous point they finally showed up—leaving us just barely enough gas to fly the planned route. BT adjusted our plan and sent Weasel and me to sit at the nearest FARP, which happened to be inside Kuwait. He and Spock would escort the 46s until they hit bingo fuel, then Weasel and I would take over escort duties if needed.

The FARP was quiet so Weasel and I kept turning on the refueling spots and waited. To pass the time we made up random stories about BT's mom and discussed them over the radio. It was an old pastime of ours and, although none of us had ever met BT's mom, she had some pretty lively adventures. We hoped BT could hear us over our discreet frequency but he probably couldn't, he was too far away.

The mission passed without incident and soon BT and Spock joined us at the FARP. They didn't sound like they were in the mood to hear about BT's mom so we wisely kept quiet. They refueled quickly and we all took off together into the gathering darkness. There wasn't any dusk—as soon as the sun set, the smoke from the oil fires dropped the curtain of night.

Excitement crackled in the short conversations between our blacked-out cockpits as we left the safety of Kuwait. The escort mission had been our cover charge—the price we had to pay to get into Iraq—but it wasn't what we were here for. Big battles, hordes of tanks, duels with AAA guns—those were the writhing strippers I'd paid to see. Now we were inside the club and the hunt was on.

But the wadded dollar bills would never leave my pocket—the strippers turned out to be toothless meth-heads well past their prime.

For nine hours we drilled holes in the night sky, crisscrossing the southern part of Iraq multiple times as we executed fruitless mission after fruitless mission. There was no shortage of requests for gunship support but they were all reconnaissance or general security missions. The grunts just wanted us overhead in case something was lurking outside their perimeter.

So far my big fight hadn't materialized—quite the opposite. Instead of blistering battles I fought tedium and fatigue. Each time we got a mission I felt a little kick of excitement—*this must be it*. After each letdown my disappointment grew a little stronger and I slipped deeper into exasperated boredom.

That boredom would soon become a fond memory.

"Hey dude, you wanna take it in?" Gash drawled, his Tennessee accent even deeper than normal from fatigue. We were heading to refuel for the third or fourth time that night.

He'd been on the controls all night dodging wires, birds, towers and the other members of our division while I tried to extract enemy shapes from the fuzzy green FLIR screen.

"Yeah, hang on a sec," I responded, jamming the map between my thigh and armored seat. Sitting back from the targeting bucket, I assumed a slightly reclined position and wrapped my hands around the controls before continuing.

"All right, I got the controls."

"Roger, you have controls."

"I have the controls." The three-way transfer of controls complete, I moved the cyclic slightly, feeling the bird bank in response as I heard Gash's knuckles against the canopy. I looked around for the landing area.

Arlington FARP was a thin, elevated strip of blacktop road on the western outskirts of the Rumaylah oil fields. Around it stretched miles and miles of absolute desolation punctuated by towering flames from burning oil wells. The scene looked kind of cool—in an apocalyptic sort of way.

Through my night vision goggles I could see billowing clouds of dust envelope first BT's and then Spock's aircraft as they landed. I loitered for a few minutes as Weasel shot his approach to land and remained clear until his dust cloud dissipated.

Rolling out on landing heading for the first time I realized that the brilliant orange flames of the oil fires were directly off our nose. I tensed as my goggles flared brightly.

Shit, I can't see a damn thing.

I tried to avoid the flames and sneak a peek at my landing spot on the road. It was no use. The intense light rendered my night vision goggles useless anytime the flames were within the field of view. I looked off to the side.

It's all good. I know my spot is clear.

Keeping my line of sight offset to exclude the flames I continued down, the comfortable shudder of the aircraft reassuring me that I was descending with minimal forward speed. Everything was just fine.

As I came through 50 feet, the flames moved out of my line of sight. I could see Weasel's aircraft again. I relaxed—we were perfectly lined up for landing. Muscle memory took over as I executed the minute corrections needed to fine-tune our approach. My mind returned to lamenting the night's unproductive missions. I hoped our luck would get better.

With the distracting flames gone the fuzzy green scene in my goggles suddenly coalesced into hard shapes and angles. My eyes started to register the fine details of the road but it was wrong—it shouldn't be happening that fast.

Too late I recognized what was happening. Alarm bells screamed in my head and adrenaline flooded my system.

"powerPOWER*POWER!*" Gash yelled, his voice increasing in urgency with each repetition.

My grip tightened on the collective as I pulled up for all I was worth. I didn't care if I ripped the driveshaft in half from the over-torque. *I need power right fucking now!*

The engines started to spool up as fuel poured into the chambers—but it was too slow, way too slow. With certainty I knew the ground would arrive before the power did. There was no doubt. We were about to crash.

With terrible speed the geometry of my perspective matched the perspective of being seated in a parked aircraft. There was nothing I could do—what I had screwed up 20 seconds ago overrode any actions I might make now.

In fear and frustration I squeezed the controls. I couldn't do anything else.

In slow motion I felt the skids compress under the strain of the collision. Lower and lower we sank until I was certain they could take no more and would snap. Once they were gone we'd continue into the ground, the blades flexing downward and slicing through the cockpit if we didn't explode first.

Aaaah shit. I cringed, waiting for the blades. *Here it comes...*

A lump of coal in my fist would have turned into a diamond.

To my amazement the skids held—even better they rebounded and tossed us back into the air like a kid on a trampoline.

Holy shit, we're alive!

Relief flashed for a split second—then I saw what was coming. The forward momentum generated by our bounce was taking us off the road. In a moment we would hit again and tumble in the soft sand. It wasn't over yet, but at least now I could do something.

I kept the aircraft level and hoped that our skids were still attached. The only chance we had of surviving the second impact was to hit and slide like a 14,000-pound twin-runner sled. I braced again as the sand got very close.

The impact never came. The power generated by the screaming turbines finally forced the wide blades to spin fast enough to support the weight of the aircraft. Amazingly the ground receded below us as Death shook his fist angrily.

Holy shit, we're flying!

Relaxing my grip on the controls slightly I began flying the aircraft again. In an instant I catalogued the shaking of our bird and dismissed the normal vibrations while searching intently for any new ones. Everything felt normal, maybe a little wobbly but that could have just been me.

I brought us around for another landing. On downwind I asked Gash how the instruments looked, so intent on keeping my eyes outside the aircraft that I didn't even want to glance at the instruments in my cockpit. I just couldn't believe that we had survived without serious damage.

"Umm, fine," he replied laconically, his level tone indicating zero concern for what had just occurred. It's one thing to almost die in a ball of flames, totally another to sound like it bothered you.

"Roger, I think I'll take this one around." I answered, trying to sound as if I hadn't just sucked the seat cushion halfway up my ass.

"Hmm, you sure?" he asked. As if I had a fucking choice.

Funny guy, I thought, *at least he isn't pissed at me for almost killing him.*

I came down the glideslope painfully slowly this time, giving Weasel and IKE enough time to verify that our skids were still attached before setting down. As I lowered the collective it seemed to me like the skids settled a little lower than usual, but I allowed that I might be a little hypersensitive. I was relieved they held at all.

Gash went through the shutdown checklist rapidly as I sat motionless in the front. The relief I'd felt turned to anger—at myself.

Great job, dildo, I thought. Quit whining about there not being any good targets and try paying attention to what you're doing.

The blades stopped turning and I hopped out of the cockpit, afraid of what I might find. The soft glow of the oil fires gave me enough light to see our bird and I scanned it nervously for damage. Incredibly, everything looked normal.

Corporal Mayo, one of our squadron mechanics embedded with the FARP team, sauntered toward me from the fuel truck. I recognized his lumbering walk even in the weak light and was happy to see him—if I'd broken anything I was sure he would find it. After a quick handshake I told him what happened. He just nodded his head. Mayo was used to pilots wrecking his aircraft. Nothing I said seemed to faze him.

"Roger, Sir; I'll take a look," and then he was gone, popping open panels and examining the components within for any signs of damage.

The rest of the division shut down as well, the initial plan of getting gas and going back out in search of work derailed by my less-than-stellar landing. After nine hours in the cockpit I think everybody welcomed the break. I just wish it hadn't been because of something I'd done. I was embarrassed—and pissed.

Cpl Mayo completed his inspection and found nothing seriously amiss. The oil level in the transmission was low and a fiberglass fairing on the tail boom was crushed when it had hit the curb, but other than that everything appeared fine. Relieved that we wouldn't have to call for a maintenance recovery team to come and fix our aircraft, Gash and I thanked Cpl Mayo and headed over to tell BT the good news. We found the rest of the division sitting in a half circle around a small shortwave radio Count had pulled out of his bag. Six questioning faces looked up in unison as we approached.

"Hard landing, overtorque and a crushed fairing near the stinger. Other than that we're fine," I reported.

"Ahh, okay. What happened?" BT asked, curious but not accusatory.

"Goggles bloomed from the fires and I didn't pay close enough attention until too late. Ground rush bit me in the ass," I answered. That I'd screwed up royally was obvious and I knew better than to try and make excuses.

Like a fart in church, my admission hung in the air—no less pungent for being ignored. My friends had all landed in exactly the same circumstances and none of them had crashed.

Can they count on me? Am I the weakest link?

Twenty minutes ago I would have laughed at that suggestion. Now...I wasn't so sure.

The unspoken question stank like rotten eggs but I was powerless to remove it. My mistake had brought it to life but I couldn't make it go away.

The quiet stretched uncomfortably. The flickering light from the oil fires made it hard to tell, but as the seconds dragged on I imagined disgust and disappointment on the shadowed faces of my friends.

Oh man, I really screwed up this time ...

Weasel was the first to break the silence. A slight tremor in his voice belied the effort it took to maintain his calm tone. Slowly he started, enunciating each word clearly into the desert air.

"I bet BT's mom could have landed it."

My dread evaporated as the night erupted with laughter and hoots of friendly derision. Weasel's quip shattered the tension and I shook my head ruefully, taking my rightful place as the butt of the joke. Although their laughter told me the crappy landing was forgotten, I still felt like an idiot.

After an hour on the deck the DASC called for us to launch. Once more into the breach...once more the mission was a total waste of time. We were never able to establish communications with the requesting unit and spent two hours flying aimlessly in the darkness.

Over the radio BT asked if anybody wanted to call it a night, to just head back to Ali Al Salem and put an end to this seemingly pointless fishing expedition. Dawn was several hours away still and there was no reason to expect that combat would flare up before sunrise. Besides, by then it would be time for the day divisions to get to work and we'd be sent home anyway.

Gash and I talked about it briefly. As tired as we were, going home early just felt like quitting. We were already here, might as well let the whole night play out. Gash let BT know that there was no reason for our aircraft to go home just yet—a bit of a lie but we weren't ready to throw in the towel.

Everybody was in agreement that we'd stay out until our replacements arrived. Instead of heading home we proceeded to Astrodome FARP for gas—Arlington FARP had just run out of fuel. While on the deck the DASC called, and it sounded like our luck had turned for the better. A unit north of Al Basrah was requesting air support to deal with some suspected tanks that were fast approaching. We had tasking and a target. Things were looking up.

The annoyances of wasted missions and the embarrassment of my shitty landing were forgotten as we flew low across the open desert, my concentration focused on the small screen that blazed green underneath the glare-shield in my narrow cockpit. With the small joystick in my right hand, I swung the FLIR left and right of our direct heading, searching along our route of flight for any enemy positions lurking 50 feet below.

Gash kept his eyes outside the aircraft, scanning between the ground and Weasel's ghostly silhouette to remain in position as the division maneuvered toward the fight. This mission had a different feel, the energy in the FAC's voice telling us more than his words as he described the sounds he'd heard north of his position. He couldn't see them but was certain they were enemy tanks maneuvering to attack. We were still miles away but I scanned the horizon hopefully, searching for the little bright spots that would indicate hot tank engines and give me what I wanted most: targets.

Twenty minutes later we arrived on-station and the FAC began describing where he thought the tanks were. It didn't go well. It can be a challenge for two people to get their eyes on exactly the same section of ground—especially when they are looking from different directions, different elevations and are using different sensors. Adding to the confusion this night were the towering oil fires scattered in all directions. The intense heat and light given off by the flames degraded our night vision goggles and FLIR image anytime they were within our field of view. Ironically, the brilliant light rendered us blind.

Trying to follow the talk-on between BT and the FAC I rapidly grew frustrated. I was wasting my time trying to see what they were talking about—couldn't even identify a large bridge that they both said was easy to spot—so I gave up. Finding the tanks wasn't really my job anyway. As –4, protecting the other members of the flight was more my responsibility than searching for deep targets. Relieved, but slightly embarrassed that I had no idea where BT was looking, I brought my sensor scan closer in and used it to search for suspicious heat sources amid the clumps of marsh grasses and bushes.

We were holding over an area that appeared to be deserted. Relying on that assumption was a bad idea though. A comfortable racetrack pattern would allow easy scanning for targets but would also leave us vulnerable to ambush from the ground. Instead we weaved and meandered like drunken sailors, sometimes turning right, sometimes left, 180 degrees, 270 degrees... The direction and duration of the turns didn't really matter. As long as we remained in the general area and didn't fly over the same patch of ground multiple times, we felt pretty safe.

It was hell on me though. With my head in the targeting bucket the random turning and weird angles had me totally disoriented in no time flat. It felt like I was peering out of a hole with binoculars—from inside a box being thrown down a darkened staircase.

Hmm. I might puke.

I sat up for a minute, seeking to clear my head and fight down my uncomfortable queasiness. Suddenly Gash whipped the bird over on its side.

"Fuck!" His tone spoke volumes and my adrenaline surged. This wasn't an 'I forgot to pay my phone bill' fuck. Something was up.

Before I could comment, Gash ripped the bird hard the other way. My helmet bounced off the canopy. He kept the turn in to the right, searching beneath us with his goggles.

"Thought I saw a tracer come up, right down there somewhere, three o'clock low." His voice was controlled but on edge. There was no trace of his syrupy southern accent now.

"Roger, searching," I replied, looking around quickly in the hopes of spotting our assailant moving in the darkness 50 feet below. Amazing how a little adrenaline settles the stomach.

If we could just get eyes on this guy it would be all over. A quick tip in and some rockets—all we had to do was find him. That was proving to be difficult. After ten seconds of frantic maneuvering Gash's voice came up on the ICS again.

"Dude, where's Weasel?" His apprehensive tone raised my hackles before the words even had time to register.

Oh shit.

We'd committed the ultimate wingman sin—we'd lost our lead.

All concerns about the tracer evaporated and I looked up from the ground. My hands flew to the controls, ready to jerk the aircraft to avoid the collision I feared was imminent. Craning my head around savagely I searched—left, right, behind, above. Each passing second made it more likely that we were converging with the other three aircraft and about to smash into their whirling blades.

The cloak of invisibility granted by the night sky turned

sinister in a heartbeat—any piece of blackness out there might turn into a seven-ton helicopter in the blink of an eye. There was no safe area to fly to, no altitude to climb to and every turn potentially placed us on a collision course or narrowly averted one. The terrible uncertainty was paralyzing.

"Searching," I replied brusquely.

He's gotta be right here, why can't I find him?

The towering oil fires that littered the area totally washed out the small infra-red lights on our division mates' aircraft. They had simply disappeared. Tense seconds stretched into minutes with no sign of Weasel or the other aircraft.

I felt like we were playing a sick mixture of Russian roulette and chicken—desperately hoping to spot an aircraft while fearing that it would happen in the millisecond before impact.

BT and the FAC were keeping up a running discussion on the tactical radio, the FAC describing the friendly positions and BT doing his best to locate them in the darkness. As dire as our situation was, we didn't want to transmit over the radio for fear of interrupting them. They were having a hard enough time understanding each other over the scratchy net and the frustration was audible in their voices. Besides, any second I expected to spot their tiny aircraft in the darkness and we could rejoin silently.

Gash kept looking with his goggles as I went back to the FLIR, swinging the sensor around level with our aircraft and searching the horizon for three small dots that would indicate the rest of our guys.

Goddamn oil fires.

The infernos caused large black blotches to erupt on my screen. Their thermal signature overpowered the sensitive heat receptors in the FLIR and made it impossible to see anything.

I ran through our options for the tenth time in as many seconds. They all sucked. If we went lower then I could look up against a cool sky to spot them, but any lower and we'd be in danger of hitting the ground. We could go higher and orbit safely until we spotted them, but then we'd be blinded by the oil smoke and exposed to radar-guided antiaircraft fire.

Shit!

"I got 'em." Gash's voice rang in my ears carrying the sweetest message I'd ever heard. Relief flooded through me as he continued "Ten o'clock, a little high, two miles."

Stowing the FLIR I glanced off to my left and instantly spotted one, then two Cobras flying in formation as Gash maneuvered to join them. I couldn't see BT's bird, but chalked that up to the additional distance between us and ignored the discrepancy. As long as we had Weasel and Spock in sight we were okay.

Oh thank fucking god, I thought as we tucked in behind them, *we're back onboard.*

The terror of the last five minutes dissipated quickly. I refocused on the hunt again, listening to BT and the FAC with newfound attentiveness.

They were describing a huge cloverleaf of ramps connecting a massive superhighway to several large secondary roads. Supposedly the tanks were hidden amid the overpasses in that area. I moved the FLIR out and expected to spot the highway easily.

Sand, ditches, scrub brush, oil fires...where the hell was the damn road?

A massive superhighway should be easy for me to see but the scene in my sensors looked nothing like what the FAC was describing. A sickening feeling descended over me.

Ooohhhh shit.

I looked again at the Cobras in front of us. Spotting the two I redoubled my efforts to locate BT, desperately hoping that I'd see a third black dot on my screen and the whole nightmare would be over. I hesitated before breaking the bad news to Gash but the screen didn't lie. There was no third Cobra, only two.

"Hey man, we're not on Weasel," I said, hating the truth behind the words as I spoke them. "I don't know where he is but there's only two birds here. We joined somebody else."

"Weasel, turn on your IR smack," Gash demanded over the radio, not wanting to believe me and breaking our self-imposed radio silence.

I stared at the closest Cobra to us, willing the small rotating infra-red beacon atop the engines to bloom brightly in my goggles and make me a liar. Never had I desired so completely to be proven wrong. Another minute went by—plenty of time for IKE to have flipped the switch. The beacon refused to illuminate.

"Oh fuck," Gash muttered, the two words aptly describing our situation.

Somehow in the darkness we had managed to lose our own division, stumble upon a section of random Cobras from someplace else and join on them. It dawned on me that the four pilots in those strange aircraft had no idea we were with them, lurking just out of sight as they maneuvered through the fires on a mission of their own.

"Just stay on these guys. At least if we're tucked in we won't crash into them," I said needlessly. There was no way we were going to detach until this situation got unscrewed.

"Weasel, Shoe."[5]

---

[5] Each aircraft in a formation uses the callsign of the Marine who signed for the aircraft to identify itself over the inter-flight frequency. Gash might answer a call for our aircraft, but he would always use "Shoe" as our callsign because I'd signed for the bird. Thus, the informal radio callsigns for our division were "BT", Spock", "Weasel", and "Shoe".

Gash broke through BT and the FAC's conversation on the front radio. Enough was enough, we needed to get back with our division.

"Shoe, go," Weasel replied quickly.

"Gimme your grid, we're tumbleweed," Gash demanded, letting him know that we were confused about our own position but without going into specifics.

Weasel hesitated briefly—probably wondering why we needed his grid if we were hanging on his wing—before transmitting his position. I quickly plugged the grid into our GPS and was amazed to find that they were almost 30 miles away.

"120, 28 miles."

"Jesus Christ!" Gash exclaimed. He broke off hard from the oblivious section. Rolling out on a heading of 120 degrees and pulling all the torque we had available we raced to rejoin our flight. Even as fast as we could go it would take 15 minutes to cover the distance. By then they could be anywhere.

I scanned the horizon off the nose. After several tense minutes I spotted them. There they were, three small pinpricks of heat against the cool night sky and we rejoined without incident. I was intensely grateful the ordeal was over.

The whole terrifying episode spanned only 20 minutes but it had felt like a lifetime. All my piss and vinegar were gone. I was...spent. Just plain worn out. I'd been so pumped up for a big fight but the alternating terror and boredom of this night had taken that out of me. I didn't care if we never got a chance to shoot at anyone and spent the whole war flying boring missions; I just didn't want to get separated again.

The phantom tanks never materialized and, carrying the now familiar feeling of another wasted mission, we returned to Astrodome FARP for gas. Enroute, Spock and Count ran into a bird. The little feathered kamikaze damaged one of their hydraulic systems and caused the heavily pressurized fluid to leak out. Astrodome was the nearest place to land so we just kept on course.

Sunrise was still over an hour away but the faintest hint of dawn lightened the horizon to the east. That was the best thing I'd seen in a long time. I couldn't wait for the sun to come up—it had been a long night.

Just before we shut down the DASC called. We had more work. Instead of the break I desperately wanted we kept turning, hot refueling to save time. Repeating the noxious concoction that had served me well so far, I stuffed another spoonful of instant coffee granules in my mouth to stave off mounting fatigue. Topping off my bitter caffeine snack with a fat wad of Copenhagen, I climbed back into my well-lived-in cockpit. I hoped that we'd knock this mission out quickly and go home: I was pretty wasted.

Leaving Spock and Count at the FARP with their broken aircraft, we launched toward the port city of Umm Qasr. I felt myself relax in the front seat, slumping lower as the comforting beat of the heavy rotor blades provided a soothing lullaby. Telling myself that we were still in Kuwaiti airspace and safe from ground fire, I indulged in a brief rest, my impossibly heavy eyelids closing without conscious effort. I let them go.

Just for a second I told myself, just rest your eyes for one sec...

The weight of my night vision goggles brought my face down

against the telescopic sight unit with startling force. The impact jarred me out of my millisecond of slumber rather rudely. Just then BT's voice came over the back radio.

"Flight, roll khaki charlie one."

"Two," Weasel responded, followed a second later by Gash. "Three."

Slowly I flipped through the long list of radio frequencies and their associated colors on my kneeboard. I found khaki and traced my finger over to the frequency. When I looked at them the numbers started to shuffle and re-arrange themselves like bugs in a cartoon.

What the fuck?

I flipped my goggles up and rubbed my eyes.

Okay, concentrate.

Starting over again I found the frequency and repeated the six digits silently in my head as my hand moved to punch the numbers into the radio. The numbers didn't stay with me though, they just squirted away like helium from an untied balloon. Confused, I stared at the radio blankly while trying to recall what I was doing.

Three times I tried to remember the numbers and transfer them from the frequency list to the radio controller.

Three times they dissipated into my foggy head and left my finger hovering over the keyboard, directionless.

"We up yet?" Gash's voice cut through my haze.

"Hmm? Naw, working on it," I replied, the insidious slide from slightly tired to worthless happening without my conscious knowledge.

"Come on man, get it in there," he responded testily. His tone sparked a flash of irritation that drove me to finally punch the last numbers into the radio.

BT was already talking to the ground unit when I finally switched frequencies, checking in and receiving our mission specifics. Somewhat belatedly I realized that I was tired—really tired—and that the coffee grounds and Copenhagen were no longer doing the trick.

It was time.

I reached into my shoulder pocket and pulled out a small baggie containing six little pills. I popped one back and washed it down with a swig of water.

Come on, work your magic.

Fifteen minutes later I was a new man. The Dexedrine tablet worked wonders, erasing my debilitating fatigue and leaving me gloriously alert. We had another 15 minutes to kill before the ground unit was going to start their assault. With new eyes I took the opportunity to watch the dawn unfold.

As I looked over the port city of Umm Qasr, my spirits were soaring. The heavy blanket of darkness lifted quickly as the sun approached the horizon and my fatigue became a thing of the past. I happily removed my night vision goggles and rubbed the sore spot where my helmet had been pressed into my skull by their weight. Under the effects of the amphetamines my mind was clear and alert for the first time in ages. I felt as though it were the first hour of flight instead of the thirteenth.

As the time approached for BT to shoot a TOW missile into the front door of the target building, we split the division. BT and Spock oriented on the large square building that dominated a city block as Weasel and I provided security to protect them from ground fire. After the difficulty of finding targets all night I was really looking forward to blowing something up that was easy to see. I watched the time carefully. Five minutes before the assault, the FAC came up on the radio.

Was he taking fire? A big fight developing? Here it comes...
My mind raced forward with anticipation.

"Go for Orkin," BT responded.

"Uhh, roger. Thanks for your help but we don't need you guys. We just took the building. You're cleared to RTB."

FUCK! Not again!?

BT's response was more measured than mine.

"Roger, give us a call if you need anything else."

We turned dejectedly toward the FARP, the cancelled mission the perfect capstone to a shitty night. We probably should have been happy that our assistance wasn't required—the lack of resistance faced by the grunts was a good thing—but we didn't see it that way at the time.

"Fuck this. You guys ready to go home?" BT asked.

"Two," Weasel responded, followed immediately by Gash.

"Three." There was no discussion. We were all ready to end this pain.

"Right. We'll swing through Astrodome, get gas and Spock, then head home." BT's plan met with universal agreement.

My little "go pill" was wearing off. Losing that boost deflated me almost as much as realizing the entire night had been a waste of time. I slumped in my seat. I didn't want to take another though, since we were only an hour or so away from finally going to sleep and I didn't want to have to take a sleeping pill to come back down. That just seemed like a bad idea. Stuffing another fat wad of Copenhagen in my tender lip I fought back the fatigue again.

Just stay awake long enough to get home, I told myself. Soon we landed at Astrodome.

I slipped out of the cockpit and shook my head at the sight that greeted me. In the bright sunlight our bird looked rough.

A thick coating of reddish, oily sand covered both sides of the fuselage and made it look like we were bleeding, which in effect we were. Like blood, you can only lose so much oil and hydraulic fluid before things don't work anymore and I was glad this mission was drawing to a close. It was time to give this bird back to Maintenance.

I climbed back into my seat as Spock and Count's blades started turning nearby. Plugging my helmet in, I heard BT contact the DASC for clearance to return to base. They answered immediately—but not with what I wanted to hear.

"Ah, negative Orkin flight. We have an immediate JTAR for you; advise when ready to copy."

BT knew we were all pretty much worthless at this time.

"Negative, we've been out all night and have a broken aircraft. Recommend you task another flight with this mission."

"Unable Orkin. You're the only flight available for tasking. Say intentions."

Well, that changes things a little bit.

Over the back radio BT polled us. "What do you say, guys? Up for another?"

"Gauges good?" I asked Gash. If we'd lost too much oil or hydraulic fluid then he'd be the first to know from his instruments in the back seat.

"Yup."

"I guess we're in then," I responded, reaching for my baggie of amphetamines.

Weasel and IKE probably had a similar conversation in their cockpit. Their delay was identical to ours before they answered BT.

"Two's up."

"Three's up."

Seconds later we were taking off. Three of us headed north

as the DASC relayed the sparse details of our mission while Spock and Count flew back to Ali Al Salem single ship.

I felt a mixture of envy and pity as their single helicopter disappeared to the south. Envy because they'd be asleep long before I would, pity because something in this mission felt different. I wondered if they'd dodged another bullshit mission or if they would miss out on something epic.

I'd know the answer soon enough.

CHAPTER 8

ONCE AIRBORNE, BT contacted the DASC for routing instructions and mission details. Their response fueled my hopes that this mission was going to be different.

"Roger Orkin 61, proceed direct Sierra. Contact Hawk on khaki. Say ETA?" The Marine in the DASC was crisp and efficient.

Fumbling through my stack of maps I searched for a control point named Sierra. I'd never even heard of it before. When I found it I thought that they'd made a mistake.

Are there even any friendly troops that far north?

"Roger. ETA 45 minutes," BT responded. Certainly they would realize they'd given us the wrong checkpoint—we were almost a hundred miles away.

Nope.

"Roger. Buster. Ground unit is in contact, with casualties." The energy was obvious in the Marine's voice—something big was happening.

I checked the grid for Sierra again, then looked for the nearest place we could get gas. The answer was not encouraging.

"BT, Shoe."

"Go Shoe," BT answered immediately.

"We've got enough gas for five, maybe ten minutes on-station up there, then we'll have to fly all the way back to Arlington to refuel."

BT paused before answering—probably checking my math.

"Shit. Well, we'll just head up there and see what's going on. If it's bullshit we'll come right home. If it's for real then we'll stay as long as we can then suck gas from an LAV or tank."

I knew that we could use the same type of fuel that the M1A2 Abrams tanks used—but I'd never tried refueling off one. I hoped it would work. If it didn't we might be in for a long walk.

Well, we'll see how this goes.

A reasonable man might have taken stock of what was going on and felt apprehension—I was feeling the tickle of excitement.

Sure we'd been flying for over fourteen hours, I'd crashed once, gotten lost, my bird was shaking like it was about to come apart, and the 20mm and laser were broken. But other than that, we were good to go.

We were down to three aircraft but that wasn't a big deal either—losing Spock and Count only cut our firepower by a quarter.

Oh, and there was the very real possibility that we would run out of gas while diving into a big fight we knew nothing about, and if we went down we'd be on our own.

Instead of chilling my eagerness, those challenges elevated the situation to something extraordinary, a rare set of circumstances that I felt lucky to have thrust upon me.

Is that all you got? Bring it, meat. Bring that weak shit to me.

It was a bright sunny morning and the amphetamines were

doing their job. Even reports of a deadly ZSU-23-4 operating near our objective were not enough to squash my building enthusiasm. All I could think about was how, out of all the aircraft in the Coalition, the only birds that could respond to this fight were our three tired Cobras. That made me feel pretty cool.

There was no answer to BT's first several attempts to raise Hawk, the air officer for Task Force Tarawa. When he answered on the fourth try his voice was stressed and quick.

"Roger Orkin, say ETA?" He didn't care what ordnance we were carrying or anything else. All Hawk cared about was how quickly we could get there.

Things must be really bad, I thought.

"15 minutes from Sierra. Say friendly enemy sit?" BT responded, asking for a situation update for all friendly and known enemy forces in the area. There was a pause on the net before Hawk's voice came back. When it did, the message sent a chill down my spine.

"When you hit Sierra just pick up Highway 7 and come north. I'm with the lead tanks on the outskirts of the city. Friendlies are on the road, enemy everywhere else. There was an ambush—we've got multiple casualties, 40 missing. Get here quick." Gunfire crackled in the background as he spoke.

"Holy shit," Gash said in a low voice. "Forty missing?"

The wheels in my head spun crazily. This is no bullshit mission—we were screaming into a full-on battle! Questions flashed through my mind.

What the hell is going on? Are there AAA guns? Tanks? MANPADS? Are we facing a platoon, a battalion, a regiment?

There was no way of knowing; we'd just have to jump in

and find out. I'd never ridden a horse but I sure felt like the cavalry right then, racing towards the sound of battle, everything else be damned.

Scanning my map again I looked for the nearest city north of Sierra. The bold letters jumped furiously in the vibrating cockpit: An Nasiriyah.

As we approached Highway 7 from the south, a line of dark bumps appeared on the horizon. Through my magnified sights the bumps became hundreds of friendly vehicles. They stretched to the north as far as I could see: giant seven-ton trucks loaded with grunts, tanks, light armored vehicles, amphibious vehicles, fuel trucks, Humvees, dragon-wagons...It dawned on me that whatever was going on up ahead was big enough to stop this huge force in its tracks.

What the fuck are we getting into?

The thought cut through my reckless enthusiasm in a flash, cleaving it to the bone and registering a millisecond of fear. As quick as it came it was gone, my frenzied eagerness rebounding to cover the slight twinge of nerves as if it had never existed.

On the horizon the desert scrub ran directly into a heavily industrialized area. The tall buildings, low warehouses and oil tanks on the outskirts of An Nasiriyah seemed to leap out of the dirt without warning. Halting our headlong rush we slowed down as the city came into view. If we could see the city, they could see us. That ZSU-23-4 could be hiding anywhere.

About a mile from the buildings we found the lead elements of Task Force Tarawa. The main battle tanks had pulled off either side of the road and small puffs of dirt kicked up quickly on the berms nearby. The little spurts of dirt popped up so rapidly I wasn't certain I'd actually seen them. Dust and dirt cleared out from underneath the tanks' .50 cal machine guns as they fired back. There was some serious shooting going on.

The situation on the radio was chaotic. Hawk was trying to answer BT's questions about where the enemy was located, but the incoming fire had driven him back into his tank for cover. He couldn't see anything. All he could tell us was that an army unit had been ambushed earlier this morning and that multiple attempts to reach the ambush site had met with heavy resistance. I could see a column of black smoke rising from two vehicles near an overpass between the tanks and the city.

Must be the ambush site.

Hawk was busy trying to coordinate another rescue attempt and told us to just keep coming until we passed his tank. His instructions were simple and to the point: Anything north of his tank and off the road was considered enemy—but to look out for the missing friendly troops.

A helmeted figure inside one of the tanks waved as we passed overhead and I noticed the orange air panel—it was Hawk. Pulling abeam Weasel and BT, we started hunting to the north, slowly closing with the first row of oil tanks and warehouses. Except for the missing troops, everything in front of us now was enemy.

There was absolutely nothing for us to hide behind. Years of sneaking around the steep canyons of Camp Pendleton had made us masters of using terrain to mask the sight and sound of our helicopters from the eyes and weapons of the enemy.

Fat lot of good that does us now.

Dry lakebeds offered more cover than this place. Our asses were hanging out for anyone with the inclination to take a shot at us.

The buildings made me really nervous—there were too many places for heavy antiaircraft weapons to hide. To stay hidden from big guns inside the city we had to stay low, but the ground beneath us was no picnic either. Shallow wadis and piles of trash could hide lots of nasty surprises. From our altitude of 25-50 feet, everything was a threat.

We took the less shitty option and stayed low. Our aircraft might be able to survive some 7.62mm, but even one 23mm round could take us apart. Small arms fire was a risk we had to absorb.

An old farmhouse lay directly in front of my bird. I searched it carefully with the optics as we approached, noting women and children peeking out from behind piles of rubble.

No threat. Next.

I shifted my scan a little deeper towards the city along the highway. My eyes lingered on the two burning vehicles whose smoke I'd seen earlier. The lead vehicle looked like a dragon-wagon but I couldn't tell what the second one was—it was too jacked up.

A seven-ton? Maybe a 'track?

It didn't really matter. Whatever it was it had been friendly and it didn't look like anyone had survived. Thick smoke billowed from the rapidly blackening hulks and their haphazard arrangement on the road seemed to indicate that they had been hit while moving. Hawk's words echoed in my head.

Ambush...40 missing ...

I looked hard at the area immediately surrounding the burning vehicles, hoping to see a group of US troops taking cover nearby.

Where are they? Maybe hiding behind the trucks?

Without knowing where they were I was afraid to shoot—I couldn't be sure my fire wouldn't hit the missing friendlies. My vantage point shifted as we moved and my hopes of a lucky sighting died. There was nothing behind the trucks, just empty, hard-packed sand. We continued around and soon I was able to see underneath the elevated bridge beyond the burning vehicles.

Oh yeah, there's my bitch.

A beautiful target unfolded before my eyes. A group of 15 to 20 men came running out of the darkness underneath the overpass, perfectly clumped together for a missile shot. The tanks couldn't see them because the high berms shielded them from view.

But I could.

I squeezed the action bar before conflicting commands stayed my hand.

Shoot a TOW, quick, before they get away!

No! The MIAs might be with them!

FUCK!

I watched helplessly as they scrambled toward the urban jungle. From their position on the battlefield there was no doubt that they had taken part in the ambush—and they were escaping! My rage bloomed and pushed its weak brother, impotent frustration, out of the nest—now I was pissed.

I was about to report their positions to BT when Gash rolled the aircraft hard right. I lost sight of where the escaping troops ducked into cover. For 30 seconds I frantically tried to get my sensors back on the area while he maneuvered to stay with Weasel and BT. When I finally did, it was too late. The enemy troops were gone.

The constant maneuvering to remain unpredictable was hampering our ability to understand the battlefield—we needed to get a handle on who was where before we started shooting. We re-set back toward Hawk's position and pulled into hover holds on the right side of his tank. Using the tanks as a starting point we began a methodical search of the terrain in front of us.

The small farm compound I had seen earlier was 50 meters in front of my aircraft. I searched it again for any threats. The mid-morning sun illuminated a bit of the interior of the biggest building and I spotted four children, several women in full hijab, and an old man crowding around the crumbling doorway. The old man shielded his eyes from the sun with one hand while waving at me with the other. I barely resisted the instinctive urge to wave back.

"Buildings look clear," I told Gash.

He moved us a bit closer to them as I shifted my scan further towards the city, the farm instantly forgotten. There were so many hiding places in front of me that anything not immediately identified as hostile simply ceased to exist.

Huh? That's a weird noise.

Perplexed, I heard vague snapping and popping sounds. They didn't seem to be coming from anywhere in particular, they were just there—all around. I scanned my limited instruments in the front seat and asked Gash.

"Do you hear that?"

It sounded like microwave popcorn two minutes in—the dull pops irregular and jumbled on top of each other.

"Yeah, I hear it. What the fuck?" he replied, sounding as confused as I was.

"I dunno dude, maybe compressor stalls?" I guessed, trying to be helpful. The popping continued.

"Yeah, but the gauges are good," he responded, his voice slow and considered as if pondering a philosophical question. If it had been compressor stalls then he would have seen indications in the Ng and MGT instruments. The gauges were normal.

I racked my brain for another likely cause, sluggishly flipping through piles of systems knowledge in search of an explanation.

BT's voice ripped through my ears.

"Shoebreakrighttakingfire!"

Gash rolled the bird almost 90 degrees right and pulled us hard to the south. In an instant I was looking down at the dusty ground, all thoughts of weird noises forgotten. The airspeed built painfully slowly and the snapping and popping chased us like angry bees as we moved away from the farmhouse.

Several Iraqi soldiers had been hiding with the family in the farmhouse and opened up on us after we had passed overhead. Luckily BT had spotted them and sounded the alarm. It slowly dawned on me that the mysterious snapping and popping had been bullets tearing the air around our cockpit. I thought I might react a little more intensely to almost getting shot—but I was just too damn tired.

Hmm, I thought, *it doesn't sound like that in the movies.*

The only reason BT and Weasel didn't immediately level the farmhouse was that they had heard me describe the women, children and old man inside. Our weapons are unsuited for the surgical work of killing Iraqi soldiers amidst non-combatants, so we held our fire. BT passed their location to Hawk and we moved out of range of their weapons.

We returned to the area where Hawk and his tanks were refueling, 400 meters to the southwest, and resumed our scan.

Within seconds of resetting near Hawk's tank I heard the now-obvious pop of rounds going past the canopy again. Hawk came up on the radio.

"You're taking fire!" he shouted, his warning making me sit up and look around quickly in search of our assailants. I saw Hawk standing in the cupola of his tank, close enough he could have hit me with a rock—underhand.

"From where?" BT responded, eager to engage. We're here to shoot. Fuck this getting shot at crap.

"FROM EVERYWHERE!" Hawk yelled, dropping into his tank and slamming the hatch closed. The rounds snapping around our birds were also pinging off his tank.

Without a word all three aircraft pulled southbound quickly and gained airspeed. This wasn't working—we had to try something different.

We crossed to the west side of the road. There was no way the missing troops had crossed the 400 meters of open ground to get there from the ambush site. If we could find enemy on the west side then we could engage without fear of hitting the missing troops. It was a welcome fresh start—the novelty of getting shot at had worn off quickly.

The terrain on the west side of the highway contained several features that could provide significant cover for ground troops. A large power plant stood half a mile west of the road, with substantial power lines connecting it to the city to the north. Beyond the power plant, muddy fields crisscrossed with ditches and berms lay in the middle ground leading up to a small village, itself still 500 meters from the industrial area that formed the edge of the city proper. A narrow jumble of one-story buildings intermixed with tall trees and bushes, the village appeared to be two or three houses deep and was about a half a mile wide. The west end of the village disappeared into a large grove of palm trees, and the eastern edge ended abruptly in a muddy field.

The power plant looked deserted so I began searching the broken terrain between it and the village. I spotted multiple holes in the ground—depressions three or four feet deep that could provide cover for a soldier or two from ground fire—but they were empty. The western edge of the fields looked clear as well, just a couple groups of people tending the crops.

Shifting toward the first row of buildings I took a quick look at the village. If there were AAA pieces hidden nearby, that's where I expected to find them. Through my daytime optics I noticed several sets of very tall power lines running east to west between us and the village.

Damn, that sucks.

They formed a fence from 15 feet off the ground to 200 feet in the air. If my TOW guidance wires came in contact with those high voltage lines the missile would get fried and go stupid. From this position I couldn't use my TOWs to engage anything inside the village or beyond—I was essentially unarmed.

Great—no gun, no laser, no TOWs. I get to just sit here and get shot at. Super.

While I scanned the western edges of the battle area BT and Weasel had located enemy positions in the central and eastern parts. Weasel called out a trench line with troops and multiple crew-served weapons. I slewed my sensors into his sector and spotted a berm of freshly piled dirt that ran the width of the muddy field near the village. Behind the berm moved what looked like very fast turtles—helmeted Iraqi troops. We could see them from our elevated vantage point but the tanks probably couldn't.

"Got em," I told Gash.

"That's good, cuz I can't see a God Damned thing from back here." The pause between the syllables of his curse betrayed his frustration—Gash didn't have the benefit of magnified sights to look through.

In fact, the thick layer of bug guts and accumulated grime on our canopy meant that he couldn't see anything to our front. I knew I should describe the enemy positions so he knew what was going on...but I just couldn't. I wasn't falling asleep tired—I just didn't have the energy to formulate a cohesive thought and transmit it. Every time I tried, the thoughts drifted away.

I quit trying.

My eyes adjusted to the new scene and I saw several rows of trench lines in the field. Men scuttled inside them bent low at the waist. Sometimes their helmets were visible and small puffs of dirt erupted in the bright sunlight nearby.

Are they firing at us or are those impacts from the tanks?

I couldn't tell but it didn't matter. BT had just gotten clearance to engage and directed Weasel to start taking them out.

An unwanted sight popped up out of the brown dirt, one small white flag amid a trench line full of troops. It waved quickly then dropped from view.

Shit, not this again, I thought.

We'd learned our lesson from the last time though. Honoring the questionable surrender we did not target the small position that had waved the flag. The ones around it were not so lucky.

Weasel placed a Hellfire into a 14.5mm machine gun nest that was nearby. The explosion drove 10-12 men out of their separate fighting positions to gather unwisely in a larger one.

Their bodies cartwheeled through the air as Weasel put another
Hellfire into their midst. I sat dumbly, watching the battle unfold
in front of me without being able to take part. I only had four
TOWs and worried that there were tanks or AAA pieces that I
would need the missiles for later. Angrily, I held my fire—what
I wouldn't have given for a cannon that worked!

After the impact of Weasel's second missile, the remaining
troops in the trench lines broke from cover and ran for the
village. Their frantic motion drew our attention and the noses
of our three Cobras shifted in unison. In seconds the soldiers
would melt away inside the town.

For most of them that was far too long.

The radio was clobbered with calls as Weasel and BT worked
the group of exposed soldiers over with their 20mm cannons
and Gash emptied most of our high-explosive rockets into them.
Many were cut down by our fire or fire from the tanks, but
several groups did make it to the edge of town.

I watched five or six of them approach a building and
realized that they were steps from safety. The hesitation and
uncomfortable thoughts I'd experienced two days ago belonged
to a different person. My frustration had fermented as the fight
unfolded in front of me. Now it exploded into cold rage.

Fuck this. They're not getting away.

Without a word to Gash I mashed the action bar on my left
hand grip. The ATTK and RDY flags flashed for a second and I
crushed the trigger to the stop.

The men had reached the first building but that didn't matter—I saw which door they went into.

The missile ignited with a satisfying roar and flew toward
the building, making small corrections to follow my line of
sight. I held my breath and kept the crosshairs glued to the

doorway, willing the dot that was my missile to continue flying straight and true.

Fifty feet from the door the missile clipped the power lines. Like a baseball bat thrown overhand it flipped end over end toward the first row of buildings. The missile detonated with the warhead pointing up, its cylindrical body transforming into a long grey needle in a millisecond. The building was unscathed but several sets of power lines fell where the missile had cut through. Their sweeping collapse generated an opportunity that flashed in my fuzzy brain.

Wires are down—shoot through the hole.

Without a second thought I mashed the trigger again. The missile came out of the tube just as Gash started to turn away—I hadn't warned him I was shooting. The missile lost guidance and detonated in the dirt about a quarter-mile in front of us.

"Goddamn it!" I shouted. The fact I was screwing up slapped me in the face like a dead fish. Gash's voice sounded loud and pissed in my helmet.

"What the fuck, dude?"

"Fucking stupid fucking missile went stupid. Gimme in constraints!" I shouted, mad at the escaping Iraqis, mad at myself for wasting missiles...and mad that I couldn't seem to articulate what was going on. I knew what I wanted to do and what needed to happen so I could do it—but the information was trapped in my head.

Luckily, Gash understood caveman speak.

He rolled back toward the building and, expecting me to fire this time, kept the aircraft within pre- and post-launch constraints. I slewed my sights back onto the door the men had run into, watching as two more men approached it from the left and two donkeys from the right. I really hoped the donkeys would keep running.

As soon as the missile launched I knew it was going stupid. Instead of the normal looping trajectory, this TOW streaked across my line of sight and continued off into the mud beyond. It never captured.

"Fuck. Firing," I warned Gash, mashing the trigger again.

"Roger."

The fourth and final missile leapt off our wing. It looked good, spiraling around the crosshairs in my sights as the missile tracked properly toward the now closed door. With relief I noted the donkeys as they trotted out of my field of view, heads up and ears erect.

In a sickening replay of my first shot the missile hit another set of power lines. As it flipped out of control I mentally threw my hands up in frustration and sat back against my seat, deflated.

First the guys escaping from under the bridge, now these guys escaping into the village—I was batting a thousand today.

Great job, dickhead.

These soldiers weren't standing around waiting for their tea to boil—some of these guys had killed Americans and tried to kill me. I wasn't prepping to sucker-punch some weakling; there were no nervous questions diverting my lethal energy this time.

This was a real fight. I was *really* trying to kill them—*and fucking it up!* That I couldn't seem to close the deal made me feel worthless.

Weasel's voice on the radio snapped me out of my little pity party. The battle was not over.

"Shoe, Weasel."

"Go."

"Buddy-lase on the machine gun nest, 355."

"Roger, standby," I replied. Weasel knew my laser was

broken, but I could shoot my Hellfire missiles at his laser spot. Quickly I flipped the switches to make it happen.

The heavy machine gun position that we had seen earlier still posed a threat. The nearest Iraqi soldiers were in a shallow ditch 30 feet behind the weapon. We left them alone—their lives were protected by a small white rag they held aloft at random intervals. If one of them changed his mind, though, the weapon could place devastating fire on the highway, not to mention knock us out of the sky. Weasel decided to discourage that idea.

Gash moved us a little in front of Weasel's aircraft off his left side and picked up a heading of 355 degrees.

"Laser on," I requested.

"Laser's on," Weasel responded immediately.

The symbols on the display in my cockpit indicated that the missile was receiving the reflected laser energy. I flipped up the flat piece of plastic that covered the firing button and pressed down hard. The roar of the missile provided instant gratification.

Less than four seconds later the position erupted in a cloud of smoke and dirt. When the smoke drifted a couple of feet east it looked like the weapon might remain operational—the missile had hit the protective berm.

Repeating the sequence I fired another missile in concert with Weasel. The missile roared off the rail and I waited anxiously for it to slam into the target. Too many seconds went by.

"Where'd it go?" I asked Gash.

Looking through the sights I could only see the area immediately surrounding the target. It was obvious the missile hadn't gone there.

"Dunno, looked like it lost the spot and went ballistic," he replied slowly, sounding almost bored. For a split second I wondered why, then remembered—he couldn't see any of the details of the fight.

BT took the machine gun out with a TOW as our lack of missiles relegated us to the role of cheerleaders. We had five rockets left and Gash owned them from the backseat. I kept looking for new threats, but there wasn't a whole lot I could do about any I found.

Weasel and BT continued to engage targets close to the road while I scanned to the west. There were no friendly troops in that direction and the trees and buildings offered lots of cover and concealment for a large enemy force. I had nothing left to shoot but could at least point out hidden threats to Weasel and BT.

Low on gas and almost out of ordnance our aircraft was really light. I asked Gash to elevate slightly—25 or 50 feet higher—to allow me to look behind the palms in the small village. He pulled some power and I searched the newly exposed terrain as we climbed.

A wide-open flat patch of sand met my eyes and an oddly shaped dark spot drew my attention. I flipped to high magnification to check it out.

"Shit! *Downdowndowndown*!" I shouted to Gash, damning the momentum that continued carrying us higher. The collective dropped as Gash tried to bring us back down but it was happening slowly, way too slowly. Each passing second was an eternity.

At first glance the squat outline hadn't looked immediately familiar to me—the wheels were folded flat to form a stable firing platform. When I saw the twin 23mm barrels pointing at us though, it got clear real quick.

As we dropped behind the trees I noticed another ZU-23, about 200 meters from the first. It was also fully deployed and pointing at us.

Why aren't they firing? I wondered.

The answer registered in my tired brain just as the lethal antiaircraft guns disappeared from sight behind the trees. I couldn't tell for certain but it looked like they were unoccupied. That would explain why we were still alive

What else was out there that I hadn't seen?

Shit! Concentrate!

I snapped back into the moment and told BT and Weasel about the AAA threats. BT triaged the threats facing our flight and told me to report if anybody moved towards the AAA guns—he knew I was basically out of ammo. They were both busy engaging targets near the road but would shift if any troops approached the ZU-23s.

Ignoring the uncomfortable realization that we were sitting ducks I continued searching: village, grove, ZU-23s, city, village, grove, ZU-23s, city...Early detection of a threat was the only protection Gash and I had.

I was relieved when BT and Weasel both called 'Winchester' a couple minutes later. With all of us out of ammo and low on gas, we disengaged quickly and headed out of mortar range of the city. It sucked to leave Hawk and his boys with no air cover, but there was nothing else we could do. We were going to be out of gas in a matter of minutes and had no idea where we might get more. The tanks we were planning on refueling from were in the middle of a firefight—not the best time for us to come begging for fuel.

The nearest FARP was over an hour away, and we had maybe 15 minutes of gas. With no real confidence that it would work, we started looking for a fuel truck in the convoy. We'd have to land close to the road and hope that a hose could reach us—and that the fuel was the right type.

BT told the DASC what we were doing and reiterated the need for more air support. They responded that the nearest gunships were still several hours away but they were sending some fixed wing sooner.

Earlier I'd been excited that we were the only birds that could provide support. But that was almost two hours ago—where was everybody?

Are we the only goddamn division flying?

They did have some good news though—Riverfront FARP had just opened nearby. The grid the DASC passed was only a couple miles down the road and we flew directly toward it. With fuel and ordnance close at hand we could get back in the fight in minutes—Task Force Tarawa wouldn't be without air support for long. Knowing that every second counted we raced for the FARP, dropping onto the landing spots without a wasted motion.

As soon as our skids touched the hastily staked fabric of the landing area, Gash and I blasted through the de-arm checklist. I saw no one nearby so I hopped out and de-armed the aircraft myself. Moments before I'd felt like we were leaving Hawk with his ass hanging out—no air cover at all—but that had all changed. Now we could reload and be back in the fight in minutes. Crazed energy flooded my body.

Where are the ordies? Fuelers? Where is everybody?

I looked around frantically for the fuel and ordnance trucks, the emptiness around me confusing my addled brain. Then I spotted them driving toward our aircraft from the convoy on the highway and it dawned on me—the FARP wasn't set up yet.

Fuck!

Two endless minutes later the trucks stopped and tired
Marines jumped out. They looked surprised to see three Cobras
waiting for them. I didn't care if they were tired, surprised or
anything else—I just wanted fuel and ordnance five minutes ago.

I shouted over the rotor noise and nearby explosions for
them to reload our aircraft. My pleas fell on deaf ears. The
Gunny in charge of ordnance operations refused to budge
on basic safety precautions. Until the grounding stakes were
pounded in and their resistance checked, he wouldn't reload our
aircraft. Even my explanation of the situation unfolding just
north of us held no sway.

*You stupid motherfucker! Don't you get it? Marines are
dying!*

I felt my anger rising dangerously.

The crazy idea of pulling out my pistol registered for a
second—but then what would I do? Instead I pushed past him
and grabbed a rocket off the trailer.

Fuck you. I'll do it myself.

Ignoring his surprised shout I carried my high-explosive
prize back to my bird. Stuffing it in my rocket pod I was thankful that I'd done it many times in training and remembered
to remove the tape that held the fins closed. It's one thing to
throw a righteous temper tantrum—totally another to look like
a douche while doing it.

I turned to run back and get another one and spun like a
fullback. Marines with rockets in their arms were barreling
toward me and had no intention of stopping. My anger abated
immediately.

I fucking love these guys!

Admiration and a deep sense of belonging swept aside my
impetuous rage—everything right in the world again.

Knowing they could reload us safer and faster than I could, I got out of their way. A fuel truck pulled up and I motioned for them to bring the hose and start fueling us. As I watched the two Marines attach the fuel hose something caught my eye—something strangely out of place amid the grime that coated my leaking aircraft.

Underneath the aft avionics compartment were two jagged holes, a little bigger than dimes in diameter and about two inches apart.

Could that be...?

The thought hung unfinished as I opened the closest panel and peered inside, finding the two holes quickly by the light they let in.

Incredulously I followed the path of the bullets as best I could and located two ragged exit holes on the opposite side of the aircraft. It appeared as if the rounds had traversed the compartment without hitting a single component within and, other than providing a little extra ventilation, had no negative impact on the aircraft. Smiling broadly I climbed up on the skids and stuck my head into Gash's cockpit.

"We got shot!" I shouted, barely able to be heard over the din surrounding us. I saw his eyes dart quickly around the instrument panel for any damage indications. Finding none a big smile flashed underneath his bushy mustache.

"Two rounds in the aft avionics compartment, in and out, no damage," I continued.

His smile broadened and he nodded his head in comprehension. Getting some bullet holes in our aircraft seemed really cool and I felt weirdly elated.

I saw Weasel climbing out of his cockpit and ran across to update him on my status. Fuse was also hopping out of BT's aircraft and motioned for Weasel and me to join him. We followed him about a hundred feet from our turning aircraft and peeled our helmets off so we could talk. The delay in getting airborne made me antsy and annoyed but I held my tongue— Fuse obviously had something he wanted to say. Weasel and I watched impatiently as he scratched out a hasty terrain model in the sand.

A minute later he launched into the best debrief I've ever been a part of. While our birds were reloaded and refueled Fuse highlighted everything that we'd done wrong, congratulated us on everything we'd done right, and outlined a solid plan for the coming fight. His calm demeanor, clear directions and brutal honesty ripped through my fuzzy head like a buzz saw and grounded my frenetic urge to just get airborne. Armed with a simple plan we shook hands and broke for our birds. The entire debrief took no more than four minutes but it would pay huge dividends.

Airborne again and flying toward the columns of smoke I felt another brief flicker of fear. A second of inactivity in the cockpit gave rise to a question that entered my mind unbidden.

How much luck do we still have?

The obvious answer held uncomfortable ramifications. I stuffed it away quickly and berated myself for getting distracted. I took another go pill, figuring that such thoughts meant I was getting tired again, and forced myself to concentrate.

When we checked back on-station we were still the only air in town. Hawk filled us in on what had happened during our absence. We found that the situation on the ground hadn't changed—but we had.

The hectic energy that diluted our efforts during the last on-station time was gone. Instead of three individual birds lashing out at targets of opportunity, we began to operate like we should—like a team.

Weasel and BT began their hunt deep, slowing to 40 knots and searching side by side from an altitude of 400 feet. The elevation allowed them to see over dirt piles and behind walls, but left them exposed to fire from everyone in the area. Gash and I stayed low behind them, tearing around like a terrier worrying a rat in a woodpile. Anybody who wanted to engage the two high birds would run the risk of getting spotted by us. We gambled that they would prefer to remain hidden—they wouldn't know that our 20mm was broken.

I checked the AAA pieces that I knew were out there first, looking them over to ensure that no soldiers had manned them while we were gone. Finding them empty I searched deeper into the palm grove and located several Zil trucks. I noted their presence and continued searching—a couple of Zil trucks weren't going to kill me. I kept looking for things that would.

With Gash and me covering their backs, BT and Weasel coldly dissected the enemy defenses in front of us. Methodically, they moved from position to position leaving smoldering destruction in their wake. Most of the fighting positions simply burped a cloud of dirt and bodies when the missiles hit, but not all. Bright orange flames gave birth to thick black smoke from two dead T-55 tanks. They'd been well hidden near the road but BT and Weasel had sniffed them out.

BT located a third Iraqi tank near the other two and destroyed it with a Hellfire. A lull descended over the radio and I took the opportunity to report the location of the Zil trucks. Unable to see them from his position, BT asked us to attack with rockets. He and Weasel would dive in and shoot where we shot.

Gash maneuvered to attack. Staying below the trees he gained airspeed while flying parallel to the palm grove, pulled up aggressively and rolled 90 degrees to the right. As he sliced the nose of the aircraft down towards the trucks he snapped us back to wings level—letting loose with high-explosive rockets as soon as the sights steadied.

I watched the geometry of the rockets as they launched off our wing. Hot exhaust gases provided just enough indication of where the speeding projectiles were located to allow me to predict where they would impact. Over the roar of the rocket motors I called corrections to Gash.

"Left left left down down down!"

I don't know if he heard me or not but it didn't matter. Debris flew crazily in all directions as his rockets kept finding their marks. Angry grey puffs and geysers of dirt erupted all around the trucks, shredding them with steel fragments. Several suffered direct hits.

Weasel and BT easily spotted the explosions of Gash's rockets and rolled in, each sending a stream of rockets into the area. To cover their attack Gash threw a couple of rockets toward the two ZU-23s in the open field—just in case. They didn't appear to be manned but you never know.

With potential threats neutralized in the palm grove we turned our attention beyond it to the ZU-23s. Elevating over the tall power lines, Gash held our aircraft steady while I put a TOW missile into each antiaircraft gun. BT destroyed a third that I hadn't seen. Seamlessly, Weasel and IKE picked up local security while we focused on the deep targets. We were flowing now, smooth, deliberate.

Several F-18s showed up on-station just as we were running low on ordnance again. As soon as BT briefed them on the known friendly and enemy locations we started heading back to Riverfront to reload. We checked off-station with Hawk.

He cleared us back to the FARP and, almost as an aside, informed us we were taking fire. Equally unimpressed, BT rogered up. We'd been getting shot at pretty steadily for the last three hours. Overexposure had robbed the experience of its ability to excite.

The scene that greeted my eyes at the FARP was a welcome one. Four Cobras were turning on the landing pads and I could see at least two other groups of helicopters orbiting while they waited for their turn. It was obvious that Hawk had plenty of help now.

We bypassed the busy FARP and headed for home. The fresh aircraft and aircrews could do more than we could at this point. I felt no regret at leaving—we'd done all we could. Physically I was numb—seventeen hours of incessant vibrations and constant stress had shut down much of my body's ability to feel.

My mind wasn't numb though, far from it.

The feeling of being a target in somebody's sights evaporated as we flew away. A huge weight I didn't know existed was lifted off my back and I felt almost dizzy with relief.

We ripped down the convoy, our blades just clearing the tops of the motionless vehicles off to our left. The Marines in the trucks were waving, cheering and snapping pictures as we tore past them. Howling like lunatics Gash and I cut back and forth above them as the tension of the battle released. In its place flowed elation, pure and intoxicating in its intensity.

We'd made it—we were in the club.

We'd stood our ground in the face of enemy fire. We'd provided support to our ground brothers when they needed it most—hell, we'd even taken battle damage while doing it. We'd undergone our baptism by fire and had lived up to the hallowed reputation of the Marine Corps. This wasn't a group of buildings sitting alone in the desert. This had been a battle—a two-way shooting match and we'd held our own. If I could have bottled what I was feeling, I'd be a billionaire.

"Fuck yeah! Fuck yeah! ..." I shouted, over and over again, each burst louder than the last. Finally the wave of euphoria crashed over my head and left me wild-eyed and panting, spent.

We reached the end of the convoy and split off from the highway. There was nothing between me and home but miles and miles of open desert. Within a couple minutes the monotony of the khaki landscape lulled me into a comfortable trance. Without warning, my adrenaline slipped away.

I fell off a cliff. One second I was euphoric, the next profoundly drained. We still had over an hour of flying ahead of us—this was not good.

Taking off my flight glove I slapped myself hard across the face to wake up. The sting was welcome, but I knew it wasn't enough.

My cheek was still warm when my eyelids grew impossibly heavy again. I pinched some nose hairs and pulled hard. Tears came in response but the pain dissipated too quickly.

This wasn't working.

How many pills do I have left? I'd lost count of how many go pills I'd taken.

Please let me have one left, just one more to get home.

I focused my fuzzy eyes on the little baggie from my pocket and smiled—two little pills remained.

It was 1330 on March 23rd when we landed in Kuwait. We'd been airborne for 19 of the last 21 hours. I lingered in the silent cockpit after the blades stopped turning, kind of puzzled. My body trembled with vibrations that were no longer there and I had to double-check that we'd actually shut down. The gauges didn't lie—the formerly living beast was motionless now, its engines quietly ticking as they cooled down. As my nerves quivered I envied the machine's ability to turn off, to just stop.

I walked off the flightline with Gash, neither of us saying a word as we completed our post-flight duties. The events of the last day were all jumbled together in my head: the long frustrating night, embarrassment at my stupid mistakes, and just when it looked like it was over—a big fight. I didn't care to untangle them though, just stuffed them in a box and pushed them aside.

What's done is done. The only thing that mattered now was the next mission.

Although exhausted, I couldn't sleep yet. Even after debriefing and filling out paperwork I knew that trying to sleep would be a waste of time. Figuring that the amphetamines were almost out of my system, I went to check email. Maybe after that I'd be able to sleep.

A long list of messages filled my inbox. Notes from my parents, relatives, brother and sister, Lena, friends…The sheer number was amazing. I read each one quickly, devouring the words of encouragement and support like an addict hitting the pipe. Memories of my loved ones from another world sliced through the dirty, gritty exhaustion in my head like a laser beam.

Powerful emotions welled impossibly fast. One second I was reading a letter from my aunt, the next my eyes swam with tears. My shoulders jumped crazily as I fought back sobs that came out of nowhere.

What the fuck?

An instant later it was over. I surreptitiously wiped my eyes on my shoulders as if removing sand and looked around guiltily. Had anyone noticed?

With relief I realized the tent was empty—nobody had seen me puss out. I rebuilt my mental walls quickly and logged off the computer. By force of will I corralled the escaped emotions and stuffed them back behind the wall, angry at myself for letting them out.

It had been easy to ignore them in the aircraft. The quiet was another matter.

CHAPTER 9

ACCORDING TO THE SCHEDULE, our division had two days off to recover from our marathon flight. I intended to make the best of it. After ten full hours of sleep I awoke slowly, staring at the dark green tent above my aluminum cot and planning my day: eat, sleep, go for a run, read a book...Other than rest, there was nothing I needed to do to prepare for the next mission yet. I refused to even acknowledge its existence.

It will come when it comes. For now, relax.

There were slight stirrings in the big tent as the other guys eased awake. I sat up and tried to knock the cobwebs out of my head, feeling the mental slowness of a hangover but without the splitting headache or cat-shit mouth. Gash, Weasel and IKE were sitting up too, their faces bemused and confused. The last time I had seen that look we were recovering from an all-night bender in Guam. The lovely bar staff at Pu's Place had tried to kill us with gin and vodka but we'd survived—barely.

The morning took on the atmosphere of a lazy Sunday back at home. With nothing pressing to do, we lingered over cold eggs and rubbery bacon, drinking endless cups of bitter coffee while the chow tent workers prepared to serve lunch. Eventually we headed over to the flightline to find out what was going on. Not knowing what was happening was nice, but only to a point.

As we walked toward the shuttle bus stop I noticed a bathroom trailer and made a beeline for it. The opportunity to crap in a real toilet was too good to pass up, and I told the guys not to wait for me.

It felt weird to be walking alone. I couldn't remember the last time I'd gone somewhere without at least one other member of the division and the crunch of my boots in the shifting gravel sounded thinner than usual. I passed a newly painted plywood sign nailed to a 2x4 in front of a tent, only the small steeple on top giving it away as the base chapel. Something made me stop.

Backing up I looked at the sign again, noting the hours that the chapel was open for business before going about my business. I'm not a church-going guy, although I was raised in that fashion, but for some reason the chapel's hours blazed white in my brain. I couldn't forget them if I'd tried.

I met up with the rest of the guys in the ready-room tent a half hour later, all thoughts of the chapel and my weird little stop forgotten. The atmosphere in the sandy-floored tent was comfortably quiet: IKE and Weasel were playing a game of acey-deucey, Count was reading a book, and Gash was bullshitting with Smitty, a buddy of ours from another division, in the corner. I pulled a couple of folding chairs close together so I could put my feet up and settled in to read my book, content, happy, relaxed.

Five minutes later BT entered the tent with an old friend in tow, JoJo. It had been a while since we'd seen JoJo and we greeted him with loud insults about his current status as a staff pogue, then fell silent. From the look on BT's face we knew something had changed—and not for the better.

"Hey, get your stuff. We got a mission." BT kicked our lei-surely morning right in the balls.

"What the fuck? We just got back. Why don't some of these other motherfuckers take it?" Gash replied quickly, tossing his head to indicate our other squadron mates scattered about the ready room.

Almost everything and everyone gets called 'motherfucker' by Gash at some point. Nobody took any offense.

Ignoring him, BT continued.

"JoJo is going to fly with Spock, Count you get to sit this one out. We're escorting some phrogs and brief at HMM-268 in half an hour."

Although JoJo was currently suffering through a staff tour, he had combat experience from Afghanistan. On top of his tac-tical skills, his easy-going demeanor made him one of the most universally well-liked Cobra pilots in the Marine Corps. Count was pissed at getting bumped off the flight but he didn't argue with BT's decision. He knew JoJo deserved a chance to get out and have some fun.

Grumbling, we got to our feet and collected our stuff. The relaxed mood evaporated as we began preparing for the flight. I sat jammed in the back of the bouncing SUV that BT had appropriated from somewhere, sullen and quiet.

The serenity of the morning had been irretrievably destroyed and replaced by something else—*Anger? Fear?* I didn't know. All I knew was that I had been happy and now I wasn't.

My mood didn't improve any during the briefing. The two CH-46s we were to escort had orders to fly ammunition up to a road intersection right in the middle of An Nasiriyah. I caught Gash's eye and saw my thoughts reflected there.

Great. Back into fucking An Nas.

From the intelligence reports, things had not quieted down there in the day since we'd left. Reports of air burst artillery, MANPADs and thick AAA fire near where the 46s needed to land were not encouraging. As if that wasn't enough good news, the weather was forecast to turn to shit.

A storm with high winds and significant rainfall was expected to hit Kuwait within the next five or six hours—just about the time we were to take off. If it had been peacetime a forecast like that would have already cancelled the mission. But it wasn't peacetime.

At least it should be a short mission. I tried to find the silver lining.

The SUV was quiet as we drove back to our squadron. There was no more joking or bitching about missing out on our rest— it just wasn't funny anymore. After loading our equipment into our birds and making sure they were ready to go we conducted our final preparation as a group—the flight brief. With that complete we split up, each of us withdrawing to prepare individually for what was to come.

I went to the flightline crew rest tent to try and get some sleep. Surprised to find it empty I unrolled my sleeping bag and climbed inside, knowing that the best thing I could do to prepare myself would be to simply fall asleep.

If only it were that easy.

Instead of restorative slumber, my mind spewed nightmare scenarios of the coming flight—each one terrifyingly realistic and plausible. Usually my worst-case fears developed slowly, building like an afternoon thunderstorm I could see from miles away.

These were different.

These fears were already fully articulated when they bloomed—

tornadoes instead of puffy clouds. They did not offer the courtesy of dwell time before reaching their frightful conclusions. I had no defense other than forcibly ignoring them—and that was not working. They were hitting too fast.

I lay transfixed as images flashed behind my quivering eyes: Gash and I shot down and having to decide between capture or suicide; Gash getting shot in the back seat and having to listen to him die slowly, powerless to help; getting shot myself and feeling my insides go cold as my blood ran onto the worn floorboards of the cockpit; a second of clarity on the jumping sights showing me that what I'd thought was a soldier was actually a woman and her kids—the instant before my missile impacts...

Fuck this.

I didn't need sleep that bad. I got up and wandered around the squadron until it was time to launch. I was still in a foul mood but at least the physical activity kept my mind from running amok.

Gash started running through the checklist in the back seat as I strapped in. The darkness of the moonless night freed me from any personal interaction with the plane captain standing nearby. Normally I enjoyed a little chitchat while going about my duties but not tonight—I was so wound up I didn't trust myself to speak. Part of the harness got caught behind my armored seat. I pulled at it in a sudden fury.

"Motherfucking piece of shit—let go mother*fucker*!" I railed as the stubborn webbing refused to budge.

I'd successfully overcome this exact issue every time I'd ever climbed in the front seat but this time it kicked my ass. With an exaggerated jerk the webbing slipped free. I buckled my harness still mumbling expletives under my breath. Gash had seen and heard my uncharacteristic explosion but remained silent. There was nothing to say.

I sat fuming in the darkened cockpit. Irritation and discontent oozed out of every pore in my body. I cursed the entirety of the universe—for what I don't know—but it was to blame for something. While I stewed, Gash got the bird running.

As the large blades began to move the strangest thing happened—the blackness that had been dominating my thoughts suddenly lifted.

Each sweep of the blades wiped a little of my anger and irritation away like an eraser on a blackboard. The vibrations of the aircraft as it came alive loosened my tenseness and I nestled into my seat, releasing myself into the bird's rhythmic motions.

By the time both engines were running, my mind was clear. I didn't have to imagine what might happen anymore—it was happening. All my worries were gone now, an annoying fly I brushed away to focus on my duties in the front seat. The reassuring sights and sounds of the aircraft induced a beautiful amnesia for anything outside my immediate surroundings—nothing else mattered. When we lifted off into the night sky, I was ready.

Two hours later we arrived at Riverfront FARP. The ammo for the CH-46s was nowhere to be seen. We parked on the refueling spots and kept turning while the 46s flew to the other side of the airfield to look for it.

We weren't far from An Nasiriyah and I scanned the horizon in its direction. If there was significant fighting then I should see the flashes on my night vision goggles. Surprisingly, everything looked calm. The uniform green color of the horizon held no ominous signs. I even noticed the bazillions of stars that looked close enough to touch.

Maybe nothing's going on up there. Maybe we can sneak in and out with no fuss.

A long stream of tracers ripped across the sky.

Shit.

The first burst seemed to wake everybody up. Soon the horizon was littered with glowing balls of fire as antiaircraft weapons of every caliber loosed their projectiles skyward.

Oh, this is going to suck.

We waited for the 46s for an hour, watching the instruments of our destruction demonstrate their prowess against the night sky. My mind flipped back and forth between equally fervent desires to just get it done, or for the 46s to break down so none of us had to go. By the time the DASC called us I didn't care which direction it went—I just wanted to get it over with.

"Costa 03, Sky Chief, state location."

"Costa 03 and flight, on deck at Riverfront," BT answered.

"Roger, have an immediate JTAR for you. Advise when ready to copy."

"Ready to copy. Be advised we are waiting for Judson 46 to pick up ammo for a re-supply mission. We're their escort."

"Negative Costa 03, this mission takes priority. We'll try to get other assets to escort Judson."

I was relieved to be stripped away from the 46s but wasn't celebrating yet—we could be jumping out of the frying pan and into the fire.

My mood brightened considerably as Sky Chief ordered us past An Nasiriyah and up Highway 7. Regimental Combat Team 1's (RCT-1) lead tanks had stopped for the night and had been taking fire from a small village. They wanted gunships overhead when dawn broke—anticipating that the Iraqis would attack at first light.

All right—this is more like it!

Dawn broke quickly and I removed my NVGs. The light of the morning was weirdly muted but I didn't think much of it. I was just happy to take the damn goggles off.

As soon as we got on-station the FAC began talking BT's eyes onto a small, nondescript mud hut where the sniper fire had originated. There were at least 20 small mud huts clustered together, one-story hovels similar in size and shape to each other. I couldn't tell which one held the snipers. After an extensive talk-on, BT said that he had the building in sight and the FAC cleared him hot. I brought my head out of the bucket to watch his missile strike.

The TOW missile leaped off his wing and smashed into a hut in the middle of the village. Good thing I was watching—the collapsing hut swallowed the bright flash instantly. The dust from the explosion mingled with the normal dust that covered everything—two seconds later you couldn't tell anything had happened.

"Great shot! Shoot the house next to it!" the FAC yelled, his voice flush with excitement.

BT dropped that hut with another TOW. The FAC must have seen activity we could not because he cleared our entire flight for rockets and guns against the remaining huts. This was what we'd been waiting for.

We'd done attacks like this at the urban training range hundreds of times—if anything, these huts were easier to see than the steel shipping containers we usually shot at. We weaved and danced through the attack in silent concert, flowing effortlessly like a pack of wolves on a caribou calf.

BT and Spock pulled off target as we rolled in to engage. Gash offset 45 degrees and gained separation as Weasel and IKE began firing. Pulling the nose up hard, Gash launched us a hundred feet up, rolled left and sliced the nose down towards the village. Just as Weasel pulled off target, Gash opened up.

Gash let loose with a burst of 20mm from the fixed forward position—finally, we had a gun that worked. The red tracers streaked just past Weasel's turning aircraft and gave the enemy no time to react against his vulnerable underside. Our deadly ballet was beautifully efficient.

As Weasel and IKE moved further away, Gash walked the rudder pedals slightly left and right, spreading the exploding projectiles along the long axis of the town. The solid hammering of the big cannon was music to my ears, the steady spacing of the explosions telling me that the gun was firing cleanly and not in danger of jamming. Bright white flashes sparkled among the brown huts as our rounds exploded.

At 1500 meters Gash fired five high-explosive rockets in quick succession. The loud 'whoosh' of each individual rocket motor blended into one continuous roar off the right side of the aircraft. The thick cloud of dust rising from the target area obscured the details as our rockets struck home. Closing to within a thousand meters, Gash fired two flechette rockets and pulled hard left to get away, the 4400 steel nails covering our pull.

We rejoined the rest of the flight over an empty area and waited for more work. I watched as the grunts, using our attack as cover, crossed the wide-open field and swept through the crumbled buildings. They cleared the small town quickly, taking 20 soldiers who'd survived our attack prisoner.

The attack had been textbook perfect. The enemy never had

the opportunity to return fire—as far as we could tell. We'd covered each other seamlessly the entire time and I felt good, like we were finally clicking. Add a kick-ass soundtrack and I was living a Hollywood movie.

I knew that there were real people on the receiving end—but it didn't really register. Mud huts, steel conex boxes, plywood targets...they were all the same. Just things to shoot at. The fact that we were doing it in combat just made it more exciting than training.

Now this is what it's supposed to be like!

High on success, but low on fuel and ordnance, we checked off-station for the FARP—it was time for us to refuel and head home. The daytime divisions should be airborne and heading up to replace us. Although it had turned into a pretty good night I was looking forward to breakfast—then hitting the rack.

Only the watch on my wrist told me that the sun was well above the horizon—the sky seemed frozen in pre-dawn haziness. It wasn't just overcast, everything looked fuzzy with a weird, orange tint. Feeling our aircraft buffeted by high winds I realized that the storm that had been forecast last night had arrived. Inflight visibility was plenty good at 2 miles so I ignored the tickle of apprehension.

Doesn't matter. We're going home.

My hopes of making it home for breakfast turned out to be a bit premature. Instead of clearing us home the DASC sent us up Highway 7 again. I wondered briefly why the daytime divisions weren't here yet then pushed those thoughts aside.

Don't look a gift horse in the mouth, dummy.

The unit we were going to support was currently in contact.

This might turn into a good fight.

An ominous orange haze met us as we headed north. Within minutes the visibility dropped as though a curtain of sand had been wrapped around our canopies.

What had been perfectly workable weather five minutes earlier now became a matter of concern. Using the highway as a hasty deconfliction measure we split the flight, BT and Spock remaining on the west side of the highway while Weasel and I stayed on the east. Looking across the highway, I could just make out their aircraft amid the brown haze and estimated the visibility at almost a mile. It wasn't too bad but I hoped it wouldn't get much worse.

I wasn't overly concerned that we'd fly into each other—that's why we kept the road between us—but I wasn't real happy either. I couldn't see for shit.

My long-range sensors were worthless in this soup. I'd have to stumble on the enemy to know he was there. What was worse was that the enemy didn't have that problem—I was loud, elevated and in the attack. All an Iraqi gunner had to do was sight in on my noise, wait until my bird materialized out of the dust and then fire—I'd never see him until it was too late.

I'd trained to kill with missiles at maximum range. But this was shaping up to be a knife fight. I squirmed in my seat as I remembered a maxim repeated by one of my close combat instructors years ago: If you're going to fight with knives, you're going to get cut.

Shit.

We were still miles from Shazam's position, the FAC we were working for, when I started to see evidence of the fighting. The

Iraqis had used the cover afforded by the dust storm to attack the Marines from close range. The narrow battlefield stretched for miles up the road but only extended 50 meters either side. A lot of violence had been condensed in that narrow ribbon.

We could have been flying over a movie set. Dull orange flames danced hungrily atop wrecked vehicles while the thick dust mimicked the insulating quiet of freshly fallen snow. The flickering tongues of fire provided the only movement—it was like the director of the movie hadn't yelled 'Action' yet. Everything looked artificially serene, like it was staged for my benefit.

Then I saw the details.

They might have been waiting for the next take, but the actors were in various states of disarray. Some were calm as though sleeping, others were missing limbs and still others were almost unidentifiable as human.

There was something fascinating about the detritus—every pile of flesh a window into the final intimate moments of someone's life. Something told me I shouldn't be looking but I couldn't stop. I felt like a peeping tom.

Beneath me flashed a white sedan with orange doors that had met its end beneath a tank. It bore a tread mark down the center as if it had been an extra at a monster truck rally.

Here and there lay clumps of Iraqi soldiers, their scattered positions betraying the desperate nature of the fighting. They may have started together, but they died alone.

Ten bodies spread out from the open door of a small bus, their mad dash to escape cut short by machine gun fire that caught even the fastest runner.

Bodies of snipers lay in their hidden positions off the road, only the strange stillness of death demonstrating that they were no longer a threat.

Something on the dusty road caught my eye. I couldn't make it out at first but then its shape became discernible as I drew closer. It was an Iraqi soldier, cartoonishly flattened by passing vehicles. He lay in the center of a large dark stain, his clothes and paper-thin body plastered into the pavement like some sick version of "Flat Stanley."

The pride and excitement I'd felt after our last attack cooled and sat uncomfortably in my gut.

Movies don't look like this.

The radio chatter snapped me out of my daydream as BT contacted Shazam.

Knock it off—get back to work.

With effort I looked out toward the dusty horizon. The enemies below me were out of the game—I needed to find those still playing.

The brown curtain of sand thickened as we flew slowly past the lead elements of Shazam's unit. It seemed a little strange to be clearing the way for armored vehicles—their heavy armor could withstand a hell of a lot more punishment than we could—but we pushed ahead anyway. Why? Because they asked us to.

I nervously fiddled with the trigger guard on the left hand grip while searching as far into the haze as I could. After the scenes on the road I was jumpy. They'd reminded me that there was a real price to be paid for losing—and we didn't have a lot going for us in this storm. My adrenaline surged at every little crackle on the radio.

Taking Fire! Uhh, nope. Just static.

I felt like a blind man who knows he's about to get mugged, but I kept walking down the alley. There was no other choice.

It's coming—don't know when, don't know what—but it's coming.

About a kilometer north of the friendly troops we came across a town. Everything was either made out of dirt or covered in it. Only their unnaturally straight lines and hard angles made the buildings stand out. The town was named Al Shatrah and it had a wide intersection in the center—a perfect ambush site.

I spotted a pickup truck with a heavy machine gun in the back and took it out with a Hellfire. From our holding pattern on the south side of the town, we located several more trucks with ZU-23s mounted in the back. Although they did not appear to be manned, we destroyed them all. Once the area looked clear of major threats, Shazam and his unit came up beneath us. We pushed into the town together.

We hadn't gone 200 meters before Shazam's voice rang out over the radio.

"You're taking fire!"

We scattered like dropped marbles. Nobody knew who Shazam was talking about, but asking for clarification didn't seem like the thing to do. When we moved north again, Shazam talked our eyes onto the building that contained the snipers.

Weasel fired a blast/frag Hellfire from point-blank range and a small hole appeared in the flat roof of the building. A millisecond later, debris and smoke shot horizontally from every window and doorway. The structure remained but anything inside was dead.

Two good targets, two good kills. My jumpiness subsided a

bit—maybe we weren't getting lined up for execution.

BT and Spock were busy on the west side of the road as well, destroying several trucks with ZU-23s mounted in the back. The fact that the heavy weaponry appeared to be deserted was comforting. The disquiet I'd felt after looking at all the bodies dissipated. Relief flooded in as the tension slipped away. This was turning into a fun shoot—just flying around in the dust and blowing up other people's toys.

All this and a paycheck too? Hell yes!

A few minutes later the lead LAVs came under heavy fire from a couple of buildings 200 meters east of the highway. I could easily see puffs of dirt rising from the buildings as the Marines returned fire. Without waiting to be asked, Gash and IKE whipped our birds onto safe firing headings. Within seconds of the Iraqi soldiers giving away their positions, we were rolling in hot.

Like clockwork Gash and IKE flowed into the attack. Firing from the back seat of Weasel's bird, IKE's rockets threw up tall geysers of dirt and smoke among the buildings. He pulled hard right and the instant they were clear, Gash engaged. The buildings disappeared behind a wall of dirt and explosions as Gash sent several high-explosive rockets and a long burst of 20mm into them. The intoxicating smell of burnt gunpowder filled our small cockpit.

Eager to press the attack we came around for another run, but stopped—the 'tracks had dropped their ramps.

Marines exploded out of their armored confines, the small figures running in short bursts between positions of cover. They moved well, no single man remaining on his feet long enough for the enemy to target him. The front of the buildings wept dust as the advancing grunts kept up a steady stream of fire. They had timed their ground assault to take advantage of the cover our fire provided, and in turn covered our withdrawal. We hadn't planned it but hadn't needed to. The common training we had all gone through allowed for instinctively synergistic operations. The sight of their attack brought a surge of pride.

We are fucking good.

It dawned on me in a flash—I'd made it. That place I'd wanted to be since joining the Marine Corps, I was there. In the cockpit of a Cobra, supporting brother Marines in combat—this was it. I refocused on the task at hand buoyed by a strong sense of belonging.

The grunts took the buildings quickly and established a security perimeter with their armored vehicles. Shazam notified us that they would be stationary for a while and had no more work. We headed south for more gas and ordnance, certain that we had just flown our last mission for the day. We'd had some good missions this morning, but I was starting to get tired. Strong sense of belonging or not, now it was really time for us to head home.

As we moved south down Highway 7 the visibility stayed crappy for longer—the storm was moving south with us. Gash fought to keep us in position off Weasel's wing as the wind shook us like a ragdoll. The weather appeared to be deteriorating and I was relieved we were done. Good missions or not we'd been out for long enough—time to let someone else have a turn.

BT checked in with the DASC to let them know we were going to refuel, then head home. We just assumed that our replacements had arrived. It was almost noon—there was no reason why they shouldn't be here.

I could have sworn the Marine in the DASC laughed when BT told him we were heading back to Kuwait. Just a little chuckle that said "Are you serious? You really don't know?"

He caught himself quickly and filled us in. Instead of sweeping in from one direction this massive sandstorm was swirling. It wasn't just bad to the north of us, but to the south as well. Ali Al Salem had been engulfed and the airfield was shut down. It could be hours or days before the storm lifted. Until it did, there would be no replacements.

We were cut off.

Well shit.

The DASC directed us to a new FARP, Camden Yards, to refuel and rearm. As long as we were comfortable flying, they had requests waiting. I couldn't know for sure, but from the silence on the radios it sounded like we were the only gunships flying in the whole country.

We didn't have a lot of options—either fly or sit on our asses—and sitting around is boring. If it got really bad then we would land and wait it out, hopefully near friendly troops. To be honest, the crappy weather made me want to stay out more—this was getting to be a good challenge, a real tough-guy operation. If we lived through this we'd have some serious bragging rights. Coupled with a fresh face-full of Copenhagen, that thought lifted my spirits as we turned toward Camden Yards.

The distance to the FARP counted down in my GPS. It showed less than 2 miles. Skimming just over the scrub brush I couldn't see a thing.

One mile. Still nothing.

Half a mile.

Is that a road out there?

At a quarter mile away the fuel trucks resembled giant bugs and betrayed the location of the FARP. We quickly took separation from each other and landed. We'd been so low we didn't really have to descend at all—just slowed down a little bit to perch on the road.

Fifteen minutes later the DASC called us with a mission—troops in contact north along the highway. Full of gas and ordnance we launched into the blustery winds.

The sandstorm was noticeably worse again. I began to second-guess my sanity.

You wanted to do this?

Gash couldn't take his eyes off of Weasel for fear of losing him. After the debacle in the oil fields, that was the last thing we wanted to do. While Gash flew the bird I scanned for wires and towers off our nose. I kept my hands resting lightly on the controls—I would only have an instant to avoid a collision even at our reduced speed.

We were about 75 feet off the desert floor. There were a lot of power lines and poles that were much taller. We couldn't fly higher though—wouldn't be able to see the ground. If we lost sight of the ground we were truly screwed.

It was disconcerting to realize that the enemy wasn't the most lethal threat out here—the wires were.

This isn't in the movies—nobody gets whacked by power lines in the movies.

—+—|—+—

Despite the danger of flying into unseen obstacles I felt

my concentration waning quickly. My helmet grew numbingly heavy. I rubbed my eyes and slapped my face to snap out of it, but seconds later found myself staring into the FLIR screen with unseeing eyes. The effects of the last long mission and this one were piling up.

One night of sleep in almost three days was not quite enough.

Just a second to rest, I thought, recock my brain and get back into the fight.

Just a second...

I snapped awake. Horrified, I looked around wildly, certain we were about to crash into something. Gash hadn't noticed.

Angrily I popped a go pill and washed it down with a swig of water from my CamelBak. Minutes later the drug pushed back my accumulated fatigue. I was back in the game.

We contacted the FAC only to find that he didn't have any targets for us. They had been taking sporadic sniper fire but, due to the thick sandstorm, he couldn't identify which buildings housed the snipers. Our being on-station had a quieting effect though, and the sniper fire stopped as soon as our rotor blades were audible to the combatants on the ground.

We remained in the area for an hour but finally called it quits. We could no longer see the ground clearly enough to identify the difference between friend and foe. Our usefulness was truly at an end.

Tension knotted my neck and shoulders as I waited to hit something. Flying by Braille we somehow made it back to the FARP. I could have kissed the Iraqi dirt when we landed safely.

Fuck. Finally.

We were cut off from home, forced to land in the middle of

a hostile country and had no idea who might be around us—but it felt *good* to be on the ground. Flying in that storm had really sucked and I was happy to be down—even if it was in the middle of bumfuck Iraq.

We had no clue what was around us. The nearest Iraqis could be 50 miles or 50 meters away, the ground might be littered with mines or it might be clear, we might have a company of grunts providing security for us or we might be on our own...The answers didn't matter though, we really only had one option—hunker down and wait. Hopefully the weather would get better soon.

Still under the stimulating effects of our go pills, Gash and I took the first watch. With our rifles and extra magazines we sat back to back in a shallow depression, 20 feet from where the other pilots lay out their sleeping bags in the dirt.

They didn't know it—but they were the bait.

We hoped that any enemy infiltrators would focus on our friends' sleeping forms so we could kill the enemy unseen. The deafening wind and blinding sandstorm meant any engagement would be at very close range but we had one advantage—we were hidden. The enemy would have to come to us. My weapon may have changed, a rifle instead of an attack helicopter, but that didn't matter. I was trained for this.

Alone with my thoughts I ran back through the events of the day, relishing the feeling that we had acquitted ourselves well. In spite of the terrible flying conditions, our attacks against the various sniper positions and technical vehicles had been spot on.

This was what it was supposed to be like. No annoying white flags, no confusion about who's playing. The FAC points out a target and we destroy it, easy as that. To top it off, it looked like the rest of our squadron was trapped back in Kuwait and couldn't come out and play.

That nobody could help us didn't really register, I just felt lucky to be where I was. If anybody was going to be out in a difficult situation I wanted it to be me. That way I'd never have to hear someone tell me about it and wonder if I could have handled it.

I probably should have been worried about when the storm would lift, but I wasn't. The weather would get better when it got better—no use worrying about it. The only thing that mattered was that nobody would get through us.

My life had boiled down to simple action/reactions and I was solidly in the moment. The past and future didn't exist—only my rifle, my best friend and the phantoms—real and imagined—lurking just out of sight.

I leaned back, increasing the pressure against Gash. He popped an elbow into my flak jacket in response.

Good—we were both still awake.

There's nothing so fortifying as knowing, without a shadow of a doubt, that your friend has your back. There are very few experiences in life that live up to the hype, but this one did. Confident that we could handle anything that might stagger out of the dust I settled in.

Weirdly enough I felt great—like all was right in the world.

CHAPTER 10

I'VE HAD SOME miserable nights, but that first night at Camden Yards really sucked.

It had started out so nicely, too. After two hours of scanning the dust for intruders who never came, I'd crawled into my warm sleeping bag and was out like a light. My fatigue was deep enough that I didn't even notice when large, muddy raindrops began falling from the sky. It wasn't until the shallow little ditch I lay in filled with cold water that my night turned to shit.

There's nothing quite so rude as being woken up by a river of cold water flooding your sleeping bag. Unsure of what planet I was on, I'd scrambled for higher ground, shedding my clammy sleeping bag like a snake dropping its skin.

Gash had gotten drenched as well and we spent the rest of the night in our aircraft, him in the front and me in the back seat for a change of pace. I hovered in suspended consciousness all night—too uncomfortable to fall asleep but tired enough to keep trying.

There was no sunrise really; the shades of blackness just

shifted imperceptibly until the world became orange. I dragged my creaking, achy body out of the cockpit at the first hint of sandy daylight. Stamping my feet against the cold I felt like death warmed over. The brightening sky did bring one good thing—at least the damned night was over.

The rain had knocked down some of the dust. The visibility was a little better and I could see a couple of hummers parked maybe 300 meters down the road—the FARP team. Relieved that there really were other Marines here with us I relaxed a bit. Maybe we hadn't needed to stand security all night after all.

As the rest of the guys woke up, Gash and I looked over our bird. Our attempts to keep sand out of the engines had been partially successful, but our cannon was hopelessly jammed with mud. There was no way it would fire again. A couple of days ago, a useless 20mm would have pissed me off. Now I just grumbled a bit. I was getting used to not having a cannon—I didn't like it, but I was getting used to it.

After a quick breakfast of Copenhagen and instant coffee grounds, we were airborne again. Shortly after we'd all woken up the DASC called with a mission. The visibility was good enough to either try to pick our way home or go support the grunts.

We didn't have to discuss it—we took the mission.

It was assumed we'd stay out until another division of Cobras relieved us. That could happen in a few hours or a few days. It didn't really matter. We had food, fuel, ordnance and water. There was no reason to go home.

With the heater running full blast, my flight suit dried quickly. Coupled with the comfort of the warm cockpit, my morning cocktail of nicotine and caffeine had erased the lingering effects of the sleepless night. I was in fine spirits as we flew north along the highway.

The adventure continues...

At first the highway looked unfamiliar—just a two-lane blacktop. Nothing about it was noteworthy until the bodies flashed beneath me. Then I remembered.

The rain had fundamentally changed the macabre scenes—the dark pools of blood had washed away and all the colors were muted. The bodies looked strangely small now, deflated, like they were sinking into the pavement.

Gone was the heat, the burning vehicles and the ability to imagine those lying there haphazardly as actors awaiting their cue. Yesterday I wouldn't have looked twice if one had stood up and walked away. Not today.

They were all still there of course, Flat Stanley, the snipers, the guys who'd tried to escape from the bus. But they didn't tell a gripping story of battle and violent struggle anymore. Their bodies looked cold and forlorn, forgotten.

The scenes didn't pull me in like yesterday—I knew what they held now and looked away without comment. I wished someone would clean them up.

Opposing sports teams shake hands when the game is over. Dead soldiers just rot.

Our FAC on this mission was Gump. As we neared his position, the visibility dropped significantly. By the time we were on-station we could see maybe a quarter of a mile in the thick dust.

BT and Spock took the east side of the road while Weasel and I stayed on the west. We moved along with the lead tank as it lumbered north, scanning as far forward as the dust would allow and trying to keep out of the wires.

The feeling of being watched made my skin crawl. Small houses and clumps of buildings materialized out of the dirt uncomfortably close—I was well within AK-47 range before I could see even big structures. I wanted to be looking thousands of meters away for threats, not hundreds. By flying in this shit we were giving the enemy the first shot.

Go ahead fuckers, better make it good.

I wish I was that ballsy. It was more like:

Oh this sucks big goat dick, this sucks moose cock, this sucks...

I was running through other well-endowed animals when a substantial village materialized out of the suspended sand. Two-story buildings showed the town to be of some importance and not just another cluster of mud huts.

I was about to check my map when something caught my eye—a series of muted orange flashes about five hundred meters in front of us.

Hmm, that looks kind of like—

"Breakrighttakingfire!" Weasel yelled, quicker on the radio than me by far.

Eyes wide, I looked over at their aircraft—and saw nothing but the belly. IKE had ripped it over on its side and was turning away from us. A split second later, Gash did the same. I cringed helplessly in my seat, willing myself to become as small as possible to avoid whatever had just been fired at us.

"What the fuck was that?" Gash shouted as we flew away from the guns.

"I dunno but it was *fucking big*," I replied. The muzzle flashes had looked like huge flaming basketballs.

Now what the hell do we do? None of us had gotten a good look at where the guns were located, but they obviously knew where we were. Poking our noses back into that hazy urban sprawl really didn't seem like a good idea.

Gee, sorry you guys missed last time. Here, try again.

Luckily, Weasel had a plan. He gave Gump a rough idea of where the guns were while we continued flying south.

Oh yeah! You guys have tanks—you find those assholes.

Weasel was a bit more diplomatic. He asked Gump to take them out.

A couple of minutes later, Gump informed us that the lead tank had engaged and destroyed several S-60 guns near the area Weasel described.

"S-60s? Fuck, that would've sucked," Gash muttered over the ICS.

"Yup," I replied, trying to sound unconcerned. The high explosive 57mm rounds from the heavy antiaircraft guns would have made short work of us—if they'd connected. We'd been really lucky and knew it.

We picked up where we'd left off and moved slowly into the town. I noted the black smoke rising from where the guns were burning—several hundred meters away from where I thought they were. If we'd been stupid enough to come back and try to duke it out I would have been looking in the wrong spot. I wondered if they would have missed twice.

BT located a manned ZU-23 on the west side of the road. The Iraqis were traversing the barrels to engage and their motion caught his eye. I looked in their direction as BT killed them with a missile.

The dullness of the blast surprised me—it looked like a weak flashlight shining though an orange balloon. I looked quickly for BT and Spock's aircraft. The ghostly shapes of their two aircraft were barely discernible even though I knew they were less than a quarter mile away.

This is getting stupid, I can't see a damn thing.

I didn't want to be the one to call it quits, but I was definitely relieved when we had to pull back to the FARP for gas. The sandstorm was picking up again and, from the activity we'd seen this morning, so were the Iraqis.

Twenty minutes later we were on deck at Camden Yards. Even though we were only ten or fifteen miles south, the visibility was better down here. Having a safe place to land made us confident that we could keep flying. If it got too bad up north we could just scoot south and land.

The momentary respite from the tension of flying in the muddy air had a rejuvenating effect. In the fifteen minutes it took to get refueled and rearmed, my attitude shifted solidly in favor of doing another mission.

BT got in contact with the DASC and they affirmed that our presence was requested again up Highway 7. The advancing Marines were facing constant harassing fire as they moved toward Baghdad.

This time I felt like a commuter who becomes immune to the sight of the homeless along his morning drive. I made a big show of ignoring the heaps of bodies on the road—fiddling with my map, checking the radio frequency, picking my nose...

It didn't work. I didn't have to see them; I knew they were there. The commuter silently defends his warm car by ignoring the flat eyes of the stoplight beggar—I did the same.

Nothing to see here, eyes straight ahead.

Their rotting presence made me feel guilty—and that pissed me off.

What do I have to feel guilty about? Not a goddamn thing— it's war, they lost. Get over it.

Confused anger swirled around the weird pangs of guilt but couldn't quite dislodge them. Like images of dead friends, I stuffed the thoughts away. Now wasn't the time.

Except for the continuing terrible visibility—and the time when an LAV destroyed a building right underneath BT's aircraft without warning—the next hour and a half was uneventful. Early in the afternoon, the grunts pulled into security halts and we got word that they were going to hold for the night. Nobody had any more work for us, so we returned to Camden Yards and shut down.

The FARP felt like home now. We knew there were security forces arrayed around us and were much more relaxed than we had been yesterday. Gash and I draped our still-wet sleeping bags over the warm engines to dry them out then joined the other guys for some MREs. The whole atmosphere was comfortable. Like we were camping.

I was digging into some Country Captain Chicken—I don't know why, that's just what the MRE people named it—when strange voices drifted out of the curtain of dust around us. Weasel and IKE stopped arguing about IKE cheating at acey-deucey and we glanced at each other uneasily.

Is this really happening?

For a moment we all froze, uncertain. Then the voices started shouting.

Skittles and meal packets hit the dirt as we scrambled for our weapons. We lay behind our rifles, sighting in on shadowy figures as they became visible atop the berm maybe a hundred meters away.

Where's the security?

The shouting figures were definitely not Marines.

The Iraqi voices repeated a phrase over and over again. At first I thought my mind was playing tricks on me.

That's just too cliché, I thought. *It couldn't be.*

But my certainty grew with each repetition. It sure sounded like 'Die, die American' to me.

For ten tense minutes the barely visible figures in the dust kept up their chants while we lay and waited.

Why are they just yelling? Why don't they attack?

I was confused—what was going on? I wished that they would open fire—at least that would settle the maddening debate going on in my head.

Do they have weapons? Are they soldiers? Maybe they're just punk kids screwing around?

The answers would determine if I would murder an innocent or kill a soldier. But from where I lay I just couldn't know. The dust had diluted the black-and-white answers I needed to shades of damnable grey. I was paralyzed by uncertainty.

An excited, impetuous voice in my head argued hard to open fire.

What are you waiting for? They're not selling Girl Scout cookies, dumbass.

The pressure built on the pad of my finger against the trigger—just a little more…I began to visualize the dusty outlines falling backwards. Then a calm, sober voice broke in.

Hold—you have no idea what they're saying. They could be

calling their goats for all you know. This whole thing might be in your head. Chill the fuck out.

I let the trigger come fully forward, my fingertip resting lightly now. I was willing to concede the first move—it was worth the risk to avoid making a mistake.

One moment they were standing there shouting—the next they were gone. The voices just dropped off to nothing and the wispy figures dissolved into the haze. We never found out what the hell was going on. The whole thing just ended.

There was no explanation, no closure. Random shouting Iraqis materializing and disappearing within our supposed ring of security...WTF?

If my life were a Tom Clancy book, I'd know everything about them. But it wasn't a novel—there was no plot development, no foreshadowing or predictable storyline to ease my fears or anticipation. I just had to take things as they came.

I stopped thinking about it.

The fun atmosphere of a bunch of guys camping was destroyed—we knew exactly where we were. Relaxing wasn't an option anymore, so I finished my dropped meal, crept into my sleeping bag and passed out. The next thing I knew it was pitch black outside and my alarm clock was going off.

When did my alarm clock sound like explosions and machine gun fire?

The question was puzzling—for about a heartbeat.

Holy shit!

Adrenaline shot to my hands and feet. I tensed in preparation to run—to where I didn't know—but I'd be damned if I was going to get shot in my sleeping bag.

As quickly as the answer to 'fight or flight' flashed in my head, reality stepped in.

The dull boom of explosions rolled to my ears from a distance and lacked concussive punch. Also missing were the snap of bullets overhead. Whatever was happening was nearby, but it didn't involve me.

The fight could only be a mile or two away. I wondered why the DASC hadn't called us to launch. Not that I was really eager to go—without the benefit of the sun the duststorm made a welldigger's ass look positively radiant. Hoping that the DASC wouldn't call us, and wondering if that made me a coward, I lay back and listened to the soundtrack of the battle.

There was a rhythm to the firing. One gun would loose a long burst, answered by another with a slightly different firing rate and tone, then the original gun would start again. Back and forth the guns talked, rarely stepping on each other but insistent in their interruptions.

There was a lull and I heard a strange, hollow, popping sound from somewhere in the inky blackness. It wasn't located with the other guns—that much I could tell—but it made their tempo change. The newcomer peaked my interest.

What the hell is that?

A string of explosions erupted impossibly close together. The duration of the explosions matched the length of the weird popping sound that had preceded it. The light came on in my head.

Ohh, that's what it is.

The sound explained why I was still in my sleeping bag and not scrambling to get airborne: There was an AC-130 overhead.

The muted report of the 40mm cannon continued for several more minutes. Soon its impacts became the only sounds as enemy positions ceased to exist under a rain of high explosive shells. A few last, desultory shots and it was over.

The low drone of the gunship's four engines stood out against the newly quiet backdrop of the midnight desert. It orbited overhead for a few more minutes, its unblinking eyes scouring the earth for nefarious movement. Finding none, the big gunship ambled off to rain fire somewhere else.

I drifted off easily despite the excitement nearby. It seems strange to me now, but at the time, the weird events of the day didn't really register. It was like I was in another universe, a place where shouting wraiths appear and disappear at will, decaying corpses normally sink into pavement and omnipotent monsters erase problems from overhead orbits. None of it registered in my tired brain beyond its immediate impact on me.

A purple-headed elephant wearing a tutu could have walked past and I wouldn't have batted an eye—as long as it didn't step on me.

Weird shit happens. Go to sleep.

Fantastically unreal was becoming my new normal.

CHAPTER 11

BRIGHT SUNLIGHT woke me up the next morning. Squinting, I dug what felt like gravel from the corners of my eyes and looked around. The deep blue of the sky and cool, crisp morning air soothed my bloodshot eyes. There wasn't a hint of dust anywhere.

This was more like it.

As soon as everybody was awake we gathered at BT's aircraft. With the good weather, we expected that the grunts would start moving north again—and the Iraqis would be waiting. There was a feeling of excitement among our small group. It would be hours before any other gunships could make it up from Kuwait. Any good fights that started early would be all ours.

The storm had halted our operations but we didn't assume it had done the same to the enemy. The Iraqis must have realized by now that we were sticking to the main highways and pushing hard for Baghdad. If it had been me, I would have used the cover of the storm to set up some nasty surprises along those roads. Today could get real interesting.

We got the call to launch and spun up quickly, checking in on the radio with BT to report the status of our birds.

My excitement for a fight cooled as I listened to the maintenance status of our aircraft. We were a mess.

With our 20mm jammed and TOW missile system broken, I thought that our bird was pretty screwed up. Then Spock and Weasel reported what was malfunctioning in their respective birds.

In addition to having a broken cannon, Spock and JoJo could only hear on their radios about half of the time. The other half of the time the transmissions just didn't come through. Besides not having a clue about what was going on, if someone called "Taking fire" they only had a 50/50 chance of even hearing the warning—crappy odds.

Weasel and IKE's bird was worse. Their cannon was jammed, one of their radios was totally broken and their telescopic sight unit (TSU) wouldn't stabilize. Of those problems, the unstabilized TSU was the most debilitating. Without the TSU, Weasel had no optics, no FLIR, no camera, no TOW or Hellfire missiles and no laser. The only weapons he and IKE could still use were their unguided rockets. Still, they were adamant they could continue fighting.

Listening to their gripes I felt better about my own bird. At least Gash and I had two radios and our rocket and Hellfire missile systems were up and operational. By comparison we were in pretty good shape. BT and Fuse's bird was in the best condition of all. Somehow all of their systems were doing fine.

With one out of four aircraft fully operational, we launched and headed north over the scrub brush. Without needing the contrast provided by the blacktop we stayed clear of the road—we'd been way too predictable during the storm.

Flying low across the empty fields and desert scrub brush felt relaxing. Sure we were still in Iraq and potentially seconds away from a big fight but, after the anxiety of flying in that sandstorm, today felt like a walk in the park.

Elevated dikes flashed below our skids as Gash maneuvered gently back and forth—considerately avoiding the small farms that popped out of nowhere. It just seemed kind of rude to rattle them on such a nice morning.

Two good-sized houses appeared off our nose. Gash aimed for the gap between them. Unfortunately a shepherd and his flock of sheep were going through that same gap at the same time. When we saw the animals it was too late—we blasted across the flock 20 feet over their heads. I craned my neck around to watch the frightened animals scatter to the winds and wondered how long it would take the shepherd to round them all up again. Gash's laugh rang in my ears.

"Fucker threw his stick at me!" he blurted incredulously, a mixture of mirth and admiration in his voice.

"Well, guess we deserved that," I answered, smiling.

I felt slightly guilty for scaring the guy's flock but was impressed by his gutsy response. Imagine, throwing a stick at an invader's attack helicopter for scaring your sheep. Had to give the guy points for having balls.

BT checked us in with Shazam again. They were about to move through a small town and wanted us to search ahead for ambushes—seems like everybody had that feeling today. BT split the division again and pushed us across to the east side.

We could cover more ground by splitting up.

We passed the lead LAV—now we were in front. The small talk and chatter over the back radio drifted off to silence as the carefree atmosphere of the transit evaporated. We weren't scaring sheep anymore. We were hunting.

If there were Iraqi forces nearby they'd had plenty of time to prepare for our arrival. The bright, beautiful day suddenly felt sinister—the absolute lack of any cover meant that we could be seen and heard for miles in all directions. My memory of the sandstorm turned nostalgic. At least then *nobody* could see.

I kept my face glued to the targeting bucket. Peering through my soda-straw field of view I scoured the elevated mud dikes, small huts and canals that led up to the small cluster of buildings in the distance. I couldn't clear everything out there—that would have taken me a week—so I stayed close to the road. Focusing only on where Shazam and his boys would travel narrowed my search but increased my feeling of being exposed. What I couldn't see had me worried. Then I remembered Weasel and felt better—he and IKE were keeping us covered with their rockets.

"Vehicle right, 2 o'clock," Gash said, intent but quiet.

"Roger."

Without looking up I slewed the sights to acquire the speeding car. The little white sedan with orange doors didn't look hostile so I went back to searching the fields.

"No factor," I told him.

"Roger."

A minute or two passed before Gash spoke up again.

"Something ain't right."

"What's up?" I asked, not taking my head out of the bucket.

"There's lots of people out and around, but nobody's waving anymore. Most folks look like they're getting ready to leave."

Before I could answer him Weasel piped up on the back radio.

"Shoe, there's a house with about six cars, bunch of dudes all standing around just looking at us, at your nine o'clock—mark mark."

"I got them visual," Gash responded before I could even slew my sensors over in that direction.

"Looks like about ten guys...civilian clothes...no weapons visible...watching us." Gash reported slowly.

They were close enough that Gash could monitor them with his naked eye. I continued searching for targets further away but I could almost feel their eyes on us. The increased tension was palpable.

Ten dudes watching us out of idle curiosity? I don't think so.

Gash began flying faster and making unpredictable turns to make us a harder target. We still had to clear the road for the grunts, but didn't have to be sitting ducks while we did it. Something wasn't right about those guys.

From the other side of the road, Fuse's slightly confused voice came across the back radio.

"Spock, BT. Are my flares popping off?"

Forgetting the group of men I looked up to locate BT's section. Time slowed down as my mind made several jumps at blazing speed—for me.

His flares aren't popping off—what else pops? I remember some pops, wonder if he's getting ...

"Break left break left taking fire!"

Fuse's voice cut through my brilliant deductive reasoning like a hot knife. There was no confusion in it anymore.

Both BT and Spock ripped their birds into hard left turns 2 miles west of us. I searched the ground beneath them for their attackers but saw nothing—only green fields.

Fight's on!

Gash set us up for a rocket run where we thought the enemy was located. In a few seconds we'd see them, just a few seconds more...

BT called us off.

"Shoe, BT. Stay east of the road and cover that side, we've got this."

It would have been foolish for all of us to concentrate on what might be a small part of a larger force, but it was tough to pull off without firing.

"Fuck!" Gash yanked the aircraft around to the north again, Weasel and IKE following suit off our left side.

Gash kept our section close to the road in case we were needed. I scanned the low brush and plowed fields on our side to make sure we hadn't stumbled into a bigger force, then shifted my attention back to BT and Spock's fight.

Their evasive maneuvering had carried them south out of the enemy's range. When I spotted them they were heading north—into the attack. Even at a distance their coordinated, purposeful movements were menacing—whoever had shot at them was about to die.

JoJo, in the front seat of Spock's aircraft, came up on the radio.

"BT, Spock. I've got four guys setting up a mortar tube, heading 350, about 2000 meters, I'm in with TOW."

I'd known JoJo for years but had never heard him use that

tone of voice. He usually spoke in a mirthful, easygoing manner that could turn any statement into a self-deprecating joke or wry observation. Now he sounded different, flat and cold. This was business.

"Roger," BT replied, his tone just as focused.

The TOW missile launched off Spock's aircraft. For a second it looked good, then careened crazily and exploded in an empty field. BT picked up the attack without hesitation.

Small, grey puffs of smoke erupted from the rotating barrels of BT's cannon and glittering brass shell casings cascaded earthward. The evenly spaced clouds of burnt gunpowder stretched out behind BT's aircraft in little puffs until the main rotor's downdraft broke them apart.

The tempo of the battle increased abruptly after BT's long burst of cannon fire—the stalk was over and the fight was joined. The two aircraft wheeled around in the sky as though their moves were choreographed. In a way, they were.

While one aircraft maneuvered the other covered its back. Their attack was a seamless weaving dance where one bird perched and turned while the other delivered punishing fire below it.

Over and over again they switched roles—shoot, move, shoot, move—until the smoke from their rocket fire covered the battlefield. BT and Spock had butted heads from time to time but it was obvious that any animosity between them was a thing of the past. Their actions reminded me of the unofficial motto of HMLA-169, one of our sister squadrons: We hate each other—but we hate you more.

The high-energy maneuvering that BT and Spock had been doing caused them to burn a lot of fuel. Five minutes after the shooting started BT called "Bingo." Weasel and I still had about ten minutes of fuel left to play with and wanted to stay to finish these guys off. BT agreed and he and Spock turned south toward the FARP, clearing the area for us to continue the fight.

Now it was our turn.

Gash rolled us toward the west and we bore down on the smoke-filled engagement area. Just as we were crossing the highway I spotted a pickup truck with a large machine gun mounted in the back. I informed Gash and shot the laser to designate for my Hellfire missile.

"45 left pull." Gash passed the attack profile to Weasel.

"Two."

I mashed the 'fire' button on the left hand grip and held the laser spot directly on the cab of the truck. As the missile roared off my wing something moved in my sights. I didn't shift my aimpoint but stared at the movement hard.

Enemy? Civilian?

I had to know—quick.

The source of the movement became clear as four men got up from where they'd been hiding. They stood up tall and brushed off their uniforms as they watched BT's section fly away. Their actions told me they figured the threat was gone. I couldn't believe it.

Holy shit—they don't know we're here!

They walked nonchalantly back to the heavily armed truck.

Come on, come on, walk faster dickheads...

Knowing that my missile was split seconds from smoking the vehicle I barely breathed.

Is this really gonna happen?

The few seconds it took for my missile to close the 2500 meters to the truck felt like an eternity. I watched the four men saunter toward their deaths, part of me willing them to walk faster, the other part staring in mute fascination.

Three of them reached the truck and climbed on. Not the fourth. He stopped with one hand on the door handle. The sound of BT and Spock's rotor noise must have quieted enough to allow him to hear us. In my memory, he turned toward me in exaggerated slow motion.

I saw him shout a warning and start to move away. The three who were on the truck leapt off like the Duke boys out of Uncle Jesse's jeep.

It didn't matter.

My missile streaked into the cab and exploded in a nasty puff of grey smoke. The three who were closest simply ceased to exist, their organic matter reduced to particles too small for me to see. The fourth, the man who had stopped and sounded the alarm, was a little further away from the blast.

His death caught my attention.

It happened so fast that I didn't see him go up, only his clothes coming back down. But they weren't just clothes—fabric doesn't fall straight down like that. Heavy pieces of him were still in them.

It looked so different from how Hollywood portrayed explosions—there they either dive for cover and survive or disappear forever. This guy didn't go away, but he was certainly gone. The tattered remnants of his torso dropped through my sights on a loop as the truck burned in the background.

The loud 'whoosh' of several rockets coming off the left side of our aircraft brought me back to the task at hand. I pulled my head out of the bucket to see what Gash was shooting at.

The field in front of us seemed to sprout running Iraqi soldiers. One second there were none, the next there was a whole mess of them. They came out of nowhere, but they couldn't go anywhere.

Gash's rockets dropped some before we had to pull off. IKE sent some rockets past us as we set up for another attack.

I craned my neck around in search of our next target and saw 10-15 runners get cut down by IKE's rocket fire.

"Truck, twelve o'clock moving fast." Gash called my attention to a pickup truck speeding away from the engagement zone.

"Searching."

Shoot, move, next target. My world became simple—threat, shoot. No threat, ignore. Mechanical.

The burning truck forgotten I slewed my sights out toward the one fleeing. Even before I saw it I knew it contained enemy troops trying to escape.

Why else would they run?

Zooming in on the white pickup I flipped up the cover on the laser designator and felt the hard plastic beneath.

The urge to fire was strong—erase this threat and move to the next, next, next. Something cut through the adrenaline of the moment though and stayed my impulse to shoot.

"Target or not?" Gash's voice was excited, edgy.

We were getting too close to the truck for me to hit it with a missile. He'd have to kill it with a rocket—but soon.

There was something in the bed of the truck and I strained to make out what it was. The part of me that had stood in silent fascination earlier, when the four men had ambled toward their deaths, now screamed in my head.

Not a weapon! What?

Just then I got a clear view of a woman and two children hunched against the rear window of the cab. They were looking at me while trying to avoid the cutting wind.

"Negative Negative, I got women and kids!" I shouted.

Without a word Gash pulled our nose off the truck like it

didn't exist. Instantly it went from the focal point of our world to background noise.

No *threat, next.*

Coming through 90 degrees of turn I started to put my head in the bucket but stopped. There were too many groups of running soldiers spread too far apart for my three remaining missiles to do any real good. Gash maneuvered toward a particularly concentrated group and set up to kill them with rockets. Without a cannon I felt worthless, just sitting there watching the show.

It was a show I could have done without.

800 meters in front of us, two figures burst out of a ditch to our right. Their olive drab uniforms stood out in stark contrast to the bright green grass and their movement drew our attention like strobe lights. Gash adjusted the nose of our aircraft slightly and fired a single rocket.

As soon as the rocket left our wing I knew its trajectory was right on. The two runners and the burning rocket motor were heading for the exact same piece of muddy green field, at rates that ensured they would arrive there simultaneously.

It was like that "Basketball to the head" video on You Tube where a kid running across the baseline of a basketball court gets knocked sideways by a Hail-Mary basketball shot. As soon as the basketball and running kid are in the picture, you know what's going to happen.

Fascinated, I watched the faster of the two runners. His legs pumped furiously and his empty arm swung hard to counter the weight of the AK-47 in the other as he outpaced his buddy. I was amazed by the detail I could see with my naked eyes and realized that we were close, really close. Questions flashed through my head faster than a camera shutter.

Were we too close when we fired? Would the flechettes

deploy or would the rocket miss him?

The heat trail from the rocket continued toward an empty patch of grass slightly in front of the lead runner. From my vantage point it looked like they converged without anything happening.

Shit, we missed.

Then, from the waist up, he just deflated.

Flesh, bone, and equipment all disintegrated into a pink mist as the warhead sent 2200 nails on slightly divergent paths through his torso.

He split in two as bits of green shirt hung in the air where his chest had stopped while his lower body continued on. His hips and legs tumbled unnaturally as momentum and twitching muscles carried them forward in a strange, drawn-out collapse. In the time it took for his shirt pieces to fall to the ground the tension of life abandoned his legs. They crumpled a few feet away as if made of Jello.

"Holy fucking shit!" I shouted instinctively, the incredible impossibility of what I'd just seen giving me an incredible rush of—euphoria. I felt an indescribable elation that threatened to carry me away.

Fuck yeah! Catching myself, I snapped back in.

Not now, later.

"Off left, off left!" I called urgently, fearful that we were about to overfly the engagement area.

Gash fired off a few high-explosive rockets and pulled hard left again, their explosions kicking up mud and smoke to help cover our pull. The first three rockets impacted behind or beyond the other runner—but not the fourth. It landed about 2 feet in front of him. He disappeared in an eruption of mud, smoke and steel.

As we pulled off target again Gash took a glance at the fuel gauge.

"Shit dude, we're bingo minus a hundred." He sounded surprised, and more than a little disappointed.

His words had the same effect as turning a hose on two humping dogs—the action just stopped.

"Fuck, roger." I was bummed too. We were doing good work here and it was unfinished. Running out of gas wasn't going to help us any though.

Over the radio I let Weasel know we were heading for gas.

"Weasel, Shoe, we're bingo."

"Roger, uhh, so are we." IKE replied, both of us lying just a little bit to cover our embarrassment of having let our fuel reach a critical state.

We turned toward Pac Bell, the nearest FARP.

"Shoe, BT." I was surprised to hear BT, who'd left five minutes ago, call me on the back radio.

"Go."

"DASC reports Pac Bell is breaking down to move north, might have gas, might not. That's where we're heading though, not enough gas to make Camden Yards and Spock's tranny is running hot."

"Roger, we'll meet you there." We didn't have enough gas to make it to Camden either. If we were going to run out of gas we might as well all be together.

A moment later Spock's gravelly voice came over the frequency.

"BT, Spock. Just lost my #1 hydraulics ... #1 engine oil temp is rising ... transmission temp is rising too."

His bird was failing. Fast.

"Roger, you want to set it down or push for the FARP?"

A split second passed before Spock answered, "head for the FARP."

I checked the distance to the FARP, 10 miles. BT and Spock must be within 5 miles of landing so they had a pretty good chance of getting there before the engine or transmission failed completely. Gash turned slightly towards their two Cobras low on the horizon. If Spock went in short of the FARP we'd be overhead to help within a minute or two.

We made it to Pac Bell with no drama and linked up with BT, Fuse, Spock and JoJo. We caught the tail end of the FARP convoy as they were about to pull out and start driving north. Lucky for us they had a full fuel tanker and several mechanics with them. As they fueled our empty aircraft we all gathered around Spock's bird to examine the damage.

There were 10 or 12 bullet holes in the bird—although it was tough to get an accurate count. Some bullets had passed through several parts of the aircraft and caused multiple entry and exit wounds.

BT and Fuse had a larger hole in one of their main blades, probably from a 12.7mm round, and Weasel and IKE had a small hole in one of their blades too. Only Gash and I hadn't been touched.

After the sandstorm and battle all of the aircraft needed maintenance, but Spock's aircraft was too badly damaged to risk flying it home. We left him and JoJo at the FARP and headed back without them. A maintenance recovery team would come fix their bird soon but we couldn't wait—the faster our birds could get patched up the sooner they could be out flying again. Right now, they were basically worthless.

We snuck back to Kuwait with none of the bravado that had accompanied our departure almost four days earlier. As banged up as our birds were, the last thing we wanted was to stumble into another fight.

It was a quiet flight home—nobody seemed to want to make small talk over the radio. It felt like the six of us had been living together for years and everything had been said. I settled in on the controls and gave Gash a break from the flying as my mind wandered.

We'd done well over the last three and a half days, really well. Not only had we weathered a nasty storm but we'd been able to help the grunts out at the same time. As monumental as the storm had been though, it wasn't what occupied my thoughts—the last battle was.

It had been a good fight, a clean fight—black and white. They shot at us, we killed them. As if to prove to myself it had actually happened, I let the memory of Gash's 'one in a million' rocket shot out of where I'd stuffed it.

Silently I sat, watching the man get cut in half and re-living the fascination and euphoria I'd felt. My pulse started to pound again with the recollection of the Iraqi soldier's violent end. I felt strangely guilty at the rush it gave me—like I was watching porn.

I wasn't gloating, but I was proud. Killing that man was exactly what we were supposed to be doing here. The fact that Gash had done it so well, so spectacularly, warranted letting the memory out and letting it run free. It formed my highlight reel and I watched it over and over again in my head like a game-winning touchdown.

Over and over again. Over and over…

The memory took on a life of its own. I'd briefly quarantined it, but not anymore. The vanishing torso flashed behind my eyes for the rest of the flight. When I had something to do, it went away, but as soon as my immediate duties left me unoccupied—there it was.

It dawned on me as we neared home. I'd fucked up—I'd let it out. Now I couldn't put it back in.

CHAPTER 12

THE UNEASE THAT I FELT on the way home didn't go away. Not totally, anyway. It seemed to come in waves of varying intensity. Sometimes I could shove it aside with little effort, other times it threatened to break through. I didn't know what it was—didn't want to know. I just wanted it to leave me alone.

Back at Ali Al Salem I settled down. Now that the mission was over I relaxed and slipped into a kind of post-flight bliss. We'd survived the last mission, done good work, earned our pay and lived up to the challenges thrown at us. The next mission was too far away to be concerned with yet, so there were no nightmare scenarios running rampant through my head. I could just—be.

One of the ordnance Marines, Sgt Collins, walked over to our bird to find out how our weapon systems had held up. When we told him, he immediately started working on the cannon. As he popped the fairings off the turret he asked how the missions had gone—he knew we'd been stuck out there for days and was interested in what had happened.

Gash and I skipped over the boring stuff—sandstorms, weird Iraqis shouting at us, shepherds with sticks—and went straight to the last engagement. Sgt Collins pulled his head out from underneath the bird to listen better. As an ordnance Marine, he lived and breathed weapons but rarely got the opportunity to learn what they accomplished after he hung them on the aircraft.

I re-told the story of Gash's rocket shot. I didn't embellish it—it didn't need any to captivate his attention. Sgt Collins' reaction reinforced what I'd been trying to convince myself the whole flight home.

"Holy shit, that's awesome, Sir. Nice shooting."

Sgt Collins was listening to me but speaking to Gash. His voice was low and respectful and carried with it a certain envy. I have no doubt he wished he could have been the one to fire that rocket.

I took his viewpoint and tried to apply it to myself. It *had* been an awesome shot, a perfectly legal killing of an enemy soldier sanctioned by all the laws of war. There was absolutely no ambiguity in this situation.

Be happy, be satisfied, be proud. I told myself. *You deserve to feel good about it.*

Walking back off the flightline I kept repeating those thoughts. If desire and repetition could have done the trick, I would have been whistling Dixie by the time I got to the intel tent.

I wasn't.

There was something about that last mission that sparked dangerously in my head—like a downed power line. I didn't know what it was. I only knew that to get too close to it was a very bad idea.

The six of us who'd made it back debriefed the mission with the intel Marine on duty, Cpl Payne. After discussing the nuts and bolts of the missions—what we'd fired, what we'd hit, what was still left out there—she asked if we'd shot any video of the engagements. Both BT and I had—Weasel's VCR and camera had been broken—and we played the tapes.

Watching BT's tape I felt the excitement of the battle all over again. I'd seen it unfold in real-time from afar, but now I had the opportunity to see it from his point of view, through his sights. BT fast-forwarded to just after they started taking fire.

The scene on the TV showed a berm next to the highway—a mound of dirt that was pockmarked with large holes. As three men walk into the picture I recognized what it was—an ambush site. The holes I saw were fighting positions and most of them contained at least one head sticking out.

The Iraqi soldiers were lolling about a bit—their attention focused on the ground forces coming up the road, not helicopters clattering in the distance. Bad mistake.

BT centers the crosshairs on the three individuals. The picture shudders for about five seconds as he opens up with the 20mm. A couple seconds later, puffs of dirt erupt in the area and several troops drop—either seeking cover or hit. Amid the flurry of activity, one Iraqi moves slowly forward, trips and then crawls toward a hole. I was puzzled for a moment, then understood—wounded.

His agony didn't last long.

BT's first burst of fire impacted high and right in relation to his crosshairs. To correct he shifted down and left and the image shuddered as he fired again. His Kentucky Windage correction was right on.

The three-barreled 20mm is great for peppering an area but it's not a 'one shot, one kill' weapon. Not by design anyhow.

The shuddering of the image stopped just before the first round exploded—exactly where the fallen Iraqi's head was. As the rest of the rounds danced among the fighting holes, I watched the puff of dirt drift away from where the headless soldier lay.

My eyes were glued to the screen. Mentally I was peeking through my fingers like a little kid at a scary movie—I didn't want to watch but I couldn't stop. I was embarrassed by my relief when it became obvious BT had been too far away for his tape to capture the details.

Now that he knew his aim was on, BT sent a long burst of high-explosive rounds into the ambush site. The dirt berm eroded under the withering fire and the remaining fighters tried to flee for safety. The screen flipped back out to low magnification as Fuse and BT flew forward on a rocket run to engage the running troops.

The entire field erupted in a beehive of activity. Little figures ran in every direction—too dispersed for effective 20mm fire but perfectly suited for flechette rockets. Fuse rolled in and fired two rockets about three seconds apart.

The first rocket hit the muddy field in front of two runners. They both froze like kids playing 'red light, green light.' In unison they turned towards the approaching helicopters and put their hands in the air.

Too little, too late.

The second rocket had been fired just before they threw their hands up—might as well have been forever. The steel nails deflated them. Fresh excitement coursed through my veins as they turned into meat.

Good shot Fuse, right on.

The video showed several more rocket runs—none as spectacular as the first but equally effective. The video ended when BT broke contact to head to the FARP.

Watching the destruction from BT's viewpoint I'd felt great—this was how I *should* feel. My satisfaction was totally appropriate for what I was seeing. They were the enemy and I was watching them losing.

The striking difference between the contented excitement I felt now and the unease I had felt earlier filled me with an immense sense of *relief*. Now I knew the unease must have been an anomaly.

Convinced that the little weirdness was a thing of the past I got up to put my tape in, eager to show what Gash and I had accomplished.

I fast-forwarded to the engagement with the truck. As the four men stood up from their hiding positions I could hear little chuckles around me—everybody knew what was about to happen. I tried to chuckle knowingly as well but all that came out was a nervous cough.

Their chuckles were the same reaction I'd had when the situation unfolded the first time. Well, almost. Then there had been a question of "Is this really going to happen?" My amazement had grown with each step they took—*holy crap it's really happening*!

Watching it the second time was different.

Now there was no question—the men walking on my screen were about to die. Without the stimulation of the unknown the whole thing lost its color. I didn't feel excited anymore. I didn't feel proud of the shot. I knew what the man would look like when he became chunks of meat. I didn't need to be reminded.

I let the tape play on silently. I blinked at the moment of the blast—

Oh gee, guess I missed seeing it again.

It didn't really work.

The falling pieces flashed through my mind anyway. After the four men died, the tempo of our battle picked up. The scene tilted crazily as Gash whipped our bird into and away from the enemy troops. We were getting close to Gash's rocket shot and I grew strangely nervous. I wondered if there was any way to avoid seeing it again.

The pickup truck with the family flashed across the screen— even now I could barely tell that they were women and children in the back. Instead of relief at not firing at them I felt sick—I'd been so close. I wiped my sweaty palms against my flight suit and waited uncomfortably for the running rocket scene.

The screen flashed solid blue and the annoying tone of the Built-In-Test came out of the TV. Relief flooded my body—I hadn't taped it.

"What the fuck?" Gash shouted angrily. "You tape everyfuck-ingthing else but miss the rocket shot? Fuck!" He was pissed.

"Yeah, sorry. Guess I missed it," I mumbled.

I wasn't sorry. Not in the least. The last thing I wanted to see again was that dude's noodle-like legs as they stumbled away from his pink mist. I hadn't tried to miss filming the shot—it had just happened too fast—but I was glad I did.

We left our tapes with Cpl Payne—she wanted to copy them

and include the footage with her intel report—and got dinner. A couple hours later Gash and I walked back to pick them up.

Night had fallen and the squadron area was pitch black except when someone came out of a tent. Then a flash of light would escape before the flap closed behind them. Gash had gotten over his annoyance at my incomplete taping of our engagement. I think he was just too tired to be pissed.

As we approached the S-2 tent I could hear muffled voices punctuated by bursts of excited shouting inside. In the pale moonlight Gash and I shrugged our shoulders and went in—it sounded like there was a party going on in there.

Jammed into the brightly lit interior of the tent was a bunch of squadron Marines—mechanics, technicians, administrative types, crew chiefs—the men and women who did the hard work behind the scenes to give Gash and me safe helicopters to fly. They were watching the footage of our last fight on the big TV screen. Nobody noticed us come in.

Without a word we slid to the back of the tent—we didn't want to interrupt. We knew how hard these Marines work to keep our birds up. They deserved a chance to see the results of their unceasing labors.

Most of them just sat there, watching the grainy footage with rapt attention. Brief cheers erupted each time an Iraqi fell or was obliterated by an explosion. At first I felt a sense of satisfaction, but it quickly turned sour.

I started to feel angry for some reason. I couldn't put my finger on why—then I heard it again.

"Fuck yeah, kill that motherfucker!"

Sitting in the middle of the group was one of the young corporals from flightline. He was qualified as a door gunner on the UH-1 Huey, but had not been out flying since the fighting had started. Scheduled to go on his first combat flight the next morning, his mouth was betraying his nervousness.

The more I heard him, the angrier I got. I couldn't have explained why in a million years. I was just getting pissed.

"Waste 'em all!" His voice rose above the din—I couldn't tune him out.

It didn't matter if they were soldiers or civilians, women or kids, he mindlessly wished violent death upon them all.

The tape reached the part where Gash and I rolled in on the racing pickup truck. My crosshairs steadied up on the figures huddled in the back. Again I realized just how close I had come to killing a family.

My dinner sat uneasily. With clammy palms I imagined again that I had pulled the trigger.

The crosshairs rapidly shift off the truck and return to the engagement area. The fact that we hadn't shot the family set the stage for one final outburst that pushed me over the edge.

"Fuck it, kill them too!" shouted the corporal.

My vision flashed red—I'd had enough. Without a word I pushed past Gash and whipped the tent flap back. Too angry to speak, I escaped into the darkness.

I stumbled in the deep sand. I wanted to choke that fucking kid, strangle him with my bare hands to make him shut up. Clenching my fists in rage I walked, to nowhere in particular, just away from the tent.

I couldn't stand to hear him again—one more goddamn word and I would have lost it.

I started throwing self-righteous questions into the blackness around me.

What the fuck was that stupid motherfucker's problem?

I wasn't ready for the voice that answered me from within.

What the fuck is your problem?

Huh? Since when did this become about me? He's the dipshit spouting off about something he knows nothing about.

Chill dickhead—he's nervous and talking a little shit, that's all. You're the one getting all sensitive about it.

My rage cooled immediately as I recognized the truth. It wasn't the corporal's ignorance that had me in a tizzy—it was something else. The same unease that had started when I let the mental footage of the last battle run through my head was coming back—stronger now.

I fought it back again.

There's nothing to be uneasy about—they were all good kills.

I knew that wasn't it but I wasn't going to go further. It was just too dangerous to open up that can of worms.

I was standing on the edge of uncharted territory—someplace I didn't know existed when I'd considered the possible outcomes of war. Death or dismemberment I was ready for. I wasn't ready to feel like *this.*

I turned away from the edge—denial is easy when you have an excuse.

Fuck it. You're tired. Go to sleep—things will look better in the morning.

I slept for about 12 hours. When I woke up I was pleased to find my prediction had come true—I did feel better. I had a long drawn out breakfast/lunch and then went over to the flightline to find out what was going on. We were supposed to have the day off and I was looking forward to going for a long run.

I got to the ready-room tent just as the Operations Officer was briefing BT on our mission. My plans for the day were smashed—we were scheduled to launch at 2300.

After the delay caused by the sandstorm, the grunts were pushing hard for Baghdad. They anticipated rolling through Al Kut late tonight and were expecting heavy resistance. Our mission was to be on-station, ready to go when they got to the city.

When I first learned of the mission I had a flash of annoyance—

Us again? What the fuck?

It quickly passed.

As tired as I was, I recognized having something to prepare for was a good thing. All morning I had forced myself to ignore the events of last night. I'd been successful but it was getting difficult. Now that I had another mission to occupy my mind it was easy. Things were good.

We went out as a three-ship that night. Spock and JoJo were still out with their shot-down bird and wouldn't be back for several more days. I had grown nervous just before we manned our aircraft, but the instant the big blades started spinning they swept my nerves away like magic. I settled into my duties calmly, pleased that I could count on the beautiful amnesia offered by the mission to clear my head.

It was a boring night. Well, boring is a relative term. It wasn't like knitting, but in relation to the last mission this one was a snoozer.

We blew up a whole battery of unmanned artillery pieces, stacks of artillery shells, a bunch of trucks and BT controlled a section of F-18s as they dropped bombs near us, but other than that it was pretty quiet. The big fight for Al Kut never materialized and we spent the night plinking away at unmanned military hardware sprinkled around the desert.

Sunrise did bring a brief thrill. Just as we were planning to head home the DASC asked if we could cover a downed aircraft. At first my excitement level blasted through the roof.

Rescue mission?! Fuck yeah!

Then the real story came out. There was no bird shot down in hostile territory, no one for us to rush in and rescue—they'd just run out of gas.

The CH-46 sat forlornly in a sandy patch of desolate countryside with nothing for miles around. The rush I'd felt withered away quickly when the boring reality became evident. Hell, we weren't even the first Cobras on the scene.

The section of gunships that had been protecting the 46 ran low on fuel and left—about twenty minutes too late. We hadn't been overhead for more than five minutes when the DASC called and asked us to cover another downed aircraft a couple miles away—one of the Cobras we'd replaced. They ran out of gas and had to set down as well.

Even having two birds to cover didn't make it any more interesting. Besides a crazy Bedouin caravan of tractors, Partridge Family school buses, donkeys, camels and a smattering of goats, we didn't see anyone for miles around. We set a solid bingo and stuck to it, letting the DASC know when we had to leave with plenty of time for them to send some replacements for us.

There was no way in hell we were going to run out of gas, too.

About 9 in the morning the DASC cleared us to return to

base. The flight back to Ali Al Salem turned out to be the most dangerous part of the whole mission. It wasn't the enemy, or the weather, or wires and towers that made it dangerous. It was the fatigue. All the long missions were adding up—I was wasted.

I knew I was flying tired. All night long I used every trick in my book to stay alert. Physical abuse worked for a time but then I grew accustomed to the face slaps and ran out of nose hairs to yank out. The Copenhagen and coffee grounds also stopped working—the simple weight of accumulated fatigue overwhelmed the stimulation of the nicotine and caffeine.

The flight home was pure tedium. At least there had been the possibility of excitement when working with a FAC—but now that we were flying home even that was gone. The combination of warm sun, light workload in the cockpit and the rhythmic vibrations of the Cobra's rotor system lulled me into a dreamlike state.

The annoying 'Dudley Do-Right' voice—the one that told me not to do things I really wanted to like "don't look down her shirt"—told me to fight it off, that it was my duty to stay awake blah blah blah.

He was easy to ignore.

I closed my eyes and slipped into blessed silence. After a few seconds of bliss, my face bounced off the telescopic sight unit. Two days ago that would have flooded my system with adrenaline and anger. Now I just adjusted my position to keep it from happening again. The little nerdy voice started screaming again in the back of my head and stomping his feet for effect.

Just to shut him up I heeded his warning.

"Hey Gash, I'm tired." I said over the ICS, trying to get a conversation going. There was no answer.

"Dude, talk to me. I'm falling asleep up here."

"Huh?" Gash groggily realized that I was talking to him.

"Dude, are you falling asleep too?"

"Shit man, I must have dozed off." Super. 200 feet above the ground and both of us are sleeping.

"Fuck this—I'm taking a pill," I muttered.

"Yeah, me too." Gash sounded as unenthusiastic as I was.

The last thing I wanted to do was take a go pill—we'd be home in an hour and then I'd be all hopped up when trying to sleep. That argument lost ground when I realized that unless we stayed awake we might not make it home at all.

Back in Kuwait, we shut down the aircraft and peeled ourselves out of the cockpit. I felt like crap, as though I'd been up for three days straight and was moving in a haze. Even the relaxation that I normally felt after a flight didn't register. All at once I felt tired, dehydrated, itchy and annoyed.

I got all my kit turned in and wrote up the paperwork for the flight. As I dropped off my flight sheets in the operations tent I took a quick look at my logbook, checking the hours written in red ink that denoted combat time.

56 hours.

I'd flown 56 hours in less than 8 days. No wonder I felt like shit. As I walked out of the tent I had to be honest—I didn't know how much longer I could keep this pace up.

CHAPTER 13

WE HAD THE NEXT three days off. I had nothing to do, no missions, plenty of time to go running, read books, catch up on letters, workout, eat meals...

It sucked.

At first it was good—I knew I needed the rest and took full advantage of it. But that only accounted for the first day. After that I grew irritable.

Instead of relaxing and enjoying the respite, I grew jealous of pilots who were out flying. They were in the mix, getting into good fights, doing good work...When they came back from their missions I didn't want to hear anything about what they'd done.

I viewed the fighting as a zero sum game—anything heroic my squadron mates did took away from something heroic I might have done. It makes no sense, not even now, but I couldn't shake the feeling that I was missing out on something.

Even having the opportunity to write emails home turned into a negative. I had received plenty of kind emails from friends and family since the fighting had started, but hadn't had time to write back. I wrote my mom and dad a long one, knowing that they would keep the rest of the family informed on how I was doing.

I didn't hold anything back. Nothing that wasn't considered classified or sensitive anyhow. With my father's combat experience, withholding the details of what I was doing and seeing would only make my parents worry even more. It's the unknown that would really haunt them.

As I wrote about the last big engagement we'd gotten into—shooting all the guys around the ambush site—I felt the unease again. It had been there all along, lurking in the background, but had been tamed by having another mission.

With time off I had nothing external to bury it under.

When I wrote about the running rocket shot—even in the factual, cold manner in which I did—I released the memory again. After I hit 'send' I tried to stuff it away, to erase the scenes from my mind.

They refused to go.

Again and again I pushed the troubling thoughts away. I tried to convince myself that they were not real, that it was something else that was making me uneasy.

I just need to go for a run...just need to take a nap...need to read a book...have a dip...grab a cup of coffee ...

Nothing worked. I might gain a few moments of engagement in a new activity, but it would soon dissipate and I'd feel just as antsy as I had before.

I couldn't release the pressure, couldn't get away from the feeling no matter how hard I tried. I began to look forward to the next flight like an addict—I needed the absorption, I needed something to occupy my mind.

I needed a combat mission so I could calm down.

On the second day of our 'vacation' my prayers for another mission were answered—but not in the way I wanted. A Huey from HMLA-169 had crashed, killing three and injuring one. Our squadron picked up their sorties to allow them a day to mourn their dead.

I felt an indecent shock of relief at the news. I hadn't known the men killed, so it was easy to ignore their tragic deaths. Our division got tapped to launch at 2300 and I slipped into a state of strange tranquility.

Now I had something to plan for, something to get ready for. All my troubling thoughts packed themselves away in the recesses of my mind. They were unruly and disrespectful when nothing was happening, but as soon as an external threat became recognized they saluted and took their seats. I felt calm and collected for the first time since returning to Kuwait.

Two hours before we were to launch the mission was cancelled. There was no explanation, no information, just cancelled. I probably should have felt relief—I wouldn't be going in harm's way tonight. It didn't work that way.

Instead I felt betrayed, like a good friend had just pulled the chair out from underneath me. Anger flashed in my head as the anticipated soothing absorption of another combat sortie was ripped out of my hands.

Fuck! Another goddamn day off? I don't need another day off, I need to get out there!

I was ripshit pissed as I headed back to tent city.

I walked off the bus and it dawned on me that I had nowhere

to go. The tent would be full of guys hanging out, reading, playing cards, smoking cigars on the back porch and generally just trying to relax. I couldn't be any part of that. There was no way I could relax right now and knew I couldn't hide it.

The anger I felt confused and embarrassed me—I had no explanation if someone asked me what was up.

Instead of going back to the tent I walked alone in the darkness. I wandered through tent city trying to clear my head.

Although getting cancelled was annoying, I knew that wasn't what was bothering me. The cancelled mission just threw fuel onto a fire that was already smoldering. As the flames crackled I decided enough was enough—I needed to figure out what was going on in my head.

Unsure if it was a good idea or not, I dropped my defenses. I pulled out the images of Gash's rocket shot out. My pace quickened as I remembered the rush of adrenaline I'd felt. Something came with it though—a faint feeling of shame.

I recalled shouting "Holy fucking shit!" as the man disintegrated. Inwardly I cringed. There was no denying it—I'd felt incredible as we cut him down.

Not now though. Memories of the euphoria I'd felt made me feel uneasy, wrong.

I remembered the four men walking toward the truck. More importantly I remembered my breathless anticipation—the giddy amazement I'd felt as they walked unknowingly toward their deaths.

I'd been like a practical joker who couldn't believe his target was really going to fall for it. But it wasn't an 'atomic sit-up,' or a soda can full of dip spit that they were tricked into drinking— my joke was a hundred-pound missile turning them into goo.

Haha, really fucking funny. Not anymore.

My thoughts jumped to the scene in the S-2 tent. I kept hearing that young crew chief spouting cliché Hollywood one-liners as he watched the Iraqi soldiers getting destroyed. My anger at him had flashed hot and fast, overwhelming me. At the time, its intensity had blinded me to the true cause.

Perhaps foolishly, I started to look for it.

Why had I gotten so upset about that? He was just repeating things that people have been saying about their enemies since time began—talking a little shit that's all.

Then I remembered *my* reaction to BT's tape. I'd felt the same way the young corporal had—excited, pumped up, happy—at the sight of men dying at someone else's hands. Realization that my reaction had been the same was really confusing.

What's going on here? BT shoots a bunch of dudes with his 20mm and I feel great. I blow four guys up with a missile and feel like shit. What's the difference? They were all enemy, their deaths are the whole reason for my existence right now, so why the different reactions?

Just be happy they're dead and move on—Fuck!

I was getting exasperated at this merry-go-round of uncomfortable thoughts. Was there any point to bringing them out? I didn't think so and began to stuff them away again—this time for good.

Then it hit me.

It wasn't the men's deaths that were bothering me. They were the enemy so we killed them—it doesn't get more black and white than that. No, I wasn't getting worked up over the deaths of a bunch of enemy soldiers.

I was getting worked up over *me* killing a bunch of enemy soldiers.

When BT or Fuse did it, I felt the rush of victory. When I did it, I felt soiled and dirty. Even Gash's amazing rocket shot made me feel weird—I didn't fire the rocket but still felt responsible for it.

This was not a welcome realization.

Years of mechanically repeating killing motions had worn pathways in my brain. Those pathways ensured I would be able to execute my mission when the time came. They had worked, and worked brilliantly. Fatigue, fear, excitement and confusion had all tried to derail my efforts, but they had failed—I killed in spite of them all.

The old me—before the war—told me to feel good, to feel successful and proud. The new me—the one with blood on his hands—just wanted to stop thinking about it.

Well, shit. Now what?

I had made a complete loop of the area and found myself back where I'd started. In front of me stood a tent. At first it was as unremarkable as the hundreds of others around it. Then I noticed the flimsy plywood steeple above the entrance.

It was the chapel.

It had been years since I'd stepped into a church—probably ever since my mom had stopped forcing me to go back in high school. I had always kept a small place open in my mind though, a belief that if I ever needed someone to talk to, some big question answered, that I could turn to the chaplain.

Well, I needed to talk to someone now.

I needed someone who could clear away the doubts in my head and let me go about my job of killing people with a clear conscience. Standing outside the dimly lit chapel I felt a wild flash of hope—an irrational belief that the answer was simple, right in front of me.

All I needed to do was talk to the chaplain and he would clear all this up. The church has a long history of sanctifying righteous killing—if anyone could put my mind at ease it would be a military chaplain.

As I had hoped, the chapel was empty save for the chaplain and one of his assistants. They looked up as I walked self-consciously down the aisle toward them, greeting me with kind smiles and gesturing for me to take a seat.

"Umm, thanks," I muttered, taking a seat on a folding chair about four rows from the front.

I sat there quietly for a couple minutes, finding my brain somehow quieted just by being in an environment that was at once familiar and strange. The chaplain and his assistant finished whatever they were doing and split up, the assistant walking out of the tent and the chaplain taking a chair next to me.

We made small talk for a couple of minutes, him feeling me out for what I was there for and me trying to come up with the courage to just say it. Finally I did.

"I guess the reason I'm here is that I don't think I like killing."

He looked at me kind of strangely, so I went on.

"I mean, I know I'm killing the right people—they're all soldiers. But what I don't know about is—am I right for doing it? Every law I know of tells me I'm right—except for one. And I'm not much of a religious guy to begin with. I guess what I'm asking is—how does God see all this?"

I sat back, relieved to finally get the question off my chest. I waited for him to respond, eagerly anticipating some ecclesiastical knowledge that would set my mind at ease. After a minute or two I looked up from the spot I'd been drilling into the floor and shot a quick glance at the chaplain.

232

Lay it on me chaps—unfuck my brain.

"Well, that's a tough question. Do you think that we are right in removing Saddam from power?" he said slowly.

I nodded.

Okay, here it comes.

"Do you believe that he is an evil person who has been doing terrible things to his people for years?"

Again, a nod.

Bring the healing power of the Lord, clear my conscience. I'll dance with snakes, speak in tongues—anything—just get me right!

"So, don't you think that you are doing a good thing by helping to remove him from power?"

I nodded again. Silence. I waited for him to continue.

Sure, yeah. He's bad—got it. What about me?

He just sat there, looking at me with a warm smile. Then it hit me with a flash—he didn't have a fucking clue what he was talking about.

That's it?! That's the biggest load of bull—

I had to get out of there. Abruptly I stood up, mumbled something and almost ran for the door. Getting pissed at a chaplain is one thing—but I wanted to smash his smug smile with my fists.

I stumbled out into the darkness as mad as I have ever been in my life. The shifting gravel beneath my boots sucked energy out of my escape and added to my fury. I hated the gravel, I hated this fucking tent city, hated the chaplain, hated—myself.

I might have been disappointed in the chaplain's answer, but I was livid at myself for even asking the question.

What the fuck did you think he was going to say? Hocus pocus you're okeydokey? You stupid fuck!

How could I have been so stupid? Of course God doesn't

want us whacking each other—you knew that. Yet you enter-
tained the question like there was some sort of loop-hole built
into the Ten Commandments that allowed good little Irish
Catholic boys to kill because they're the 'good guys.'

My anger turned mean, nasty.

You don't have the luxury of feeling bad about killing—you
gave that up a long time ago, dildo.

You're here, you're in it. You better unfuck yourself quick
and quit whining like some puss.

Amid the self-flagellation, part of my brain remained coldly
rational. It was the part of me that solved problems, that broke
obstacles into manageable sizes. While the finger-in-the-chest
lunatic continued venting in the background, the rational voice
laid it out for me.

Okay, you don't like killing. Now what?

This war was far from over. If I kept flying I'd have to kill
again—of that I had no doubt. There were only two options—I
could either quit, or stomp the unease once and for all.

I knew I didn't have the balls to quit.

That only left one option. My seething self-anger turned red
hot but I didn't try to cool it down. I needed this pain, needed
it to harden the resolve I had found lacking. I held my hand
against the flames and welcomed the agony.

The lunatic and rational voices stopped competing. Twisting
their logical and emotional messages into unassailable common
sense they joined forces. When they spoke again they formed a
unified front—there was no more dissension.

I knew right then—this is how it's gonna be.

Put this away. Put it so far away that it will never come out
again. Do it. Now. If you let this weakness out again you might hes-
itate, might get yourself or your friends killed. You owe it to them.

It was one thing to assume risk for myself. There was no way I was going to let my mental weakness increase the risk for my friends.

I'd die first.

I stuffed the unease into the hardest, strongest box I could fashion in my head. Molten anger flowed around it, sealing it closed.

I held onto the anger and humiliation longer—I needed to suffer, to make this so painful I never tried to do it again. As my resolve to ignore the unease hardened to steel, the unified voice fired a parting shot.

This is war. Do your fucking job, or else.

I'd reminded myself of this little tidbit before—a little exhortation to try harder, some rough encouragement to concentrate on what's important. But this wasn't a playful reminder anymore. This time it was different.

This time it was a threat.

CHAPTER 14

SO, IF MY LIFE were a movie this is where a really cool montage of action shots would appear. I was bloodied, seasoned and had weathered my little bout of nerves—this is when I should sprout a determined gleam in my eye and start laying down some serious death and destruction. No qualms, no worries. Hero time.

Yeah, right.

I'd settled the uncomfortable question of "Am I right to kill?" by ignoring it completely. Looking at that question honestly was not something I was willing to do—the potential answers were too dangerous. Besides, I'd already made up my mind that the answer didn't matter—I was going to keep killing until someone told me to stop.

Years of training and self-discipline had taught me to push distracting thoughts aside and focus on the job at hand. Couple that ability with the concept that only anger and disdain for weakness are appropriate feelings for a Marine to have, and I was solidly armored against my own unease.

That's not to say I didn't have to keep working at it.

A couple mornings later we found ourselves on the outskirts of An Numaniyah, covering a friendly tank that had a track blown off by an RPG. We'd flown all night again—the front lines of the battle were now a four-to-five hour flight from Kuwait—to be on-station when the sun came up.

As we flew toward the city I could see columns of black smoke rising into the clear morning air. BT got contact with Wolfie, the FAC, and he filled us in on the situation.

About an hour earlier, 2nd Tank Battalion had entered the city of An Numaniyah on their way to Baghdad. As Wolfie's tank crossed a bridge an RPG knocked off one of its tracks. The 60-ton behemoth ground to a halt. Sporadic sniper fire from the surrounding buildings kept the recovery vehicle from being able to pull the stricken tank out of danger or repair the broken track. As rounds pinged off his tank, Wolfie calmly asked us if we might be able to locate the snipers. His tone made it sound like it was just another day at the office.

...the printer is out of toner...we're trapped in our busted tank while everybody nearby shoots at us...did you catch the Padres game last night?

From our low altitude we could barely see Wolfie's position. Tall eucalyptus trees formed a barrier between the surrounding farmlands and the city itself, making it difficult for us to see inside the city except along the major roads. We weren't about to go blasting into the city though. By this point we'd all taken battle damage at one time or another. The shine of counting bullet holes in our birds had definitely worn off.

Remaining over open farmland we searched the city with

our sensors. We slowly cleared the terrain below our aircraft of potential enemy threats and got closer to the buildings with each pass. It was not an easy task.

Abandoned Iraqi military equipment littered the surrounding area. Some of it had been destroyed, but the majority looked simply abandoned. An early warning radar site, complete with control trailers and transport vehicles, lay beneath us. I scanned them for threats but they looked pretty benign—the doors of the trailers hung open and some of the vehicles looked like they'd been hit with 20mm fire.

Several burning armored vehicles slowly melted into the asphalt nearby—victims of an earlier Cobra division. Amid the columns of thick smoke from the dead vehicles we spotted some heavy machine gun emplacements, M-1939 cannons and ZPU-4s spread about the area. They all *looked* abandoned.

There was so much stuff strewn about that we could have expended all our ordnance on it and barely make a dent. As much as I didn't like flying 50 feet over lethal AAA guns, we really had no choice. There were just too many to avoid them all. Until someone tried to bring one of the weapons to bear against us, we'd just act like they weren't there.

BT and Spock worked with Wolfie to try and spot his snipers while IKE and Gash maneuvered our section behind them. We kept BT and Spock covered while they looked for targets inside the city.

Gash was doing his best to make us a hard target, aggressively maneuvering our aircraft unpredictably while staying in position to support Weasel and IKE. I kept my head in the bucket through all the gyrations, peering through the sights as they twisted and turned along with the aircraft. I couldn't keep my eyes in an area for more than two or three seconds before we whipped around in a different direction.

My stomach protested at the violent rolling and pitching of my sight picture—but I kept my mouth shut. Foiling the aim of any hidden Iraqis trumped me trying to keep my breakfast down.

Weasel came up on the radio—he'd spotted a Zil truck parked inside the city with a ZU-23 mounted in the back. It was just an informative call, letting us all know that it was there.

I looked where Weasel described and spotted the twin barrels of the AAA gun pointing skyward from the back of the flatbed truck. There was nobody on the weapon but plenty of people in civilian clothes were moving around it. They didn't appear to be concerned with the gun. Most of them ignored it as they moved along their way.

It was just another in a long line of potential threats. We went back to searching for active ones.

We got within a kilometer of the city while watching the ZU-23—too close. We'd only spotted one AAA gun inside the city; there were bound to be more. Gash pulled hard to stay with Weasel and ducked a little lower as we scooted back toward the safety of the countryside.

Taking a break from my nauseating duties, I stowed the TSU and sat back. The tension knotted in my lower back from the new position, then released a little. I willed my head to stop spinning. It felt like I had been staring through binoculars while riding on a merry-go-round.

Do I have anything I can puke in?

I ran through my options. I didn't have anything big enough. Just as I realized that I might barf on the floor something registered deep in my brain.

There was no cognitive thought. The reptilian part of my brain—the primitive mush that governs breathing, hunger and sex—just took over.

My reflexes fired before I knew what was happening.

I yanked the cyclic backwards—ripping the controls out of Gash's surprised hands.

"What the fu!...oh." Gash's shout died on his lips.

Our skids couldn't have missed the power lines by more than a foot. Rolling to the left I let the nose fall downward to avoid unloading the head, then passed the controls back.

"Wires. You have the controls," I said, impressing myself with my composure.

Wow, you sound a lot calmer than you feel. My heart was pounding and I had to force my hand to release the cyclic.

"Roger, I have the controls," Gash drawled as if we hadn't come within inches of getting cut in half. It wasn't his fault we almost ate the wires—our canopy was again covered in soot and bug guts.

The realization of how close we'd come to getting slapped out of the sky faded almost as soon as it hit. The incident was just background noise—one of a thousand things that could kill us out here. Before the wires were a hundred feet behind us they were forgotten.

Good thing, too. A few minutes later we had plenty to keep us occupied.

BT and Spock were talking about which building they thought the snipers were in when Weasel cut in. The calm urgency in his voice was unmistakable.

"BT, Weasel. I lost the ZU-23."

My guts twisted in a knot—this was not good.

Shit—manned AAA gun and they know we're here.

I quickly scanned the parking lot where the Zil truck had been—yup, empty. Gone too were the civilians who'd been wandering the streets.

The race was on. We had to find and kill the big gun before whoever had taken it knocked us out of the sky.

Through the 13x magnification of the optics, my eyes spotted movement between two tall eucalyptus trees. It was a man seated on—I couldn't quite make it out—something. His hands spun rapidly in front of his chest as though pedaling a bike. My confusion mounted.

What the fuck is that stinky doing?

It wasn't until bright orange flashes obscured my view that it became clear—he was traversing the 23mm cannons. The truck and gun were almost completely hidden behind the trees and he was firing at us through the light foliage.

Dirty trick. Good one though.

"Break Left Break Left Taking fire!" Weasel's warning call rang out over the back radio.

The first burst from the gun must have gone right between BT and Spock's aircraft—they were within 400 meters of the gun when it opened up. Miraculously they escaped.

Weasel brought our section back inbound—straight toward the still firing AAA gun. I watched as two men in civilian clothes jumped off the truck and began walking nonchalantly away.

Oh no you don't. That's not how this goes.

With cold efficiency, Weasel threaded a Hellfire missile between the trees. It destroyed the ZU-23 and dismembered the two men trying to sneak away.

Wolfie, using the exploding truck as a mark, cleared us for rockets and guns against a building nearby. It was the one that housed the snipers who had been hampering the recovery efforts.

Pressing our attack home, Weasel rolled in on the building with his 20mm. Gash followed with ten high-explosive rockets. The multi-story building crumbled under the impacts.

We never knew if we got the snipers—but things quieted down enough that Wolfie's tank was soon repaired and moving on toward Baghdad.

A few hours later we were back in the same area. Friendly units were moving through the city and wanted gunships on-station for cover. Each one that came upon the narrow bridge where Wolfie's tank had been hit had their 'Spidey sense' go off—the bridge was a perfect ambush site.

We'd done a thorough job of scanning the city from the west—but that was only one side. BT decided to reposition to the south of the city for a different vantage point. The city was small enough we could continue around and peer inside from each cardinal direction. Comfortable that the threat resided inside the city, as long as we stayed a couple kilometers away from the built-up area we felt pretty safe.

Keeping the city on our left side we flew southeast. From my seat I could see the other three aircraft spread out toward the city. Weasel was a couple hundred meters away, but BT and Spock were a couple kilometers. With the bright sunny day there was no reason to fly close to the other section—as long as we could see each other we were close enough.

I relaxed back into my seat. The radios were silent and the green fields looked lush and healthy below us. I drank in the scenery and my mind drifted away.

Just a couple drops of water and this place grows like crazy.

Miles of farmland spread out in all directions, the individual fields split by raised dirt roads and irrigation ditches.

Wonder what it's like to live here? Mud hut, cow, tractor parked on a dirt mound—what else do you need?

"Shit! Taking fire right underneath me mark mark!" BT's excited radio call ripped me out of lala land.

I jerked forward so fast my restraint harness locked.

Fuck!

By the time I could release the lock and got my head in the bucket BT and Spock were turning hard to get away. IKE and Gash had already whipped our section around to engage. Nothing needed to be said—this was tactical maneuvering 101. Basic.

"I got a bunch of infantry in the field at my six o'clock, probably 30-40 of them." BT filled us in on what he'd seen.

His voice sounded slightly incredulous, like he couldn't quite believe what had just happened.

"Roger, in from the south," replied Weasel.

Through my sights I spotted several figures get up from the tall grass and run toward a ditch at the edge of the field. Our 20mm was broken again—I needed to get Gash's eyes on them.

"I got 'em, runners heading 010, maybe 2000 meters," I shouted. If Gash could just see them they would be easy to cut down with rockets.

"I got nothing." Gash's voice betrayed his irritation.

"There, right fucking there!" I shouted—my powers of description failing me at a critical moment. All I could think about was that these guys were going to get away if we didn't shoot quick.

"Where the fuck is there?" Gash shouted back.

"Off the nose—in the field!" Fucking worthless. I might as well have shouted—"In Iraq!"

IKE fired some rockets and pulled off left. Gash sent a couple rockets in the general direction of IKE's shots and pulled off too. This wasn't working. I used the brief respite while we flew away to hatch my plan.

The bug-splattered windscreen meant Gash was basically blind. If the 20mm wasn't tits up then I could shoot the men with that—but it was. I needed some way to mark the men for Gash so he could kill them with the rockets.

Aha!

"If I can get eyes on I'll hit them with a TOW," I told him.

Gash grunted in response, his neck craned over his left shoulder like mine in an attempt to see where BT was firing.

A minute later we were heading back toward the battle. I jammed my eyes against the foam eyepads and searched the field in question. Wisps of smoke drifted across my line of sight, remnants of BT and Spock's rocket attacks. I knew I was in the right general area.

Movement.

I slewed the crosshairs and found three men standing in a ditch.

Are they worth a missile?

I only had four shots—needed to make them count.

A fourth man ran up, unaware he'd just screwed his friends.

I mashed the action bar and barked "Gimme constraints!" at Gash.

He kept the symbols in his HUD aligned. I'd swerve to avoid a squirrel on the road, but I mashed the trigger without a second thought.

The burning motor rotated slowly around my line of sight as the missile's flight controls made slight adjustments. The dead men in my crosshairs pointed animatedly at something in the distance.

I had no concerns about killing, no thoughts about whether I should be doing this. I just wanted them to stay tight—to hold each other would be best—so I could get them all with one missile.

As we closed to within 1000 meters the missile reached the group. It passed close enough to one guy that one of the missile's fins hit him as it passed. He flinched a millisecond before the explosion ate them all.

The missile buried itself in the berm the men were huddled around. The eruption of smoke and mud highlighted their position quite nicely.

"Hit there, hit there!" I directed Gash, needlessly.

He fired seven or eight high-explosive rockets into the shallow ditch, spreading their impacts out to cover the largest area possible. IKE and Weasel must have located another group to work over, because their impacts were on another trench several hundred meters away from ours. There were pockets of troops all over the field—including beneath us.

"Off left, Off left!" I called quickly. A flash had caught my eye and I recognized human figures lying in a ditch beneath us—some firing directly up.

Gash pulled hard left and broke into...laughter.

Laughing?

"What's up?" I asked once we were far enough away.

"Just as we pulled off I saw a dude try to jump a ditch. Dumbass looked at me instead of where he was going—busted his ass hard, AK went flying, must have broken some ribs.

I laughed a little too—it felt good to release the tension.

We made a few more runs on the field, firing a few rockets each pass as we searched for any troops who might still be alive. Anything that moved got rockets thrown at it.

It felt weird. We were in a fight, shooting people who had tried their best to kill us, yet the whole situation was pretty calm. There was no shouting on the radio, no heartfelt epithets. I felt almost devoid of emotion—it was just business. The only thing I remember thinking about was how bad these dudes screwed up.

If they'd just let us fly past them unmolested we never would have seen them. They died because somebody decided to try and sneak a few rounds into BT and Spock. I couldn't be sure we killed them all but it didn't matter. Any we missed were caught in the artillery barrage that pulverized the area after we left.

An hour later we shut down at Qualcom FARP. Qualcom had been an Iraqi superhighway until very recently. Everything for several hundred feet either side of it had been bulldozed and C-130 transport planes were landing on the long stretch of road between overpasses. We parked on part of the cloverleaf on-ramp.

I was just turning off our radios when BT made one last transmission.

"Hey, when you guys shut down come check my bird out." He sounded sort of strange—like he wanted to laugh but couldn't quite clear his throat to do so.

I wondered what was going on.

After tying down the blades and grabbing some water, Gash and I walked over to where BT's bird was parked. The rest of the guys were already there.

BT and Fuse were standing next to their aircraft, looking up at BT's cockpit and shaking their heads. When we got closer the reason became clear.

In the lower third of the canopy, on the right side of the aircraft, was a neat hole where a bullet had punched through. It had continued upward on a diagonal through the cockpit. The slightly larger exit hole was in the middle of the center panel.

That bullet—and the shower of exploding plexiglass—provided the first indication to BT and Fuse that there were fighters underneath them. They'd gone from zero to *Holy Shit* in about a heartbeat.

How did it miss BT?

I wasn't the only one wondering how he'd survived.

Fuse pulled out a piece of string while BT climbed back into his seat. BT held the blue string between the entry and exit holes, smiling wryly as the path of the bullet became clear. Without a doubt, if BT had been looking through the sights it would have hit him squarely in the side of the head. Luckily he'd been sitting back—relaxing like me—while we transited to the other side of the city.

We snapped some pictures of BT smiling, fingers in the bullet holes, and joked about how he needed to go buy a lottery ticket. As strange as it may sound, the whole incident seemed kind of funny. Laughing in the face of death is part of the warrior ethos and it did serve to relieve the stress of the morning's fight. After all, nobody had gotten hurt.

Standing with my friends, making fun of a buddy's brush with death and enjoying the midmorning sun, everything felt comfortable and right in the world. My mind relaxed and I enjoyed the simple pleasure of being alive—for a moment.

Once relaxed, my mind went straight to where I'd been preventing it from going. In a flash I remembered a story my dad had told me about his tour with VAL-4 in Vietnam.

VAL-4, a Navy squadron of OV-10s, had been in-country for several months before any of their airplanes got hit by ground fire. The Vietnamese gunners had a hard time adjusting to the speed of the OV-10—faster than a helicopter, slower than a jet. When they did start coming home with bullet holes they were in the tail section—at first.

My dad and his squadron mates who weren't flying that day heard the call on the radio. The copilot had radioed ahead that he'd taken fire and couldn't raise his front seater on the intercom. He had the twin engines pushed to the firewall and was racing back toward Binh Thuy. In the time it took for him to get home, most of the squadron had gathered near the runway.

My mouth felt full of ashes as I remembered how my dad's voice would change when he told what had happened next. It was always the same—a calm, matter-of-fact tone that betrayed the depth of emotion buried with the memory.

The copilot landed and stopped the aircraft on the runway. As the aircraft rolled past my dad he could see his friend in the front seat, slumped forward over the stick. He didn't move.

Lt Pete Russell was VAL-4's first combat fatality. A single

bullet had penetrated the cockpit, passing just to the right of the bulletproof center panel and hitting him in the head.

Lt Russell's death and BT's narrow escape were two sides of the same coin—*heads you win, tails you lose*. The years and miles that separated them were inconsequential—the game was the same.

The realization that things could have ended very differently for BT flashed unbidden in my head. Oh, I was well aware that each and every one of us could come home dead on any flight—that's not the point.

Knowing it could happen is one thing—seeing it is another.

Looking at BT smiling in the cockpit I could see the other ending. I could see him slumped forward in his straps, head lolling about as the big blades ground to a screeching halt. I wondered how in the hell we would pull his 200-pound body out of the seat.

And then what?

One thing was for sure—we wouldn't be snapping any fucking pictures.

I didn't want to look at bullet holes anymore. I didn't want to be reminded of the other side of the coin. I know it's there, isn't that enough?

Mumbling something about forgetting my dip in the aircraft, I wandered away.

Put it away dipshit—don't think like that.

I had to get my head right, and fast. We could get a mission at any moment and I needed to be ready—not moping around like some whiny bitch.

There it was—the anger. Using it again I berated myself for getting all weirded out.

Yeah, dumbass, you might die. Wanna cry about it?

A couple minutes later I was straight again—the other side of the coin was hidden from view. I was relieved that my rebellious brain responded well to high-school bullying.

We flew another mission that afternoon—more reconnaissance around An Numaniyah—but nothing happened. Well, almost nothing. When we were flying back to the FARP we passed the field where we'd fought earlier. I noticed some movement in one corner of the field and took a closer look.

Standing on the edge of a ditch were two older men in loose fitting robes and headscarves. Their demeanor, and the presence of several women and kids, told me they were not a threat. As we got closer the men turned, their faces broke into big smiles and they waved at our approaching aircraft.

Arrayed around the men were 15 to 20 bodies—some of the soldiers we'd killed. The men were stacking them up, cleaning their fields. It made sense—why wait until they started to stink? But I was kind of surprised they were doing it so soon.

The old men and two of the women waved and smiled as we flew past. I waved back—but didn't smile. I didn't feel victorious or proud.

I just felt dirty.

The big fight for Al Kut never materialized. Our ground forces just skipped the town entirely on their way to the capitol. After a surprisingly restful ten hours of sleep at the FARP, I awoke the next morning ready to go. For some reason I slept much better on the concrete underneath my dripping helicopter than I did in my warm cot in Kuwait. Go figure.

Another division relieved us and we got back to Ali Al Salem a little before noon. After filling out all our paperwork for the flights and dropping off our gear, we met back up in the intel tent to debrief. LtCol Heywood happened to be in the tent at the same time.

I hadn't seen him since the first night of the war—he'd been flying almost as much as we had.

The CO joined us as we played the tapes of the engagements in the VCR. He gave Weasel a solid slap on the back for killing the ZU-23—I was still amazed by how big the muzzle flashes looked. As the tapes played on, he congratulated us for the kills and let us know that the actions of our division were receiving attention up the chain of command to the Wing level.

It was nice to hear our efforts were not going unnoticed by our higher ups, but we really didn't feel like we'd done anything out of the ordinary. Everybody was doing good work.

I was a little nervous when I put my tape in. I wasn't sure how the CO would view my hitting the men with a missile. It wasn't that I was worried about having killed the wrong guys— they were obviously fighters. It's just that I used an expensive missile against a low-value target.

I pressed play.

"Whoa, Shoe! What was that? Why'd you shoot those guys with a TOW?"

LtCol Heywood said it with a smile but it didn't extend to his eyes. I knew he was serious. He might very well have to answer the same question if one of the generals up the line didn't like what I'd done.

"Well Sir, my gun was broken, and Gash couldn't see them

through the bug guts on the windscreen. Putting a missile into them was the only mark I had. I wasn't gonna let them go."

He thought for a second, then clapped me on the shoulder.

"Good thinking." His smile got wide and included his eyes.

"You guys are doing great stuff, keep it up. First that 19-hour flight at Nasiriyah, then staying out for four days in the dust storm, now this. You fuckers—you're my Loco Ocho!" He laughed.

I was relieved that there was no more discussion of the missile. I didn't quite know where he might go with that one. He stood up and motioned for us to come outside.

"Let's get a picture. Me and my Loco Ocho," he said expansively, handing his camera to Cpl Payne. We gathered around him in the bright sunlight.

We were a ragged bunch—dirty faces and oily hands, sweat-stained flight suits, long mustaches and out-of-regulation hair sticking up every which way—but our smiles were wide and bright.

The intense peaks and valleys that had come to characterize my emotional responses continued—I was either pumped or depressed. At least I didn't need to hide feeling stoked.

I was on top of the world right now. Standing with my friends I felt my chest swell with pride. We were Marines doing our job the best way we knew how. That our boss noticed and appreciated it was icing on the cake.

It doesn't get much better than that.

CHAPTER 15

FOR THE REST OF THE DAY I remained in a good mood, coasting on a successful mission and praise from my boss. I wasn't *thinking* about anything, and that made for a very relaxing afternoon.

That all changed after dinner.

As we were leaving the chow tent, the President came up on the TV screens. He was addressing the Marines at Camp Lejeune, North Carolina. Gash, Weasel, IKE and I stopped to listen to what he had to say.

He started by mentioning how well things were going with the war, how great the troops were doing, and thanking all of us for our dedication and sacrifice. He went on for a while, stopping and smiling every few seconds to allow the 'Oohrah's!' and clapping to die down—a wartime president talking to a group of Marines is likely facing his most adoring crowd ever.

It felt like he was talking to *me*. He spoke of events that I had played a role in, about things in my world. His praise felt very personal. As the President reached the end of his speech, his topic turned to victory. He congratulated us on the goals we'd achieved and urged us to redouble our efforts until victory was fully ours. Then, smiling and waving, he departed the stage to tumultuous applause, stopping to shake hands along his exit route.

When the speech started I'd felt a rush of excitement, of motivation. When it ended though—when he spoke of victory—the feeling turned sour. Walking out of the tent I felt distinctly uncomfortable.

After the emotional betrayal I'd felt leaving the Chaplain, anything that made me feel uneasy got shitcanned immediately—I don't have to sniff a carton of curdled milk to know it stinks.

This feeling was a gallon of milk forgotten in the back of my car for a month—no way in hell I was going to open it up.

I pushed it away, trying to deny its existence.

After a shave and a shower I climbed anxiously into my cot. This was the worst time—I didn't have anything pressing to keep my mind occupied. There was nothing to hide behind.

Sleeping in Kuwait was my own catch-22. I had to relax to sleep, but relaxing released uncomfortable thoughts from their holding cells and I couldn't sleep. I much preferred sleeping in Iraq—there, I didn't have to relax.

This night was no different. The President's message kept running through my head. It brought with it the vague unease that I'd felt before. I don't know why, but in the darkness I dropped my defenses. I let the feeling come out and tried to figure out what it was.

It didn't take long—victory.

The President's mentioning of victory had screwed me.

I'd done a great job ignoring any thoughts of what might happen *after* the war. It was my way to avoid thinking about getting killed. Any rumination about future events brought with it the caveat—*If you live that long*—that rotted in my gut.

The only way to avoid that question was to not think about the future. Stay in the moment—that's safe. I'd worked hard to stay in that safe zone.

Now I was screwed.

Thoughts about life after the war, about returning home a veteran like my father, getting married, having kids, growing old—actually *living*—came flooding into my head. I didn't want them there and tried to push them back. It was futile.

The part of me that believed John Wayne's characters were real was growing tired of what it considered whining.

What's the big deal? Enjoy the fantasies and move on. Shit.

Problem was, we hadn't won yet.

My thoughts about the future fluttered about like happy butterflies—until a punk-assed kid named Random Death smashed them with a tennis racket.

The comfortable images of Lena and me growing old together were savaged by recollections of the bullet that passed through BT's cockpit. It could happen at any time, to any of us. There was not a damn thing I could do about it.

I tried to force my mind to go blank, to stuff the images of a happy future back into the darkness. I wanted to find them someday but not now. Not when there was such a strong possibility they would never come to pass.

That realization was too painful.

Somewhere in the night I fell into a restless sleep. I should have just walked around all night, the result would have been the same. When I awoke I was exhausted.

That morning we learned that our division had the next two days off. Normally such news would have made me antsy and irritable—too much time to think. Not this time, though. Shortly after noon a truck pulled up to the squadron. Stacks of bulging orange bags were carried enthusiastically into the ready-room tent—mail call.

It felt like Christmas morning. Guys milled about the stack of boxes hungrily, scanning each box in search of their name. The chatter was loud and good-natured—as if our mothers could hear us through the tins of cookies and wet wipes. The mail got distributed in seconds flat.

I had several boxes, as well as a few letters. I took the letters outside and found a spot amid the sandbags to be alone.

It's funny, nobody bothers you when you are reading a letter. Any other time, someone sitting alone is not going to stay that way for long. Passers-by say hello, mates stop to chat about random stuff, hecklers in the distance shout taunts—all of that ceases when an envelope is ripped open.

As soon as a solitary person pulls out a folded piece of paper and starts reading they disappear. Everybody recognizes that when a person reads a letter they are not here—they've escaped. Respecting that moment is unspoken law.

I sat for a while, cloaked in that strange veil of invisibility, reading letters from my uncle Tim, my mother and father, and a couple of friends from my trail crew days in New Hampshire. There was nothing earth-shattering in any of them, but right then they were the most important papers in the world to me.

I read each letter several times. Memories blossomed into a spider web of happy thoughts and recollections of past events that were totally disassociated from the present. The mental escape they provided made those letters more valuable to me than their authors could ever imagine.

Later that evening, after dinner, the tent took on the comfortable atmosphere of a summer camp bunkhouse. Yeah, we had gas masks and pistols—but other than that it was just the same.

The warm thoughts of home and boxes full of goodies—coupled with the knowledge that we were not tasked to do anything for the next 24-hours at least—gave everything a rosy glow. I hadn't felt like this for a long time.

The tent was filled with my squadron mates sprawled out on folding chairs, writing, reading, playing acey-deucey or just listening to headphones. I caught up on my journal and wrote a few letters back home. I even had a chance to start a book that my father had sent along—"The Island of the Sequined Love Nun" by Christopher Moore.

If my brain was an overactive border collie, that book was an off-leash dog park. The delightfully strange tale of a South Pacific cargo cult, organ thieves, transvestites and a talking fruit bat provided a safe haven for me. My thoughts could run anywhere they wanted within the confines of the story and wouldn't hit up against anything disturbing. I dropped the leash and relaxed—it was like Iraq didn't exist.

After a few hours we turned the lights off and went to sleep. I was almost nervous when I lay down—is this comfortable calm going to last?

It did.

My mind didn't race as I stared into the blackness. I closed my eyes and tested the waters carefully—nothing danced across my eyelids.

Ahhh.

Without effort I slipped into a deep sleep.

Steel-toe boots make a distinctive sound when whacked against an aluminum cot. It is not a pleasant way to wake up.

What the fuck?

I sat up quickly in the darkness, unsure what planet I was on. Someone was standing in front of me and I focused on the dark silhouette.

BT.

Of the thousands of possible reasons why BT might wake me up in the middle of the night, none of them were good. Instantly I was awake.

"You up, Shoe?" he asked in a low voice.

"Yeah, what's up?" I could see the dim outlines of Gash, Weasel, Count and IKE sitting up in their racks. I'd been the last one to be awakened.

BT paused and cleared his throat.

"Sammis and Ford are dead, the rest of their division is on their way back in." His voice was low and steady, controlled.

In the five seconds I'd been awake the possible reasons for the midnight wakeup had been running through my brain at breakneck speed. Now they stopped. In their stead flashed the smiling faces of my dead squadron mates—then nothing. The silence of the tent oozed into my brain like a heavy fog.

"We're heading out in the morning to replace them. We brief at 0630," BT continued.

He unknowingly dangled a lifeline in front of me. I grabbed

it without a second thought and my brain shifted into gear. It skipped totally over the fact that two of my friends had been killed and went right to the next mission.

I let it go—it was safe there.

"No word yet as to what happened, they went down south of Baghdad during a CAS (Close Air Support) mission. The grunts are securing the crash site now. We'll know more when the rest of them get back."

He paused for a moment to see if anyone had any questions. Nobody did.

"Try to get some rest; we'll probably be out for a while." With that, BT shuffled off to his rack and lay down. The creaking of his cot was the only sound.

Gash exhaled slowly and let out a single word.

"Shit."

There wasn't anything else to say. We all lay back down—0300 was way too early to begin the day. We were briefing in a little over three hours; mourning was a luxury we couldn't afford. We needed the sleep.

I locked Ben Sammis and Travis Ford away in my mind. I didn't think of them as dead, didn't think of them as alive. I just didn't think of them at all.

Minutes earlier they had been unremarkable among the multitude—just two squadron mates out flying like hundreds of other guys I knew. I knew that I needed to stuff them back into the crowd—to strip BT's words away from their faces. I retreated behind forced ignorance and barricaded myself in.

The fact that their flight ended tragically was the only thing that had changed. If I just tuned that fact out then everything was fine. In my head they were still out flying—and would be forever.

I slept. I actually fell back to sleep and didn't get up until my alarm went off.

When I look back on their deaths, my reaction—or lack of reaction—is troubling to me. How could I have not felt anything? They weren't my closest friends, but they were good guys and we had shared some laughs. I knew they had families who were devastated, that their loss was overpowering and real. Yet I ignored it with an ease that still makes me feel guilty.

It just isn't normal to shut memories of people away as if they never existed.

Or is it?

The more I thought about it, the more it made sense. I'd been through that pain before when Teddy had died. Only then the knife had cut much deeper and I didn't have anything to cauterize it with.

When Ben and Travis were killed I was prepared to face that blade again—indeed I had expected it for some time. That preparation allowed me to parry the thrust.

I still got cut, but the receipt of another mission seared the wound and stopped the bleeding. It left a nasty scar, but I was alive.

That's the point.

You do what you have to do to protect yourself and keep going. But it comes at a cost.

I still can't recall what they looked like alive. When I think of them, I can only see their faces in a picture.

At our 0630 briefing the mission was cancelled. Our sister squadron had picked it up to give us time to deal with the crash.

I was pissed. I didn't need time to deal with the crash—I needed a mission to *not* deal with the crash.

I fought throughout that day to stay focused on my book, running, cleaning weapons...anything other than Ben and Travis. It wasn't easy. They had been well-liked by everybody and the atmosphere in the squadron was stifling. There were no smiles, no jokes. Everybody was glum and somber. The next mission couldn't come soon enough.

Midmorning on the 6th of April we got airborne again. The squadron was still packing Ben's and Travis's gear away, making preparations to send their bodies home and planning a memorial service. I had to get out of there.

The unceasing reminders that they were dead were becoming impossible to ignore. They made remaining in Kuwait more dangerous to me than Iraq. Flying north, I had the distinct feeling that I was escaping something. But I didn't dwell on it.

That was the beauty of being in the cockpit—I didn't dwell on anything.

We stayed out for three days. There wasn't a whole lot going on. We blew up a huge stockpile of artillery ammunition, took some fire while covering Shazam and his unit as they crossed the Euphrates River and got caught in another nasty sandstorm—but other than that it was pretty uneventful. The scariest part of the whole three days was when a helicopter almost landed on top of us at the FARP while we were sleeping.

When we returned to Kuwait we found out why things had been quiet. Orders had come down that prohibited helicopters from providing close air support within urban areas.

Turns out that so many helos were getting the shit shot out

of them that the higher-ups were getting worried that they wouldn't have any left. Makes sense—26 out of our squadron's 27 aircraft had taken battle damage since the fighting began. That more of us hadn't been killed was plain old dumb luck.

In addition to the orders keeping us out of the cities, there was another reason why things were quieting down. There weren't many big Iraqi Army units left. There were still some irregular forces operating, small groups that hit and then melted away, but the large-scale units were choosing to surrender rather than fight. Baghdad and Tikrit had yet to fall, but there was a feeling that it was only a matter of time.

We had three days off. Three days of solid intelligence reports of Iraqi forces surrendering, light resistance in the urban areas and small-scale skirmishes. I could almost hear the clock ticking down to the final seconds of this war.

And I was sitting on the sidelines.

The feeling that this adventure was drawing to a close made me anxious. I should have been happy but wasn't. I didn't want it to end—then what would I do?

I carried a bucket load of fears into battle but had hidden them away. I only felt the strain of that suppression when I *wasn't* getting shot at.

When the bullets were flying the entirety of my being was concentrated on surviving and doing my job. There was nothing to suppress.

There was something so totally absolute about being in combat—a beautiful intensity in which there is no past, no future, only now—that is addictive.

I'd taken a hit off the crack-pipe and a loud part of me wanted more.

Sitting in Kuwait I felt the opportunity for that last battle slipping away. Every positive report that came back sent me further into an angry sulk. I ran a lot and tried to keep my mind occupied but it wasn't working. All I wanted was one more mission.

When it came I felt like a new man.

Once I knew we were heading out, the unease settled down. It wasn't much of a mission—we were just supposed to pre-position up to a FARP site close to Baghdad and wait to be called—but it was better than sitting on our asses in Kuwait. At least up there we had a chance to get lucky. Maybe someone would shoot at us.

The mission was a non-event.

We made the most of it though, dropping off candy, smokes and chewing tobacco to the Marines at the various FARPs. Gash's folks had sent him a huge box of goodies and we took it upon ourselves to distribute them. It was a good feeling to be able to spread a little happiness to those guys—there was no way we could have done what we did without them.

We spent the night at Three Rivers FARP and got a full six hours of uninterrupted sleep on the concrete parking ramp. On Easter morning we checked if there was any work for us, and receiving a negative response, launched out to return to Kuwait. Another division was enroute to replace us and would stand the next 24-hour alert period.

There were no reports of any enemy activity going on anywhere. The lack of chatter on the radio sounded strange in my headset. We detoured slightly towards An Nasiriyah, flying low over the trenches where we'd fought just three weeks before.

Except for calling out burned tank hulks, nobody really talked as we poked around our old battlefield. It wasn't respect for hallowed ground that stilled our radio banter. Rather it was the sheer weirdness of being here, yet not being shot at.

Last time I'd seen this place it had been through a veil of fatigue, fear, adrenaline and confusion. Flying into the area I wondered if I would feel antsy or jumpy. I didn't. Somehow I knew there was no threat here anymore.

Packs of mangy desert mutts lolled around in the dirt, uninterested in the twisted remnants of the AAA guns except for the shade they offered. The area was devoid of people and the hostile energy that characterized my memories of the battle was noticeably absent.

Except for the blackened scars on the road and buildings, it was hard to tell that anything had happened here. The shifting desert sands had already started to fill in the trench lines and shell holes. I didn't see any bodies—either the dogs or local citizens had cleaned them up.

The whole scene looked calm and tranquil. A little mortar and paint on the buildings and all the markers of the battle would be gone. It wouldn't take long and the whole event would slip into history.

I didn't contemplate when *my* markers would be erased.

I couldn't—I didn't know I had any.

A couple of hours later we landed at Ali Al Salem. Watching another division of Cobras take off I felt the now familiar irritability start again. I knew what it was—they were heading off to a potential fight and I wasn't.

I hated being in Kuwait. I hadn't even filled out my paperwork from this flight yet and already I wanted to be heading north again.

Then we heard the news.

It was over. Baghdad had fallen and the last major Iraqi Army unit surrendered. To top it all off, our squadron had orders to start packing up—we were to be among the first units heading home.

Antsy-ness, irritability and mental blinders about the future all fell into the sand at my feet. I didn't want to go back to Iraq—now that nobody was going to get into a good fight I didn't give a shit about flying north again.

I could tell from my friends' reactions that we were feeling the same relief, although to an outsider it might have been invisible. There were no throaty cheers or high-fives to mark the occasion. A slight exhalation, an easing of the tension out of our shoulders and sudden contempt for the gas masks that had been our constant companions for months were our only reactions to the news.

We didn't know it at the time, but that Easter flight would be our last flight together. Soon we would all have orders elsewhere. Ground tours, schools, command—the normal track of military careers would cause our paths to diverge. While we would remain close, the intimacy we'd taken for granted when we'd relied implicitly on each other for survival would soften as wives, children and normal life regained their rightful places in our lives. Almost all of us would return to combat in both Iraq and Afghanistan, but not together, not like we were in the beginning.

CHAPTER 16

THE LIFE I HAD refused to think about was now laid out before me.

I had a future now, a future I was free to envision and enjoy without fear of having it violently taken away. Coming home, I ran headlong into that future, sprinting forward with abandon—there was so much good in front of me that I couldn't wait to grab it all.

Life, fuck yeah.

Iraq, my 96 hours of combat flight time, the whole three weeks of "major combat operations" got stuffed into a box and put away. It was over, done with. There was nothing in the box that needed attention.

I hit the ground running. Lena was still in Okinawa and would be for another month. Although I could have hung out with Gash, Weasel, IKE or BT, I didn't want to intrude on their homecomings. Sitting around in Lena's apartment in Del Mar and waiting for her was not an option either—I needed to keep moving, to start *enjoying* life again.

The first thing I did was load up my kayak and go up to Big Sur. There was a kayak surfing competition up there and I decided to compete at the last minute. Two days after getting off the plane and three weeks after my last combat mission in Iraq I was kayaking in the cold Pacific waves. The two worlds couldn't possibly have been more different.

There was absolutely nothing about my environment that even remotely hinted at anything military—yet that was where my mind was. I was the only short-haired guy for miles in any direction, kayaking amid the natural splendor of the California coastline, and the only things I could think about were flying, fighting and Iraq.

The people in the competition, some of whom I had kayaked with before, were effusive in their thanks for my service. Even folks I didn't know would come up and shake my hand—the word of my recent return having made the rounds. It was nice, but left me feeling disconnected.

People would ask how it was.

How the hell am I supposed to answer that? I didn't know how it was. I did my job, stuffed shit away in my head and drove on.

But you can't answer a caring face like that. These people genuinely cared, yet they couldn't have a clue what they were asking me.

I remembered a stock answer that my parents' neighbor had given when asked about his Vietnam tour—"It was nice." He gave it not to be glib, but because the person couldn't hope to comprehend what it really was like. Any efforts he made to explain it would be in vain.

I had to learn the lesson myself though and tried to explain it the first couple times I was asked. Each time the listener's eyes would glaze over and I found myself getting angry. Not at them, but at myself. The experiences were so intense, yet I couldn't communicate them. Anything that came out of my mouth sounded trite, cliché or outright inadequate. I quit trying.

"We were busy, really busy." I began answering.

It worked. The well-intentioned person would nod knowingly, shake my hand and walk away. They were absolutely ignorant of what I really wanted to say—just like I was.

I didn't want to process any of the events in Iraq. I wanted to move on with my life and have them fade into the past—but I still wanted others to comprehend the immensity of what I'd been through.

Well, you can't have it both ways.

Amid the crisp, clean air I felt the pressure build inside me. There was a swirling cloud of powerful emotions—laughter, sadness, fear, anger—just aching to be released. More than once that weekend I was thankful for my dark sunglasses when tears welled up out of nowhere. I wanted to open a valve and let it spew but I couldn't. I didn't know how.

Something told me that what I was doing was dangerous. By even attempting to tell people what it had really been like I risked waking a sleeping dragon. I'd lived it, but hadn't come anywhere near processing it. To try and do it in a two-minute conversation with an acquaintance was foolhardy.

Move on. Leave it alone.

I began to wall up the room that held my box of Iraq memories. Those emotions were too strong to bring out—nobody who hadn't been there could possibly understand. Knowing that I couldn't explain them even to myself made me frustrated and afraid. Instead of facing the dragon I tiptoed away—convinced he wouldn't hurt me if I left him alone.

Now he just had to sleep forever.

I only stayed for half the weekend. After a day I just couldn't take it anymore. I didn't understand it—I love kayaking, love being out in the waves but I couldn't relax. For some reason I couldn't enjoy my surroundings and took no solace from the friendly companionship of my fellow paddlers.

I didn't make any excuses, I just packed up my tent and left. Right then I would have given anything to be back in Iraq. At least I wouldn't have been confused.

I went home but didn't stay there. I traveled on the East Coast, attended my little brother's graduation from college and commissioning in the Marine Corps, spent time with my family, visited friends in New Hampshire and went hiking in the Mahoosucs. As long as I kept moving, I felt great.

Everything about that trip was geared toward having fun. Steak dinners, good beer, good friends, family...It all felt so good that my mind didn't wander.

I really tried to answer questions asked by my friends and family—none of that 'we were busy' stuff. I felt I owed them that much. I told them about the long flights, about some of the fights we'd gotten into, about Ben's and Travis's deaths...

At the time I was pleased that I was able to talk about such things as matter-of-factly as I did. I thought that was a good indicator that I was dealing fine with the events. I knew that *not* being able to talk about things indicated being disturbed. Well, that wasn't gonna be me.

What I didn't recognize was that I was only recounting facts. I told the nuts and bolts of what we had done, where we'd been, who'd shot whom...I might as well have been giving a debrief to the S-2 Marines for their intel reports.

My recollections were devoid of emotional tags—I'd stripped those from the events and hidden them away deeply. All I was doing was recounting the physical actions. The emotional responses generated by those events were safely tucked away. I was conscious of their existence only enough to know to stay away from them. As long as I ignored them they couldn't hurt me—I'd convinced myself of that.

Lena came home and life moved on—in the best way. Our relationship had been somehow strengthened by the year we'd spent apart. I had tried to keep her up to date with what I was doing in Iraq via the SIPR net—the classified email network—and felt I'd done a pretty good job. When she returned from Okinawa I didn't feel that there was any backlog of information that I needed to tell her about the fighting. I'd written to her after almost every mission and assumed she knew what I had been through—and understood it. The future was what interested me now—not the past.

After the dust settled from the homecoming parties, vacations and family visits, things settled into normalcy. Not that we really had any clue what 'normal' meant. After the last year, 'normal' was definitely open for interpretation.

Let's just say that we were getting back into the swing of life in the US. We could go grocery shopping, surf, run, drive our cars, watch the sunset...We could do all the fun things we used to take for granted until they became impossibilities. Even mundane daily events came with a flash of enjoyment.

Lena and I went back to work—me up at Camp Pendleton, she at Miramar. Saturday and Sunday regained their importance in our lives—on deployment every day was Monday—and we established a predictable, comfortable routine. Everything settled down in our little slice of heaven.

Except for me.

The little apartment we shared was gorgeous—quiet, open and relaxing. The dark wood floors creaked soothingly and lent the room a reddish glow in evening light. Ocean breezes tickled the curtains through the open windows, bringing with them the earthy smell of pine trees and eucalyptus. It was the perfect place to sit quietly and listen to your heartbeat, to let your mind wander and simply be.

I couldn't stand it.

All day long at work I would feel fine, yet the moment I entered the tranquility of our home I'd get antsy, nervous. As soon as I walked in the door after work it would begin—a maniacal drill instructor screaming in my head "RELAX—RIGHT FUCKING NOW! RELAX!"

At work I was a Marine, an officer, a pilot. I had responsibilities, things I had to do and people counting on me to accomplish them. When I got home I had none of that—no distractions.

While I was operating as a Marine my mind was harnessed to a heavy wagon, pulling it along steadily even as my motor was straining. It was in balance—the load, the screaming engine— each negated the other. If only I could have stayed engaged all day, every day, I would have been okay.

When I got home though, when I took off my uniform, the

hitch would disconnect. My brain, unencumbered by the heavy load, would scream off uncontrollably.

The most maddening part was that it didn't go anywhere identifiable. Gory images of death and destruction didn't flash before my eyes. I never thought I'd seen Sammis or Ford. I didn't have nightmares about any specific event or experience—yet I *felt* like I had.

Instead of being able to relax I had nebulous feelings of anxiety, of having to do *something,* but without any idea of what it was.

In the quiet of our house my pulse would pound and my knee would bounce. A lump would build in my throat. I'd stand, walk around, move. I couldn't stay in a conversation with Lena—my responses would drop off to grunts or nothing at all. When I noticed, I'd try to jump back into the conversation, but it was just on the surface. My mind wasn't there. I didn't know where it was, but it wasn't there.

I tried mindless entertainment—tried watching TV. That was even worse. My eyes would follow the movement on the screen; part of my brain would comprehend what was happening in the story, but emotionally I was somewhere else.

Intense emotions circled unconsciously through my head. I wasn't aware of them—but I reacted to them. That they were unrelated to anything in my current surroundings did nothing to reduce their very real impact on me. They were like swirling ghosts—invisible, ethereal, yet scary.

External silence became my enemy, internal silence my impossible dream. The unease didn't come calling every day. In some ways it would have been better if it had. Then maybe I wouldn't have been able to deny its existence.

The unpredictable periods of relative calm offered proof that

I was okay, that nothing was bothering me. Then the unease would swing back with a vengeance and I'd have to quickly fabricate an acceptable reason for it.

I could have understood it if something really bad had happened to me in Iraq. Then it would have been totally normal to be a little screwed up. Random intense emotions could be explained if I thought I'd done anything to earn them. But I hadn't.

While I could convince myself that nothing was bothering me, I couldn't deny that the energy was there. Its presence was unmistakable and I had no idea how to get rid of it.

Well, that's not totally true. Having a drink or two seemed to help.

If I had wanted to look for justification it was all around me. Images of a Norman Rockwell "dad" character smiling over his Tom Collins, the drinking culture of the Marine Corps and my own comfortable history of getting pissed all paved the way for me to have a drink as a way to take the edge off.

It's as American as mom and apple pie—when the man comes home from work he has a drink and relaxes. Shit, why didn't I think of that before?

So I did. I began coming home from work and having a drink. It worked perfectly—the waking dragon took a hit and went back to sleep.

I was able to relax a bit, enjoy a conversation with Lena without my mind spinning in circles, and when the time came to go to sleep I dropped right off.

Win-win. This coming home from war stuff isn't as bad as everyone made it out to be. I was golden.

But then one drink didn't work so well.

Must have had a bad day, I'd tell myself. *Go ahead, have another. You deserve it.*

My pours got thicker and thicker—*it just tastes better with more gin, that's all.*

At first my slightly buzzed persona was engaging, relaxed and funny. I laughed with Lena about things that had happened in our day, made her eyes roll with my hair-brained, get-rich-quick schemes, and stayed on the wavetop level of life events—everything was glowing, good and fun.

Over time my slightly inebriated mood changed. The happy-go-lucky attitude lasted for maybe the first drink before turning dark. I would withdraw into myself. My mind, unable to ride the wavetops, slid down into the troughs. Once it went down there, it didn't come back up.

Maybe I just need another drink...

I was doing a good job of hiding it—from myself and Lena. Usually I was getting into bed about that time of night so it wasn't a big deal—I'd blame my melancholy on being tired.

I was starting down a slippery slope—one that led to a very bad place—and was totally ignorant of the danger.

But Lena wasn't.

Now, before you think this is some "After School Special," remember who we're talking about here. We're Marines. Marine pilots. Warriors. We drink and party with enthusiasm and abandon today because we might be dead tomorrow. If I want to have a drink or two to relax it's nobody's fucking business but mine—that's how I saw it anyway.

Lena and I had been deployed together. She'd seen me

dancing on the bar with "girls" in Thailand—hey, it's hard to tell—climbing a 60-foot tent pole in the Darwin Officer's club in my underwear and blissfully peeing on myself before jumping fully clothed into a pool in Singapore. When measured against the no-holds barred partying of Marines on deployment, having a cocktail when I came home from work was like a pimple on a hog's ass. Yeah, it ain't pretty—but look at the rest of it.

I was looking at drinking from a gross-tonnage point of view. I'd drunk much more than this at other times in my life—college, flight school, deployments—and was fine. Hell, I used to drink in a night what I now meted out over a week. That's all that matters right? Alcoholics guzzle bottles of cheap vodka on their way to work in the morning—I had this under control.

Thank god for Lena. She saw something I was blind to—the shift in my drinking habits. I wasn't drinking to have fun or to be social. I was drinking to escape. In that regard it didn't matter if I sipped a glass of wine or downed a half-bottle of gin. Either would be cause for concern because I was *depending* on the alcohol to give me numbness—to take the edge off.

She brought it up gingerly. Good thing, too. If Lena had confronted me about drinking too much, she wouldn't have had a leg to stand on—I'd held her hair before while she puked.

She started by refusing my offers to pour her a drink, preferring a beer or glass of wine—and then only one. She brought up an article in one of her Glamour magazines about the health effects of too much alcohol and said that maybe she would cut back on her drinking.

Fine by me. Her subtle nudges were buried beneath my insistence that everything was good, under control. This was temporary stress, just need to relax a bit. Nothing to get all worked up about.

If she didn't want a drink, that was fine. If she was worried about long-term health issues, great. I still chewed Copenhagen on the assumption that I would die long before mouth cancer had a chance to get me. Some spots on my liver? Whatever.

I ignored her increasing reluctance to indulge with me. Calming that itchy irritability was worth a little tension between us. I could deal with the knowledge that Lena didn't like how much I was drinking—I couldn't deal with being so goddamn amped up all the time.

So that might have been it. I could have continued for years that way—outwardly happy and well-adjusted at work, mildly buzzed at home. What was the harm in that? As long as my work didn't suffer and I didn't break any laws, why should I have felt any concern about it at all?

The slippery slope toward alcoholism was not clear to me at that time—that was a disease for other people, not me. I wouldn't comprehend how close I'd come to the edge until after I started writing this book.

If it hadn't been for Lena I would have lived on—possibly for the rest of my life—seeking solace from something I didn't comprehend by running for a drink anytime the unease came to visit. That was the easy way, the cheap fix. It would also have been a really shitty way to live.

Lena wasn't willing to live that way.

It came to a head several months later while we were vacationing in Monterey, CA. We'd planned to camp in Big Sur but cold rains and a very numbing surf experience made hanging out in a clammy tent unattractive. We got a nice hotel room instead. After warming up we went out to explore the town.

The rainy day was perfect for touring the aquarium and meandering through the tourist shops.

I'd been in good spirits. I loved the smell of the ocean up there—salty and kelpy with a not-unpleasant hint of sardines. I imagined it smelled a lot like a burp from one of the barking brown slugs that littered the seawall.

The riotous sea lions, dampening fog and gentle tinkle of sailboat rigging created a soundtrack that could have come from a hundred years ago. I envied the romantic image of a fisherman, working in this environment and earning a living off the bounty of the sea. It sounded so simple, so fulfilling. I suspect it's not, but the atmosphere of the quaint town and the swirling coastal fragrances let me overlook the reality of such a life and enjoy the fantasy.

I drank it in like a sponge. The vast ocean has always intrigued me and being near it kept my mind engaged and entertained all day. Sure, I lived close to the ocean in San Diego but it was different. Down there it was blonds, tanned beach bodies and endless summer. Up here the ocean was cold, dark and mysterious. The town's fishing heritage gave it an edge that fudge and T-Shirt shops couldn't quite wipe away. I could live there, happily.

To top it all off I got to spend the day with my beautiful fiancée—oh yeah, Lena and I had gotten engaged. Things were going pretty well.

After walking all day, pulling up a bar stool at the London Bridge Pub seemed like a great idea.

Wrong.

Moving into the second pint my mood darkened. The happy thoughts about fishing and the allure of the sea disappeared without a trace. In their place came the bouncing leg, uneasy silence and short, curt responses.

I found items of intense interest pinned to the walls of the warm pub. Staring at old newspaper clippings and pictures of celebrities, I withdrew. It was like Lena wasn't there.

We had dinner and I had a few more drinks. Although it was early, Lena proclaimed that she was tired and wanted to go back to the hotel. That was the last place I wanted to go.

I knew she'd picked up on the shift in my mood and would ask me about it. I also knew I didn't have an answer for her.

Walking arm in arm through the wispy fog I felt a gulf widening between us. This wasn't good—none of this was good—I needed to avoid this conversation. I knew it was coming and didn't want to go there.

By the time we got to the hotel I had my plan. It was early and if she wanted to go to bed that was fine—I wanted another drink.

Hey, I'm on vacation.

I dropped Lena off and picked up a six-pack and a tin of Copenhagen at the corner store. Like I'd hoped, Lena was in bed when I got back. Moving quietly through the room I went out on the balcony to sit by myself in the dark.

The misty damp night was a perfect companion for my melancholy mood. I wasn't irritable anymore—I was past that. I stared over the sleepy town from the sixth floor, not really seeing anything as the thick blanket of numbness enveloped my brain. I had achieved my goal. I wasn't itchy, the compelling need to act was gone and the unease was asleep. I was calm.

And drunk.

I didn't notice the sliding door open. The flimsy plastic chair beside me was empty and then Lena was sitting in it. Wordlessly she pulled her feet up and hugged her knees, wrapping herself in a blanket to ward off the chill.

After a few moments she broke the silence. Her face was warm and concerned, but her steady voice held an edge.

"Hey babe. How're you doing?"

"I'm okay," I mumbled, the big dip of tobacco in my lip distorting my speech almost as much as the alcohol.

That's what she had been waiting for, fearing and expecting. I didn't disappoint.

"Dan, you're not okay. You're sitting out here alone and drunk in the cold instead of warm with me in bed."

Ah, shit, here it comes—you drink too much blah blah blah.

"You've been like this more and more often since you got back. I'm worried about you."

She looked at me to see if I was listening. I caught the movement out of the corner of my eye but kept staring down at nothing. Sensing that I wasn't going to volunteer anything, she continued.

"If you were doing okay after what you had to see and do, you wouldn't be normal. *Normal* people don't kill without regret. *Normal* people don't bury friends and never think of them again. *Normal* people don't move on from something as traumatic as combat without baggage."

She spoke slowly and with conviction. She'd obviously been practicing this speech for some time and was delivering it with a punch.

This wasn't the nagging I'd been expecting—that would have been easy to answer with anger. She was tickling the dragon's nose.

"What scares me is that you are not willing to deal with the baggage, preferring to get drunk even though it makes you more miserable." She paused and took a deep breath.

What she said next hit me right between the eyes.

"I love you Dan, but maybe we should put the wedding on hold until you sort this stuff out."

A bolt of fear shot through my hazy brain.

What?

My breath caught in my throat and I glanced up at her quickly, hoping that her face would give some indication that I'd heard incorrectly. The set of her jaw matched the tone of her voice. Her mind was made up.

Fuck.

The ball was in my court. It was my choice to make.

For a while neither of us spoke. I sat with my head down and my eyes welled up with tears—*an effect of the alcohol* I lied to myself.

Something about her statement resonated with a nagging suspicion I'd worked hard to suppress. I couldn't verbalize why, but I knew there was something wrong with how I was drinking. Until she labeled it important enough to make a stand, I'd been able to delude myself with ironclad reasons why it was fine.

I'm just relaxing...

I'm only having one...more.

It's nobody's business but mine...

My logic rang hollow now.

In the space of a few seconds I realized I could hold onto those excuses and lose her, or quit lying to myself. One thought surfaced above the clamor of hurt pride and soggy reasoning in my head.

I don't want to lose her.

I wanted to need *her*. I didn't want to need alcohol.

Without preamble I blurted it out.

"Babe, I don't know what's wrong with me; I don't know what's bothering me. All I know is that I want to marry you."

She responded quickly to the gap in my defenses. When she

spoke her voice was devoid of the steel it had held when she delivered her ultimatum.

"You don't have to fix it right now, or even next year or the year after. I just want you to take it easy with the drinking. You're a good, kind man who's had to do some pretty crappy things. It's going to take time to get over them but drinking yourself into a stupor isn't going to help. You can't run from this, can't hide from it, but you don't have to do it alone."

She paused for a second.

"You can't keep me out anymore. If we're going to get married, you have to let me in."

My eyes flooded with tears and I turned to hold her tightly. I didn't trust myself to speak—but she knew what I was saying. She returned my embrace and I felt like I'd just been given a death-row pardon.

Losing her was something I had never considered possible. The fog in my brain lifted and I swiftly and decisively swore to myself that I would change my behavior—and totally missed the point she was trying to make.

Issues with combat? Nope, not this guy.

I'd cut back on my drinking to avoid losing her, but admit that I wasn't the personification of all that is manly and strong? Bullshit. I wasn't going there.

It would be years before I could see the truth in her words.

At the time, I didn't see my experiences as having been traumatic enough to warrant any aftereffects. I measured my experiences against those of other Marines and came up short.

I hadn't stormed the beach at Iwo Jima, fought hand to hand in the Chosin Reservoir, or withstood the siege of Khe Sanh. I'd never had a buddy blown up next to me. I'd never been showered with gore or had to hold a friend while he died screaming. I'd never had to listen to someone being tortured to death. As far as bad things that could have happened, I'd pretty much escaped unscathed.

Well, I would cut back on my drinking if that would help me keep Lena, but I'd be damned if I was going to admit that anything was bothering me.

Everybody else I knew was fine, and some of them had gone through some *really* nasty stuff. Nope, I'd had a good tour and was ready to move on. I'd just have to figure out a way to do it without drinking—so much.

So, without addressing any of the root causes, I made a decision to quit the only coping mechanism that dissipated my nervous energy. I'm no psychologist, but that sounds like a recipe for relapse if you ask me. That's what might have happened if it weren't for two things: the Marine Corps gave me the opportunity to live a jarhead's wet dream—and I got totally addicted to spearfishing.

Spearfishing hit first. Inspired by the massive fish I saw swimming in the Monterey Aquarium I looked at the ocean in a whole new light. I had spent a lot of time surfing and kayaking above the waves, but when I realized what was underneath, I had to get down there.

At first I'd bring home a sand bass, maybe a kelp bass or two, but usually not. Even on days when I carried nothing home for our table I wasn't empty-handed. I'd wrangled something from the sea, something infinitely more valuable than a twitching meal.

Contented exhaustion.

There was something about being in the water that soothed my nervous energy. Balancing the calm required to hold my breath against the intensity of hunting prey took all my concentration. It was effortless. The excitement of what I might bump into and the challenge of operating in an alien environment kept me cemented in the present. There was no past, no future. There was only the next dive.

I soon found myself going out for a dive anytime I could. If I got off work early—or just left early—I'd hit the water on my way home for an hour or two. Sometimes I could pull Weasel away from his newborn son long enough to join me, but more often than not I swam out alone. I preferred it that way.

Once beyond the surfers I would catch my breath and relax. Finning slowly on the surface I'd peer into the murky water, looking for the slight change in color that betrayed the presence of a reef. When I saw the bottom become slightly darker I'd dive, kicking once or twice to get below the surface and then relaxing. The lead weights around my waist pulled me down as the air trapped in my wetsuit compressed under the pressure.

I'd flare out a couple of feet above the bottom. The grasses and sandy patches got my attention first—the jawline of a halibut or the fat head of a cabezon were dead giveaways of a good meal. If the bottom beneath me was empty I'd look up, searching horizontally for any inquisitive fish coming to check me out. I'd hang motionless for as long as I could, enjoying the ebb and flow as the waves passed through me, before heading back up to the surface to breathe.

Over and over again I dove. Each time what greeted me under the waves was interesting and new: an octopus slinking across the reef, a sand bass eating a small lobster, what I thought was a little halibut turning into a five-foot-long guitar-fish. I might see nothing for two hours, then on the twentieth dive I'd come face to face with a 200-lb black seabass.

The draw of the unknown was powerfully addictive.

My desire to dive and fish provided a great reason not to drink to excess the night prior. On the weekends I would dive first thing in the morning, often getting out of the house before Lena was out of bed. If the conditions were good I'd stay out until the shivering robbed me of all my oxygen and I couldn't dive anymore.

The more I dove, the better I got at holding my breath. The better I got at holding my breath, the more fish and lobsters I brought home. I absolutely relished the challenge of freediving and loved the tangible rewards I was able to bring home.

It didn't hurt that everybody I knew thought I was crazy for doing it. It's tough to find something that Marines find crazy, and I enjoyed my friends' surprised reactions when I'd talk about my latest underwater adventure. I guess the idea of diving for hours into the cold Pacific in search of dinner just didn't resonate with some people—go figure.

They focused on hypothermia, sharks, shallow water blackout—the little things that could kill you out there. I thought about that stuff too, but instead of scaring me off, it made diving all the more attractive.

Of the possible things that could kill me, the chances of running into a Great White shark were the least likely—yet they were the most alluring. As much as I enjoyed the beauty of the fish and the physical challenge of freediving, it was the tingle of the unknown that I was really after.

Slipping beneath the waves I knew, without a shadow of a doubt, that I was no longer on the top of the food chain. Each foray into the depths tempted fate. Spearfishermen and women call him the Taxman, or the Man in the Grey Suit—always with respect. Those powerful sharks rule the alien, underwater universe where we trespass.

It wasn't hard to imagine big sharks nearby when I was diving. Not being able to see them didn't mean a thing. They might be hidden in the murk and I'd never know it until they made their move. The water was a one-way mirror though—they'd know exactly where I was. The slight fear I felt was constant.

It fulfilled a need I didn't know I had.

Over time, the effects of my diving became obvious. The anxious feelings that used to assail me when I got home from work came less frequently. My mind didn't disconnect anymore at the first hint of silence in the house. I could have a beer with dinner and still feel calm and relaxed.

When the unease did settle upon me I wasn't unarmed anymore. Without realizing it, I would mentally deflect the feeling by planning out my next dive, or by recalling some of the neat stuff I'd seen on the last one. Even when I would get snappy and irritable it didn't last. At the next opportunity I would escape to the cold water and everything would smooth out.

After I started writing I recognized the role spearfishing played in my return from combat. I knew nothing of it at the time—it was fun, exciting and a good workout. I didn't need any other reason to go diving. In hindsight though, I can see exactly what it did for me.

If my combat experience had been heroin, the constant low-level fear of being eaten by a shark was methadone. The pure intensity of combat was not something that I could walk away from—I'd unknowingly tried to quit cold turkey with predictable results. Through dumb luck I stumbled upon a way to 'step down' off the rush of combat.

Even though the duration of my combat experiences was relatively short—three weeks—those experiences had been pretty intense. The irritability and *need to do something* were left over physiological responses from Iraq. Even if I had recognized them at the time, there was nothing I could tell myself in order to make them stop. They were physical responses—they needed physical actions to dissipate them.

Freediving provided an environment where the nervous energy being pumped out by runaway processes in my brain could be put to good use—keeping me alert and safe underwater.

The time I spent in the water gave me hours where elevated alertness was desirable. This effectively harnessed the energy that had driven me to seek numbness from a bottle and expended it in a natural and appropriate manner.

When I would finally stumble out of the water, shivering uncontrollably and mumbling to myself, whatever reservoir of neurotransmitters that had kept me twitching on the threshold of 'fight or flight' for hours was totally depleted.

I could actually relax.

The chemicals that kept me *on* had become background noise in my daily life, a solid, static racket that couldn't be ignored—only adapted to.

I can see now that the only choice I had in the matter was

whether my adaptation to the overabundance of those chemicals was healthy or not. I got lucky—Lena likes lobsters.

The calm I enjoyed after spearfishing was proof that my adjustment was working—but it might not have been enough. I couldn't stay underwater forever. Luckily, diving wasn't the only ingredient in my inadvertent recipe for coping.

The Marine Corps also played a large role in helping me move past my first combat tour.

They gave me a second.

CHAPTER 17

NOW, BEFORE I GIVE the impression that the Marine Corps forced me to go back into combat, let me be perfectly clear—I would have paid *them* for the opportunity.

After only a couple of months at home, my memories started to shift. The incidents of gut-wrenching fear, disgust and paralyzing uncertainty all faded into the background. What remained were camaraderie, intense excitement and the feeling of doing something important. The positive memories of my flying tour soon towered over the negative ones.

Before long I came to see combat as an adventure again—something I was eager to get back into. Normal daily life provided emotional highs and lows but they were just that—normal. Combat emotions are incredibly potent and, once felt, make all others pale in comparison. There's something powerfully addictive about combat—it provides the searing heat that lets you freebase emotions and gives you the rush.

My second combat tour brought the rush, big time.

Shortly after returning from Iraq I began scheming to get back. I didn't want to go back in a flying capacity, though—I'd done that already. No, I was looking for something else, something exciting, dangerous and new.

Through luck, good timing and a reputation for not being a bag of shit, I landed my dream job—Forward Air Controller with Marine Corps Special Operations Command, Detachment One.

Det One, as we came to be called, was a new unit. Brand spanking new—like *didn't even have a building of its own* new. It was a temporary unit created to prove a concept—that the Marine Corps could provide a significant added value to the United States Special Operations Command (USSOCOM).

Marines had been serving individually with USSOCOM for years, but this was different. Det One was the first Marine unit designed to operate independently within the special operations community. Its success or failure would determine the future relationship between the Marine Corps and USSOCOM for years to come.

In my totally unbiased opinion, it succeeded brilliantly—but that's another story.

The Marines selected to populate the nascent unit were the absolute best. The original 86 members were hand-picked by Colonel Coates, the Det's Commanding Officer, and he unabashedly took only the cream of the crop. The Boss, as Col Coates was known, had been in the Marine Corps since slightly after

Christ was a corporal. He knew everybody and filled his 'once-in-a-lifetime' unit only with proven warriors he knew and respected.

He didn't know me from Adam.

But he knew Hobbit—the same Hobbit who would command my brother's squadron at the time of his crash. He had worked for Col Coates before and the Boss loved the tenacious, wiry, foul-mouthed Hobbit like a son—okay, maybe not a son but like a good dog. Okay, a reliable watch—never mind.

The Boss knew and respected Hobbit, and Hobbit didn't think I sucked too badly. When it became apparent that the Det needed a second pilot to act as a FAC, Hobbit vouched for me and the Boss gave me the nod. After the uncrowned elite of the Marine Corps were painstakingly selected to man the unit, I slipped in under the wire.

Within a couple of days of checking in I found myself humping a heavy rucksack through 10,000-foot mountain passes in Bridgeport, CA on a mountain warfare training exercise. Even as my lungs wheezed and legs cramped, I couldn't believe my good fortune.

I was in heaven.

I worked directly for Hobbit and he quickly filled me in on what was expected of me. Officers usually have to balance a bunch of jobs at once—you have a primary job, like being a pilot, and fifteen secondary jobs like Printer Fixer Guy or Fun And Games Officer. The most important one—training for war—sometimes gets shelved behind ordering flowers for the Wives' Club tea party. I worried that with so few officers at the Det, I would be inundated with all sorts of extraneous crap. Hobbit had a different plan.

My job was plain and simple—learn. In a very short time, the Det would be in combat somewhere. I would not be stuck in an office while operations were taking place. I would be on the operation. My job was to become an asset on a mission, not a bumbling, stumbling liability.

I had a lot to learn. Measured against the decades of specialized infantry and reconnaissance experience of even the most junior operators at the Det, my six months of basic infantry training at TBS were laughable. I didn't know shit about the recon world, but I had one thing going for me—I knew it.

I kept my mouth shut, listened to the professionals around me regardless of their rank and absorbed information quickly. The new material—new weapons, new targeting equipment, new tactics, new comm gear—took time to learn, but soon I had a working knowledge of all sorts of deadly stuff.

I was becoming a valuable member of the team, doing things that were exciting and challenging. I couldn't wait to go to work in the morning.

A constant stream of new challenges at the Det kept me engaged at work, and hours of spearfishing and freediving filled the void when I wasn't. The appropriate/inappropriate high energy cycle was still there, but I was using it to my advantage. By remaining constantly engaged, I started to regain some balance in my life.

Physically, I was sliding into a good place.

I felt like I had everything under control. And I did, for the most part. But as the loud and boisterous physical aftereffects of my first combat tour dissipated, their absence revealed something that had been hidden. I didn't quite know what it was—just a sense of unease that bubbled up in my rare unguarded moments.

It was nothing overpowering—nothing that kept me up at night—but it was there. I recognized its presence even as I refused to acknowledge it—like a well-heeled traveler consciously ignoring the hostile stares of impoverished locals.

It made me uncomfortable because it was *different*. The physical reactions I'd felt—the nervousness, irritability, disquiet—all seemed to fit. They were tangible reminders of the excitement I'd felt in combat, and on some level they made sense to me.

Whatever this was, it wasn't on the surface. It was like my baseline emotional state—the one I reverted to when not diving, exercising, working or anything else—had been fundamentally changed.

And not for the better.

There was something unsettling about the insistent unease—I could force it down into the depths of my brain but could never get it totally out of my mind. It always lingered there, deep below the surface, waiting.

It only came out when I was by myself—a characteristic that made it easy to hide. As long as I was engaged in something, riding above my emotional baseline, things were as good as they'd ever been. I was happy, energetic and comfortable with my place in the world. But when external stimuli disappeared, it seeped in.

I didn't try to figure out what it was—something told me that would be very dangerous. I steered well clear of any introspective thoughts. I was going into combat again soon and knew that mental preparation was just as important as physical. Now was not the time to entertain any thoughts that might degrade my ability to do my job. Combat requires cold efficiency amid raging emotions. I knew that, and knew that the type of combat I was likely to get into would be more savage than what I'd already experienced. In a world where split-second decisions mean life or death, I was not about to handicap myself with some weak-minded bullshit. Doing that would be a sure way to come home in a bag.

No. Irritating unease could go fuck itself. I had work to do.

As our deployment date approached, the details became clear. We were going to Iraq to conduct special operations missions in and around Baghdad. I was excited and nervous—in 2004, Baghdad was a seething mess of beheadings, car bombs, rockets and mortars.

Cradle of civilization my ass.

In my mind the potential trauma of six months of sneaky ops around Baghdad made the dangers I'd faced in the cockpit seem like child's play.

I wouldn't have a clean, powerful helicopter to deliver death and destruction from afar. No, this time I'd be down in it—in the shit, hookin' and jabbin', where the rubber meets the road...I'd be in the place described by all the cliché terms for the dirty, gritty, dangerous world created when men live only to kill each other.

I thought my first tour a warm-up—the second was going to be the real challenge.

The idea that ground combat was the true test of a warrior had been driven into my head by movies, books and the Marine Corps itself. Platoons of jogging Marines don't chant jodies about blowing up tanks or dodging wires and bullets in a sandstorm. Instead, the selfless act of jumping on a grenade to save your buddies is shouted from thousands of raw throats on Marine bases across the world. The desperate situation that requires the ultimate sacrifice is heralded as a good thing, an opportunity for real heroism. Dying didn't matter. Being remembered as a hero did.

There were scenarios in the cockpit where things could get really dicey, but those seemed to pale in comparison to what could happen on the ground. No, it's ground combat that Marines hold up as the true test of courage.

I felt a need to experience the toughest trials. I had to prove I could handle them—because I believed I could. It was *on* the battlefield—not above it—where I imagined I could face them.

It wasn't just bravado that made me seek more severe experiences. I needed something to drive away that undercurrent of unease, something that would overpower it and flush it from my system without me having to process it.

I needed mental Draino.

I came to see my FAC tour as the way to dissolve the persistent hairball of disquiet—one way or another.

If I came back from my ground tour unscathed, then I was free and clear, because I'd survived something universally recognized as truly traumatic. That would *prove* that I was fine and the unease was inconsequential. I could ignore it forever and move on.

On the other hand, if something really bad happened, I'd have an excuse to feel all screwed up.

Either situation would be better than the status quo.

As it stood, I considered the anxiety a betrayal—a weakness that undermined me as a strong warrior.

Well, fuck that.

If the price of protecting the self-image I'd worked so hard to create was ignoring a little unease then it was a no-brainer—I'd hide it forever. I was strong enough to do it too.

As events drew down to 'lasts'—the last time I'd have to fill up my car with gas, the last time I'd dive, the last good meal before deployment—my excitement mounted. I didn't have to think about suppressing the unease—my mental state was nowhere near baseline.

I was gearing up for action and was entirely focused on the challenges ahead. Like a clarinet at a Judas Priest concert, the restlessness was overwhelmed and absorbed into the general cacophony of my nervous exhilaration.

Less than a year after I'd left I was back in Iraq, stepping off the plane in Baghdad.

The next six months were awesome.

That might sound weird, but it's true. The deployment was everything I'd hoped it would be and more. Working as a separate task unit underneath a SEAL Task Group, the Det executed over twenty direct-action missions in and around Baghdad, fought in al Kut and an Najaf, protected a Vice President in the Iraqi Interim Government and assisted other coalition units with highly specialized intelligence, reconnaissance and fire support. And we did it all without losing a single man.

I got to go on all the missions, sneak around in the dead of night and help make bad people go away. My ground combat experience was terrifyingly incredible, intensely satisfying and almost completely devoid of the moral ambiguities that had sullied my first tour.

I got to do things I never thought I'd have an opportunity to do. Yes, I'm a Marine—but I'm a pilot. Pilots don't usually get to do the things I did.

I got to sneak through sleeping Baghdad neighborhoods in the dead of night.

I got to feel the rush that comes from seeing a bullet hit the wall where my head had been moments before. I'd actually giggled at the sting of plaster on my cheek.

I got 'salty' enough to act really blasé about indiscriminate rockets and mortars—right up to the point where they almost dropped one on my head. The white-hot fear from the soft, evil whistle of that round consumed me and I'd tried to burrow into the asphalt like a mole. Nobody acts cool when they're *really* close.

I learned that Iraqi puppies are cute. Iraqi dogs are uglier than sin.

I learned that the real danger of climbing a house in the middle of the night in Baghdad doesn't come from falling or getting shot—it comes from electrocution. Every goddamn house was draped with arcing, jury-rigged power lines with stolen electricity flowing from cartoonishly overwhelmed transformers. I hated climbing through that shit.

I learned that people who get shot by snipers usually fall out of their shoes. Really, they die shoeless. It's weird.

I learned that smearing peanut butter on the inside of a porta-john's door handle is really funny—unless you're the one who grabs it.

I learned that Iraqi mothers don't want the men who blow down their doors in the middle of the night and take away their husbands to give their crying kids Jolly Ranchers. Somehow it's worse than ignoring them.

I heard the call to prayer punctuated by automatic gunfire so often that the two sounds are inseparable in my head.

I learned not to sit on body bags—especially ones that had been dragged to the Hummer. They leak.

I learned that Apache 30mm rounds don't penetrate thick masonry walls. Good thing, too, since we were behind them.

I learned that I could hear the fins of a JDAM (Joint Direct Attack Munition) click menacingly as they steered a 2000-pound bomb over my head. What if they clicked when they should have clacked? Don't worry about it.

I got to live a warrior's dream—experiencing the breathtakingly intense highs of combat at a tremendously low cost. There was always the 'what-if' factor—what if they're waiting for us, what if the house is booby-trapped, what if…But the caliber of the men I was working with made the 'what-ifs' much less worrisome than they otherwise might have been.

As good as I thought I was, the men around me were better. Sometimes it's really comforting to *not* be the best. There was no doubt we could handle any threat that popped up.

That's not to say there wasn't fear involved—there was. While I can't remember feeling fear out on a mission, there were times back in garrison when it would slink into my thoughts. It was different though, almost academic.

Tying my boots just before jocking-up always seemed to spark uncomfortable questions.

Is this the last time I'm going to need to put a boot on this foot?

Wonder if I'll have two hands to tie my laces in a few hours?

Is this the night?

The questions never hung around long—there was too much

to do. Radio checks, final briefings, vehicle mount-up, and before I knew it I'd hear the platoon sergeant, Top Oakes, come over the radio as we approached the gates—

"Eyes. Lights. Sights."

With his quiet reminder that we were now in hostile territory, lasers flicked on, each man double-checked the electronic sights on his weapons and the whine of diesel engines spooled up into a menacing roar.

We were five blacked-out Hummers screaming into the night, bristling with weapons and focused intently on our target. We would bring our prey home with us, alive if possible, dead if not. The choice was theirs to make, and most chose wisely.

The six months in Baghdad passed quickly. When we did rotate home, I began to take stock of what we'd done, and more importantly, how I was dealing with it.

This second homecoming was different from the first. Then, the war was fresh and new. Everyone in the States wanted to know someone who was fighting in it. By shaking a service-member's hand or buying them a beer, people felt connected to a grand victory over a dictator and tyrant. When I'd come home the first time, there was a patriotic fever sweeping the nation. Those of us with short hair and tans were rock stars.

A year and a half later it was different. Units came and went to war without fanfare. Families cried and hearts were ripped in two, but it was personal suffering. Coming home was the same. The celebrations and tearful reunions marked the end of profoundly painful separations and months of sleepless nights, but only for those who'd remembered the ones who'd been gone.

It may sound weird, but coming home without the attention

was easier. We landed in Miramar, drove up to Pendleton and turned in our weapons. Then we went home.

That was it.

Sand marked the spot in Lena's apartment where I unpacked my gear, but besides that, there were no visible reminders of the world I'd come from. I preferred it that way.

I monitored myself pretty well after my second tour—checking the results of my little litmus test to see if I was all right. I tested the waters carefully and let my mind wander on a tight leash. The only thing I noticed was a little of the old irritability when things got quiet at home, but that didn't last for very long.

I had my coping mechanism in place for that—diving. Again I found solace beneath the waves. On my time off, and sometimes during work, I went diving whenever I could.

I got a bigger speargun, rigged my kayak so I could paddle out to the kelp beds, and worked off my nervous energy in pursuit of bigger fish and lobsters. I sought deeper challenges and routinely found myself more than a mile offshore, drifting alone amid the underwater jungles of kelp. My nervous alertness was again consumed by the slight tingle of danger.

Besides the slightly heightened level of alertness that I expected, there was only one other little weirdness that stemmed from my second tour. It happened a couple of months after our return—well past the time I thought it would—and caught me totally unaware.

I was driving home from work one sunny afternoon, zipping down I-5 in uncharacteristically light traffic. My mind wasn't anywhere. I was zoning out and listening to the radio, driving

75 mph on total autopilot.

I was approaching the overpass for Mission Avenue. There is nothing peculiar about that overpass. In fact, it is pretty unremarkable in all respects. Overpasses like it span highways all over the world, from California to...Baghdad.

Overpasses were always danger zones in Iraq. Grenades could be dropped from above, bombs could be chiseled into the concrete, gunmen could hide behind them and spray us as we drove past .... There were no limits to the bad things that could happen near an overpass. There are a lot of them along Route Irish—the main highway from the airport to the Green Zone. We'd driven that route a lot.

We had standard actions when going under an overpass in Iraq. The vehicles were staggered across all available lanes of traffic, and each driver would go into the overpass in one lane and switch in the middle, exiting in another lane to frustrate any attempts to drop nasty surprises on our heads.

Gunners, of which I was one, scanned upcoming overpasses for any activity and, upon exiting the overpass, immediately covered the backside of the bridgework in case anybody was hiding there to engage us. It was like clockwork and we did it hundreds of times during the deployment.

None of that was going through my head that pleasant afternoon. I was thousands of miles from Iraq both physically and mentally—right up to the millisecond before I went underneath Mission Avenue.

Motion on top of the bridge caught my eye—a construction

worker walking out from behind a street sign. The yellow hardhat and orange vest made him easy to see but that wasn't what my brain registered.

In the blink of an eye I was back.

One thought screamed white-hot through my head—

Threat!

Unreasonable fear flooded my veins. The synapses in my brain ordered me to swing my weapon around and engage—

Quick! Before he opens up. Shoot!

But my hands weren't gripping a 240G. I didn't have a laser spot to put on his chest.

Nothing felt right.

My brain's frantic orders hung in the air—I couldn't follow them.

I froze.

Gripping the steering wheel I blasted through the underpass in white-knuckled terror.

There wasn't a single coherent thought in my head—no *Shit!* or *Fuck!* giving voice to my fear. Instead I fought back the overwhelming urge to get out of my speeding car—to just be anywhere other than where I was.

When nothing exploded and a hail of bullets didn't chase me out of the darkness, the terror released me. Mentally, I snapped back quickly. Within a mile, I convinced myself it never happened.

It took several more miles before my cramping forearms reminded me to release the wheel.

I was on pins and needles for a couple of days, waiting for some other weird shit to hit me.

Is this how it starts? Was I going to start seeing bodies in the street? Have screaming nightmares? Had I failed my test?

To my immense relief it was a one-time occurrence. Besides that one flash of overwhelming terror, I never felt anything like that again. I brushed it off as an aberration—it didn't fit, so I ignored it.

I saw my ground combat tour as a pass/fail test. Failing would have meant I came home with clear-cut symptoms of PTSD. In that case I was prepared to seek help.

Passing was anything less.

There was no middle ground, no room to acknowledge unease short of incapacitating PTSD. It was all or nothing.

Well, I didn't have it all. I must have nothing.

CHAPTER 18

SO THAT'S IT. I'd been to combat twice, returned with no physical or psychological wounds and was doing fine. Hell, I was better than fine—I'd escaped injury, been honored with medals and had some pretty kick-ass adventures.

On the outside, I'd say I was doing pretty flippin' awesome. So would anyone who knew me.

Inside was a different matter.

In the years following my last combat tour, I maintained my stubborn belief—I carried no baggage. Along the spectrum of possible outcomes of my combat tours—happily victorious or dead/seriously wounded—there was no middle ground. I put myself solidly on the happily victorious side.

No wounds, no screaming nightmares equaled I'm good. In my mind, that *proved* I'd gotten over Iraq, that I'd moved on.

I did come to recognize that my hyper-alertness and irritability were related to the intensity of my combat tours—but I thought I'd handled them. I assumed my victory over the physical hangover from combat was proof positive that I was fine, even as the low-grade rumble of unease continued unabated.

The disquiet stopped by at the weirdest times—most notably during TV shows. There was something about watching someone else's emotions playing out on the screen that weakened my walls. One second I'd be laughing, then next my throat would constrict. I'd have to look away from the screen to stop the tears from welling up.

Then I'd get mad.

When did I become such a douche?

Even the cheesiest, most overly sentimental bullshit was able to reach into my heart and rip me to pieces. I'd watch commercials where some dildo buys his wife a luxury car for Christmas and find myself tearing up at her joyous reaction.

What the fuck is that about?

If I'd been honest with myself, I would have understood why. I would have seen that my brain was like a kennel where I kept my emotions chained like unruly dogs. They sat quietly in their little cages until they recognized the bark of the actors' emotions—then all hell broke loose. Snarls, growls, howls and yelps echoed through my head as *my* emotions—angry at being trapped for so long—got riled up and threatened to break out.

But I wasn't interested in being honest—I wanted to be fine.

I'd run up and down the kennel and browbeat the emotions into submission. True anger at myself provided the energy—this was not going to happen, not to me. As long as I could snarl and bark louder than they could, I had control.

You'll behave because I fucking said so.

If they were going to conspire to overwhelm me at strange times, then I was just going to have to put a stop to it. Who ever heard of a decorated war vet getting sentimental about TV commercials?

That wasn't going to be me. I knew exactly what I needed to do.

Stuff it away. Smash it down.

If you don't give it a voice, then it will stay hidden. Hidden is good.

If I can ignore it, then nobody will know. Nobody will know I'm weak.

That was all that mattered.

For five years that *was* all that mattered. I got out of the Marine Corps, got a good job flying for a civilian company and kept the lid on my pressure cooker tightly closed.

I was ready to slip into some idealized concept of a hero and live happily ever after. Inside I would have been a mess, but I could have dealt with that. Internal misery was a price I was willing to pay to maintain my self-image as a warrior

Then, in the aftermath of my brother's crash, I locked eyes with my son as he crossed his legs and leaned against the kitchen cabinet door. What I saw in that 18-month-old version of me turned my world of self-serving deception on its head.

Since when does being strong mean hurting your son?

I finally decided to face what was bothering me, for his sake and mine. There was only one problem—I had no idea what it was.

I tentatively broached the idea of writing something, its definition nebulous and unstructured, to Lena. Her reaction surprised me.

Instead of a kind word or two of support—something along the lines of "That's nice Dear, could you pass the salt?" she'd said, "Thank god—finally." I realized then that she had known for a long time that I wasn't quite myself. She just never pressed the matter, knowing that to push me to acknowledge something I didn't want to see would be futile.

Now that I had brought the subject up she jumped whole-heartedly behind the idea. Her support and encouragement moved the thought of actually *doing* something out of the abstract and I began to explore the dusty boxes of memories stuffed away in my head.

I sought refuge in our basement. When my son, and later my daughter, was napping I'd descend into the moldy darkness and write. Pouring over Gash's and my journals and re-watching my gun camera videos, I reconstructed each flight moment by moment.

My writing started very mechanically—a cold retelling of facts without emotional color. I caught myself quickly, though, knowing that I had to dig deeper. I had to allow myself to feel *now* what was unsafe to feel *then*.

It wasn't long before I realized I was on the right track. It started small—just a sense of accomplishment and unusual serenity on days when I wrote. It didn't have to be much, an hour, maybe a page or two. The duration or amount of mea-surable progress didn't seem to matter. Just the simple act of putting words on paper felt good.

On the days when I couldn't write the opposite was true. I'd get moody, snap at the kids and withdraw from Lena. The contrast in my mental state was noticeable and hardened my resolve to keep working at it. To stop writing would only put me back on course to the bad place—emotional coldness punctuated by unpredictable outbursts.

No way—I wasn't going to be that kind of dad.

Eventually I got through the first draft. I was really pleased with it. Not because it was a work of literary genius—it most certainly was not—but because it provided a crucial first step toward understanding the unease. I knew I was on an indefinite journey and all I could do was put one foot in front of the other.

But I was finally moving.

With the luxury of time and distance—both from combat and the military's cultural stigma against 'feelings'—I began to understand how my actions and experiences in Iraq had actually made me feel.

That seemingly small step brought with it the first flicker of comprehension of what I'd been through. It also fueled introspective thoughts I never would have entertained before.

In the heat of the moment—when missiles strike home, bullets snap overhead and lives are snuffed out in milliseconds—introspection and emotional awareness exist only in Hollywood fantasy.

I'd survived and been successful expressly because I'd controlled my emotions and reactions in combat. I'd caught them, stuffed them into a box and built a wall around them—just like I'd been trained—and went back to work.

What I hadn't recognized was that those emotions still

existed—my refusal to acknowledge them did nothing to dilute their potency. All I had done was deprive them of an anchor to hold them in place by separating them from their associated events.

What I didn't understand was that when you strip them away from their original events, strong feelings and reactions still maintain their power over time. Mine didn't fade even as the war slipped further into my personal history. My denial sustained their rage for years behind the walls I'd built—hidden but not unfelt.

My rock-solid compartmentalization had been a godsend— it had helped me survive combat.

But it came with a cost.

Relentlessly, the swirling emotions had probed my defenses, exploiting any weakness they found immediately. I didn't know it, but I'd been locked in a fight that required increasing exertion on my part to just hold even. Ironically, the harder I fought to control my emotions, the greater the pressure they exerted to escape.

And sometimes they got out.

It was those little escapes that gave rise to disconcerting emotional responses. It was like I was trying to shake a little salt out—and the whole lid would fall off. I'd relax my defenses for a brief moment while watching TV—and the next thing I knew some totally random shit would come pouring out and kick me in the teeth.

What the fuck?

I lost confidence in my own responses. To protect myself, I controlled all my emotions—good, bad, indifferent. It didn't matter which. Entertaining any of them seemed to have negative repercussions. It was safer to not feel anything than to risk being ambushed by feelings I didn't understand.

But putting it all down on paper re-attached the emotions to the events that gave them birth. The act of writing let the poisons drain away, and the pressure against my walls seemed to dissipate.

Small emotional responses stopped triggering something bigger. I started to feel things without danger of being over-whelmed. I began to think I'd achieved a state of equilibrium. The walls were still there—I hadn't taken them down—but at least they weren't in danger of exploding from the pressure.

That left me with a choice to make: Trust that the walls would always be strong enough, or go all the way?

Mentally I was holding a sledgehammer. Did I have the courage? There was no halfway anymore—it was all or nothing. *Live in denial or face it?*

Maybe it was distance from active duty, maybe it was being a father, maybe I'd eaten bad clams...I don't know exactly how it happened, but it did.

My concept of strength had changed.

To deny the unease became weakness, to face it fortitude. More than that, stopping would be cowardice—it would mean gambling my family's future to spare myself a little discomfort. *Fuck that.*

The walls were well built but they didn't stand a chance. I was on a mission and smashed them to kingdom come. As the mental dust cleared, the questions came out. Slowly at first, almost uncertain if their freedom was a joke or not. They were the simple ones, the surface-level questions that had been jailed with the hardened criminals—guilt by association.

Was the war right?

I don't know why that question ever ended up in my head. To a Marine, the concept of deciding whether a war is right or not is the same as mental masturbation—there's no point to it. I'd decided years ago that I would support and defend the Constitution of the United States against all enemies, foreign and domestic. I didn't swear to follow orders only if I agreed with them or to second-guess those appointed over me. The war was legally authorized and fully sanctioned by my elected leaders—that was all the justification I needed.

Right or Wrong? Come on dude, you would have stormed the Vatican if the President had declared war on the Pope. Don't play the hindsight game. You did your job, that's it. Next.

The easy questions gave way to ones that were more complex.

Why didn't your 'test' work? Why were you still screwed up from your first deployment after having a pretty easy time coming back from the second?

That question stirred some thought. I had believed that my ground tour had been more traumatic than my air tour—until I remembered that the nagging unease had actually existed *before* I went back the second time.

Slowly I realized that the premise of the test was fundamentally flawed. It was based on my assumption that the experiences I'd had on the ground were, by virtue of being more dangerous and exposed, more traumatic than those in the air.

But they hadn't been.

That little tidbit of information came as a surprise to me. How could a ground combat tour *not* be more difficult to deal with than one in the air? It didn't make sense—until I stopped looking through the filter of how I *thought I should* see them.

Then things started to come into focus.

At first glance my ranking of the potential for disturbing aftereffects was logical. On the ground, I would be exposed to every danger known to the modern battlefield and would be operating in a small group far from help. The whole experience should have been way more distressing than sitting behind the controls of a powerful machine.

Then I dissected those thoughts a little.

Had I really been exposed more on the ground?

The surprising answer was no. On the ground I was one of many. Fifty of the best gunfighters in the Marine Corps were all around me. The chances of someone getting a couple of rounds off before one of us cut him down were pretty damn slim.

But when I thought about being in the cockpit, the opposite was true. There I had felt truly exposed, all the time. In the air I was visible for miles in all directions, near deaf and basically blind underneath and behind me. My only defense was the enemy's crappy aim. At 50 feet any dickhead with an AK should be able to knock me out of the sky. Going higher was even more deadly—heavy AAA guns and missiles love elevated targets. Every flight was a gamble and there was no way to avoid all the risks. We *had* to take a bite of the shit sandwich. How big a bite was up to us.

What if someone had shot me? Or if I'd been blown up? Then what?

Easy. On the ground with the Det, we had some of the best corpsmen the Navy has ever created moving along with us—I was never more than a few seconds from lifesaving help. Our "docs" were incredibly skilled and I had absolute confidence that they would take care of me. If I survived the initial wound, there was no doubt in my mind that they would keep me alive. No doubt at all.

And what if I'd gotten shot in the aircraft?

I might as well have been alone. Although Gash was with me in the bird, five feet of electronics and instrumentation separated us. There was no way he would be able to help me out—he couldn't reach me to apply a tourniquet, hold pressure against a wound or dig for a spurting artery. Unless I could help myself, the chances were high that I'd bleed out from an otherwise survivable wound.

No, when I looked honestly at the relative exposure I'd had during each tour, it was clear—I'd been in much greater danger in the air.

That was an interesting realization but I knew it wasn't what was bothering me—it was too out in the open, too acknowledged.

Danger in combat is expected. Fear is an appropriate reaction to deadly situations and one that I had fully expected to experience. True courage is continuing on in spite of fear—you can't have one without the other.

I had no problem admitting I was scared.

Well, what the hell is it then?

I knew the answer was close at hand but wasn't sure how to find it. Figuring that it had something to do with a difference between my two tours, I focused my attention there.

What could have made combat in the aircraft more difficult to deal with than bursting into insurgents' homes in the dead of night?

I began to see that my combat tours were very different experiences—and not in the ways I thought they would be.

I thought I'd fought twice in the same war. Nothing could be further from the truth.

Oh sure, I was in Iraq both times, but that was where the similarity ended. In the year between my tours the enemy changed, the fighting changed and my weapons changed.

I was the only constant.

Using my second tour as a litmus test to determine if I was 'over' my first one suddenly seemed extremely naïve.

I'd based my self-assessment on a confident comparison of apples to oranges because they were both round-ish. It wasn't until I actually *looked* at them that I saw the differences.

The enemy was totally different. During the invasion there had been the question of "Is this guy about to surrender or not?" There were situations where it was totally possible that the men I found in my sights were conscripts abandoned by their superiors. They might have been completely unaware that we were even at war. There's no CNN in a sandy hole in the middle of the desert.

I had to face the possibility that some of the men I killed might not have deserved to die.

That wasn't the case on my second tour. Then we were fighting the insurgency. Every single insurgent made a conscious decision to become my enemy—they picked up weapons when they could have left well enough alone. They chose. There was no doubting their culpability in their own deaths.

That wasn't all. Not only was the nature of my enemy different, the mechanics of how I killed them were, too.

At first glance I thought that wasn't a big deal—the end results were the same. I was so certain of that fact that I almost blew past the issue without really considering it. Something made me take a second look.

Were the end results really the same?

That question was like a lever craftily hidden in my mind. I inadvertently leaned against it and a whole wall rumbled and split in two. A secret place opened up to me, a place where dangerous thoughts were held incommunicado.

Oh shit.

Even before I entered the hidden room my thoughts became different—they flowed where they wanted. Internal barriers were dropping like flies and realizations rushed to fill the gaps.

The end results were the same for the guys I killed. Not for me, though. The results were very different for me.

It wasn't the dying that bothered me. People die every day and I don't get overly upset about that. There was something about *doing it*, actually carrying out the killing that sat uneasily with me.

I was so close, so close to figuring out what was bothering me. It was on the tip of my tongue—but I just couldn't quite spit it out. The answer lay in that hidden room but it wasn't going to make it easy for me. I had to go in.

This was the last thing I wanted to do. That room held questions that, if I asked them, I would have to answer honestly. Whatever the answers were I'd have to deal with the repercussions.

There was no bullshitting in there. It was the center of my soul, the foundation of all that is *me*. Did I really want to screw with that?

Quit now. Maybe you made this whole thing up. Maybe your kids will thrive with an emotionally unpredictable Dad, or maybe you'll piss Lena off bad enough she'll leave you and find someone better...

That voice could be a real prick sometimes—but it served a purpose.

I went in. The questions were waiting. They'd been waiting for years.

So what's the difference? Killing is killing—isn't it?

Outside of this room I'd been convinced it was. Inside though, I wasn't so sure.

On the ground I killed by proxy. I directed aircraft to shoot or drop bombs on certain things I knew to contain enemy personnel. I killed with my radio.

In the air I spotted the enemy, decided whether he should live or die, and then killed him as efficiently as possible with missiles, rockets or guns.

The difference became blazingly obvious to me.

In the cockpit it was *my* fingers that kept the crosshairs on a man's chest, *my* decision to fire the missile, *my* actions that turned another human being into goo.

I did it. Me. I killed—that's what was different.

Like one clue that leads to another, this realization brought a host of memories back to the forefront of my mind. They were contained within the sturdy capsule I'd buried the night of my failed talk with the Chaplain and hoped to never see again.

Now I dug it up.

Inside were all the emotions and thoughts from that sunny morning after the long sandstorm, undiluted by the passage of time.

All the suspense, elation and horror I'd felt when killing the four guys at the truck came spilling out. I felt my pulse race again as Gash cut the man in half with a rocket.

I remembered feeling confused at the contradiction between how I'd felt watching footage of BT killing some troops and footage of me doing it—chest-thumping elation versus secret guilt.

I recalled the discomfort I'd felt when the young Marine was spouting off and talking shit about the deaths on the video screen.

I'd never allowed myself to answer why that mission affected me so. Now I knew.

It was the first time I saw, without a shadow of a doubt, that I personally killed someone.

In hindsight I can see how close I came to screwing up—really screwing up—in the aftermath of that mission. I'd almost gone into this room while still in combat.

That would have been disastrous. At the time I'd still had a job to do, more killing to accomplish, before I could safely entertain my *feelings* about anything.

There had been nothing the Chaplain could have said to ease my mind. In a strange way, his inept attempt to justify my killing had been exactly what I needed. I came to see that my worthless talk with the Chaplain hadn't been worthless at all—it put a stop to my flirtation with ill-timed introspection.

FIDO—Fuck It, Drive On.

After the wrath I'd directed at myself for thinking the Chaplain was some sort of happiness fairy, FIDO had become my mantra.

Don't think about it. Don't think about any of it. Just do your job and make it home. After that you can think about it all you want.

Promises to process later worked well—really well. I went back to my job of killing the enemy with, if not enthusiasm, at least cold effectiveness.

The problem was that I never did process anything. I left the thoughts trapped in their boxes and built walls to lock them in. I would have left them there forever—a hazardous waste site in my mind. But the damn things started leaking out.

Well, I was processing them now. It wasn't any easier than it would have been then, but it was a hell of a lot safer to do it in my basement than in the cockpit.

—┼—

I stayed in that hidden room for several weeks, uncovering things and dealing with them as best I could. I had long conversations with Lena and my dad, talking about what I unearthed in there. Even if we didn't arrive at any conclusions, just airing the questions out seemed to help.

I cleared out the backlog of memories and questions. Just when I thought the room might be empty, that there was nothing else left to deal with, I found it.

It was a menacing box—squat, nasty and covered with dire warnings. As much as I wished I could flip off the light and close the door I couldn't. I knew it was there—I had to open it.

Oh fuck.

This was it. Without a doubt I knew this was it. If my denial and fundamental unease were a pearl, this was the grain of sand in the center.

Good people don't kill.
I killed.
What does that make me?

There was no way to answer that question. Oh, I could create any number of qualifiers that were absolutely true—I'd only killed lawful combatants, I was only doing my job, I killed in the name of freedom and justice...

None of them came close to answering the question.

I've said it before and I'll say it again—I'm not a religious guy. But I do believe I'll be called to answer for the actions I've taken during my life. So when I come face to face with whatever god there is and it asks—

"Did you kill?"

How am I supposed to answer that?

"Wellllll yes but..."

There's no 'but'. It's a pretty fucking simple question—yes or no.

I have to answer yes. So where does that leave me? Am I going to be reincarnated as a dung beetle? Tossed into the fires of hell? Made to push a boulder up a hill for eternity? Am I fucked?

I wish I had strong enough faith that a priest could tell me to say a bunch of prayers and all would be forgiven—but I don't.

What does that make me?

No person can answer this question. No one can explain away what I've done in terms that don't sound trite and shallow.

After learning it was unanswerable—before I'm dead anyhow—I wished I could stuff the question away again. But that's not how it works. Its undeniable presence made me uncomfortable—like a dying man watching a vulture land nearby. I knew it wasn't going to go away. It would always be there until I wasn't. Then the question would be answered and there wasn't a damn thing I could do about it.

It wasn't just the potential of eternal fuckage that concerned me. Closer to home was another concern that, given my secular nature, was harder to accept.

How can you be having problems dealing with killing? What warrior doesn't take pride in vanquishing his foe?

This had been the first thought that escaped when my dad told me about Dave's crash—the bullet of self-hatred that slammed into my chest. Subconsciously this question had existed since I'd killed my first Iraqi soldier, but I'd refused to acknowledge it. The implied answer—that not reveling in the slaughter disqualified me as a warrior—formed a steel jacket around the question's lead slug.

I'd been out of the Marine Corps for years, but it still formed the basis of my identity. I earned my place among the heroes of that organization and am proud of what I accomplished. Nothing could change that—but this realization came close.

Identifying myself as a warrior had meant everything to me. I'd worked hard to feel confident in bearing that label—and a strong component of that confidence was the belief that I possessed the mental fortitude to carry out my duties and be ready for more.

I wasn't somebody who didn't want to go to war. I never had my innocence ripped away from me in a spray of gore. Being in situations where I had to kill people was no accident—I'd eagerly sought that challenge for years.

I come from a family of warriors and I joined the Marine Corps—a warrior society. Up till now I was confident that I had upheld the highest traditions of both my family and the service. Regardless of what direction I went after I left the Marine Corps, I'd felt confident that I did so as a warrior.

Now the evidence before me suggested otherwise.

I felt like I was struggling with something that others breezed past without a second thought—weak by comparison.

Was it all bullshit? Was I a poser—a fake? Real warriors don't get weepy years after doing the exact thing they were supposed to do.

What the hell is wrong with me?

There was no relief associated with uncovering the root cause of my unease. No deep sigh of comprehension and then on to 'happily ever after'. Instead of unscrewing my head this whole writing project seemed like an adventure into pointless self-flagellation—and not the good kind either.

I found myself in uncomfortable and uncharted territory—alone in my distress.

Well fuck. Now what?

I had no idea it was coming, but an event was looming that would bring all this together. It would prove my question wasn't a sign of weakness. Instead, I would recognize it as a burden common to warriors since war began. I'd be free of self-doubt and ready to move forward confident of who and what I am.

But the price of gaining that awareness was high.

Way too high.

CHAPTER 19

I GOT THE NEWS around noon on a sunny July day in 2010—almost a year after my brother's crash.

It was feeding time at the zoo. Both of my kids were strapped into their highchairs and giggling as the warm breeze through the open windows made my daughter's hair stand up like Kim Jong Il's. I loved watching them interact—having one kid was awesome, two blew my mind.

The phone's insistent ringing interrupted the happy scene—I almost ignored it.

Checking quickly to make sure nobody was choking I picked up the phone. My annoyance evaporated when I checked the caller ID. It was IKE.

He'd switched over to the Marine Corps Reserve a couple of years after the invasion. We'd stayed in touch via phone calls and random emails since then. I was glad he'd called—it had been a while.

"Today's the worst day of my life." The background noise told me IKE was driving as he spoke.

Hmm, that's not how IKE usually starts a conversation...

"Really? What's up?" I asked. He sounded a little strange, but not like a man under great duress. I figured he was screwing with me.

He wasn't.

"Weasel's dead. I'm on my way to tell Mae." His voice quivered a little at the effort of saying her name. I could almost see him trying to blink away sudden tears as his words struck home.

I froze—physically shivered, ice shooting through my veins. *Where the hell is Weasel? Oh shit—Afghanistan.*

"Oh shit. Fuck—What happened?" I stammered—unconsciously stalling with curses as I tried to formulate a cohesive thought.

"He was shot down, him and Sugarbear. Both dead."

Sugarbear had been one of our instructors when IKE and I first learned how to fly the Cobra.

My mind started racing—I had a million questions but knew there were no answers. Information concerning crashes comes out months later, if at all. Silence stretched uncomfortably across the phone line as I tried to wrap my mind around what had happened.

IKE's voice snapped me out of it.

"I'd totally forgotten that he put me down as his CACO (Casualty Assistance Calls Officer)—I'm driving behind the CO and Chaplain to go tell Mae. I had to call you first."

This time I caught it and was confused—why tell me before Mae? Nobody gets to hear it before the wife. IKE continued.

"I wanted to know if you had any pointers for me, man—seeing how you did this for Jaymie when we lost Teddy."

His voice was getting stronger as he talked. Like Dad going to tell my mom about Dave's crash; IKE had a mission, something to focus on.

"Oh fuck, man, I'm sorry as hell you gotta do this."

I was stalling for time—I really had no advice for him. How do you tell your best friend's wife that she's now alone with two young sons? Having stumbled through something similar did not make me an expert. I jumped on the first recollection that came to me.

"You gotta hold it together for her. Her grief takes priority, man—you've gotta just *be there* for her. When you get home though, when it's just you and Carol, you have to let it out. You have to grieve, too."

It felt like I'd just recommended putting a band-aid on a sucking chest wound.

Brilliant.

"I don't know how I'm going to do this. Shit. We're here—I gotta go." He sounded like a condemned man. I knew the hell he was walking into and my heart went out to him.

"Jesus brother, I'm sorry."

"Yeah. Me too. I'll give you a call when I can." He hung up.

I sat on my stool facing the kids' highchairs and pressed the phone into my stomach.

Then I cried.

Flashes of Weasel's smiling face beamed out from the years we'd been friends—diving together, deployed together, kayaking, mountain biking, running, drinking…Ever since we'd mooned our Navy swim instructors during the first stages of flight school thirteen years earlier, we'd been tight. Like most buddies, we could go months without contact, then out of the blue the phone would ring and we'd pick up right where we'd left off.

No more. Never again.

The tears ran down my cheeks freely. My chest heaved and jumped as I breathed between sobs. I let it go, let the sadness come out. I wasn't about to try and stop it—the last thing I wanted to do was compartmentalize this one.

What I wouldn't have given for someone to start shooting at me right then—or the house to catch fire, or a tree to fall on the car, or anything else that would dislodge my brain from memories of Weasel's smiling face.

There was no relief—no threat to focus on, no distraction. My time to suppress tragedy with action was past—now I just had to face it. It wasn't being strong to stuff it away and drive on anymore, not in my life.

I wanted my son to see this. I wanted him to see me cry, to see me visibly suffering for something that truly hurt. I wanted to give him a good example to follow—that meant teaching him that strong men do cry. Hiding that truth has fucked up more men than the penis-tuck scene in *Silence of the Lambs*. Well, not him. Not if I can help it.

Through my tears, I checked on the kids. At 7-months-old, my daughter was happily oblivious, but my son knew something was up. He was watching me with a strange half-smile, like he was trying to figure out if this was some sort of new game.

Their little faces stabbed me in the heart. In a flash I thought about Weasel's sons, Justin and Ryan.

The crushing vice of sadness clamped down again as I glimpsed the immensity of their loss.

I'd lost a friend—they'd lost their father.

It would be some time before I could hug my children without tearing up. The feeling of their little knobby backbones and tiny ribcages under my hands ripped the scabs off my wounds of grief. The joy I felt at holding them brought with it searing guilt—Justin and Ryan would never feel their daddy's arms around them again.

That was the worst part. I could comprehend that my friend

was dead—we were Marines, it's a risk we assume. What I couldn't wrap my brain around was the incredible price that his family was forced to pay. That was just too much.

For the first time in my life, I allowed myself to grieve. Really grieve—past the shock response. It wasn't intentional—I had actually been in the process of walling up Weasel's memory when Mae stepped in and broke the cycle.

She asked me to speak at the funeral.

As much as it terrified me to do it, writing and preparing that eulogy kept his memory fresh in my mind. Mae's request allowed my grief to run its course and subverted my natural tendency toward immediately burying all painful recollections. I stayed in the house of pain for much longer than I wanted to—and benefited greatly from it.

It would be foolish of me to try and encapsulate the pain and sadness that Weasel's death injected into the world. He was, as is so often the case, the best among us. Death has the unique ability to bestow sainthood on just about anybody—faults slip into the ground with the body while virtues swirl in the minds of the survivors. That's not how it was with Weasel.

He was the perfectly balanced Marine. Somehow he did everything well—family life, professional life, faith, triathlons, friendships…There was no chink in his armor, no weakness that would have betrayed him later in life. Many of us can do one or two things really well, but everything else suffers from neglect. Weasel did them all—and made it look effortless.

I'll refrain from describing the huge church overflowing with mourners at his funeral or the joyful reunions with friends I hadn't seen in years that ran headlong into the reason we had gathered.

Over and over again happiness smashed against grief and manly hugs were held longer than simple greetings demanded.

Those memories are cherished ones for me, and for all who shared in Weasel's life and death. I can't do them justice so I won't try. I'll leave it at this: It was a great funeral, befitting a great life. When I go, I hope half as many people even know about it, let alone stop their lives to reflect on mine.

A couple of things happened when I was in California for the funeral that didn't register until after I got home. The intense emotions of that trip, both good and bad, created a cacophony of feelings that I couldn't begin to process. It wasn't until things settled down and I started writing again that I remembered them.

The first was something that Gash had said. It scared the shit out of me.

I know him about as well as I know anybody. We'd grieved together when Teddy died, almost died together in a freak sand-storm off the coast of Djibouti, weathered the trials of our first combat tour together—shit, we'd shared more life experiences than most married couples. I knew that he was feeling really messed up about Weasel's death—we all were. I didn't realize how bad it was until the day I left.

He drove me to the Carlsbad airport for my flight home to the East Coast. I asked him how he was doing—amid the hustle and bustle we really hadn't had a chance to talk. There are some things that you wait for a little privacy to bring up with a good friend.

His answer stung me.

"I still haven't cried. I want to—I just *can't*."

He said it without an ounce of pride. He desperately wanted to let it out, but couldn't. Years of denying his emotions had created thick scar tissue in him—I could see it only because I knew he'd loved Weasel at least as much as I had.

Fighting grief is like struggling against an amorous gorilla— better to just get it over with.

I thought about how much I'd gained by being able to cry, by embracing my grief and letting it wash over me. Only by not struggling against the grief was it able to run its course. Eventually I came out on the other side—the place where I can remember my dead friend and smile.

Gash was stuck in the bad place—the place where happy memories of our friend kick him in the balls over and over without remorse.

The thought of Gash carrying that load really scared me. Add to it that his marriage was failing, that he was living thousands of miles away from the most important people in his world—his daughters, and that he was leaving for his seventh combat tour in a couple of months...The weight crushing his soul must have been staggering.

This was not good.

I had to go, the plane was not going to wait on me. Something popped into my head as I grabbed my bag, a warning I couldn't ignore. I wanted to explain it away as horseshit, as absurd, as something that couldn't ever happen—but I knew it could. Anybody who ignores this warning does themselves and their friends a disservice. I had to say it.

"Dude, you gotta let it out. Find a way. I hate to even say this— but if someone told me six weeks from now that you'd suck-started your pistol I wouldn't be shocked. I'd have to say 'Fuck, I knew it.' Don't do that to me, man, don't make me deal with that too."

He gave me a scary little smile—an ambiguous smirk that either said "How'd you know?" or "You're out of your mind dude; I'd never off myself" with equal clarity. I'd hit on something but had no idea what.

"Just call me before you do anything stupid." I left it at that.

"Yeah, no worries, mate. I'm good."

I really hoped he was.

The other thing I unpacked with my suitcase was a conversation I'd had on the night of the funeral. It struck me as important at the time, but I didn't see just how important until later.

After the interment and reception at Point Loma, a bunch of us went out to a bar for some drinks. It had been a stressful day and we were ready to relax and enjoy each other's company for a bit.

We found ourselves in a sports bar owned by a friend of a friend. Pitchers of beer were on the house and about fifteen of us took over a corner of the room surrounded by big screen TVs.

Among the old squadron mates and friends, I spotted another familiar face. It was Colonel Heywood, now retired. He'd kind of fallen off the face of the earth after commanding our squadron during the invasion. I'd wondered what he had been up to. He looked just the same as I remembered—short-cropped salt-and-pepper hair, weathered face and a commanding presence with a quick and easy smile. It was good to see him.

A while later I felt a meaty paw land heavily on my shoulder.

"Hey Shoe, how the hell are you?" I was surprised—not because Col Heywood was growling in my ear but because I could understand him. His characteristic mumble was replaced by a surprisingly coherent Rhode Island accent.

"Ha! Shit Sir, I'm doing great. How about yourself?" My face split into a big grin and I turned to shake his hand.

I don't know if I would have noticed it before having kids myself, but there was something paternal in his demeanor. It felt like I was talking to my dad.

It made sense. Those of us who had served under him were like his kids—he'd watched us grow up in the gunship community, seen us gain our footing and strike out confidently on our own. He'd borne the fear of sending us into combat, shared in our exhilaration when we returned safely and buried us when we got killed. Such are the burdens of a good commander. I wasn't surprised at all that he attended Weasel's funeral.

We chatted for a few minutes about how incredibly Mae was dealing with things, how the ceremony was really nice and how great it is—circumstances notwithstanding—that we were all able to get together again. Then he turned serious.

"So, you're really doing okay?"

"Well, shit—no, I mean, this whole thing sucks, but I think I'm handling it okay," I stammered.

"Because I was watching you at the burial—you looked kind of different, I don't know, just different." His ruddy face showed his concern.

I was surprised—I thought I'd hidden it pretty well.

Besides the normal introspection associated with burying a close friend, there had been something else percolating inside me. I couldn't quite shake a sense of shame when I looked around at friends I'd served with—some who'd spent much longer in combat than I had. They all looked like they were doing so well. Their apparent invincibility to the unease that had been dogging me gave teeth to a question that lingered.

Everybody else is fine. What the hell's wrong with you?

I hadn't talked to anyone about what I was writing—or even that I *was* writing—other than Gash. This just wasn't the time or place to go into it and besides, I didn't have a clue what I would tell them. I kept the fact that I had spent the last year *thinking* about my past hidden from everyone. Even to me that just sounded weird.

I wasn't sure if I ever wanted them to know about the unease I harbored or the questions I couldn't resolve. I feared that knowledge would make them think less of me, weaker somehow. It was my dirty little secret, my shame to hide.

I looked at Col Heywood quizzically, letting him continue. I wasn't going to volunteer anything and it looked like he had something he wanted to say.

"Not many people know this, Shoe, but I've had a really rough time dealing with things."

Huh?

I leaned closer to combat the noise of the bar. I wasn't certain I'd heard him correctly.

He read my actions and understood my surprise.

"Yeah, I never expected it either. Everything was fine right up until it wasn't. Happened almost three years to the day after Ben and Travis were killed—I just lost it. Totally lost it. I don't know how to describe it other than a complete mental and physical breakdown."

His voice was strong and steady—whatever he'd lost, it sounded like he'd gotten it back.

I still didn't say anything, just kept looking at him. Of all the people I'd thought might have suffered mentally, he was not one of them. He kept going.

"I spent three months in the hospital, getting help for something I never thought I'd need help with. I mean, I was raised a good Catholic boy—then I killed a bunch of people and expected that everything would be fine. Oh, there was other stuff too—alcohol, family issues and all that, but at the root was the killing. It's just not natural, what we did."

I kind of looked down and found something incredibly interesting on the floor—hiding the surprised tears that threatened to flood my eyes.

Heywood had trouble dealing with the killing? How's that possible?

He'd been the quintessential combat leader—tough, compassionate and outwardly impervious to the demands of leading men in combat. His revelation floored me.

"One thing I swore to myself, Shoe, when I got better, was that I'd keep an eye open for other guys having problems. I never saw it in myself until it was almost too late—and even then had to have my face shoved in it. Well, I see some of that in you."

I was really glad I was looking down at his shoes—his words were cutting deep.

"I just want you to know, if you ever need to talk about anything, gimme a call. I've been through it, probably more stubbornly than anyone else, and I might be able to help."

When I got my feet underneath me again I told him about my writing, about how I was having some problems but felt like things were pretty much under control.

I'm not sure he believed me but he wasn't going to press. He knew that dealing with issues like ours has to come from within—it can't be forced on someone or dragged out. Pressing would have activated my defenses and I'd have thrown up walls again.

Someone else joined our conversation and we changed the subject. I filed it away amid the small talk—something to chew on later.

In the months that followed the funeral I returned to writing. I was working on a new draft and was struggling with the question of 'Why?'

Why should anybody want to read what's going on in my head? What am I trying to say? What's the point?

It's not a dramatization to say that I almost quit right there. There's more that I want to do with my life than sit in my moldy basement and write a book that may never leave my computer.

Then I got my head out of my ass.

The realization didn't hit like a thunderclap—it kind of oozed into my mind. One day I was able to look at myself from a slightly different perspective, almost like an outside observer. Then things started to make sense.

I'd spent a full year examining how *my* experiences impacted *me*. The end result of that personal odyssey was predictably alienating—it made me feel like I was the outlier, the weak one.

In my hubris I imagined that I was different—the only person ever to suffer for actions taken in combat.

That's about the stupidest thing I've ever believed with all my heart.

I'll never say that anything good came from Weasel's death—ever. That would be asinine. I will say this, though. The intensity of the loss felt by his friends provided an arena free of testosterone, of external and false impositions of what popular culture says a man should be. Bullshit fell away at that funeral and true feelings were expressed. In this arena, I realized something simple yet profoundly difficult to see—

I am not alone.

Gash can't cry. A friend whom he spent years with, whom he served in combat with during both 2003 and 2004, whom he included in his closest ring of friends gets killed and *he can't cry about it?* Find one goddamn thing that's all right about that—just one, I dare you. There's nothing. It's crippling, it rips him open from the inside, yet he clamps it down. He must hold it together. Until he can't—then what?

He doesn't have the option of sitting around in his basement for a year, pouring over his past and extracting meaning from tragedy. No, all he gets is another combat tour. Seven combat tours. I can't even remember seven vacations.

Gash showed me I wasn't alone. Col Heywood showed me what I could do about it.

If someone as strong and resilient as my old CO can admit to having trouble dealing with combat, then surely I can do the same. Through his admission of pain he legitimized mine—and gave me an example of how I might help others. After our conversation, the shame that had burned in me at the funeral began to morph into something else—a sense of duty.

All thoughts of not writing, not digging anymore disappeared. That would have been as despicable as Barnes leaving Elias in *Platoon.* I could no more not tell my story than I could leave a wounded comrade on the battlefield.

I began to believe there was something universal in my story, something that might be able to help my brothers and sisters still suffering the echoes of combat. If I could figure out what it was, then maybe I could do for others what had been done for me. Maybe my story could legitimize someone else's pain, maybe I could help others understand that they are not alone.

Okay, so figure it out.

One day it happened. I wish I could say my epiphany took place in a church, or watching my children playing, or in a deep conversation with my wife—but no. It was in a gas station.

I was getting some work done on our car and brought the laptop to do some writing while I waited. I didn't really feel like writing though, so I found myself surfing the web.

I started researching the definition of 'warrior' in other cultures and languages. Shit, humans have been killing each other forever. Maybe somebody in the past figured this stuff out.

I'd lived my life to date either seeking to define myself as a warrior, or defending my self-perception as one. I never bothered to figure out what being a warrior meant—I took the definition that was provided.

The Oxford Dictionary told me it was "a brave or experienced soldier or fighter."

Okay, got that.

Hollywood told me it was Chuck Norris, John Wayne and the Spartan 300 all rolled into one.

Easy enough.

I might be stretching it a bit on Chuck Norris—nobody could be like Chuck—but other than that I figured I'd pretty much met the popular definition of a warrior. Then the punk-ass in my head spouted off again.

But none of them ever had questions about killing—you did. So you're not a warrior after all are you? Puss.

He had a point. In the definition of a warrior that I sought to emulate there was no room for the type of thoughts bouncing around in my head.

I just didn't recognize that my definition was pure horseshit.

After scrolling through what seemed like thousands of links to video games with 'warrior' in the title, I stumbled upon something that caught my eye.

It was a loose translation of the term used by the Mohawk Indian tribe to describe their warriors. It turns out that there is no direct translation from their language to ours, but the word they used means something along the lines of:

One who bears the burden of peace.

What? That's it? Now I'll be the first to admit that I know slightly less about Native American culture and linguistics than, say, rocket surgery, but I kind of expected something more descriptive.

These guys were among the fiercest warriors in a land of fierce warriors. They fought with knives, clubs and fists. They didn't get to pop dudes with missiles from two miles away—they felt the hot spurt of lifeblood on their face when they killed. These guys knew killing. I expected that their definition of 'warrior' would denote something of that knowledge.

Then it came to me—it did. It totally did.

These guys knew more about killing than I ever would—shit, they knew more about the subject than just about anybody. They'd encased that knowledge in a package of sounds that some linguistics scholar had translated the best way they knew how.

And here it was—the knowledge I'd been unknowingly searching for—in simple, unadorned terms on my computer screen.

One who bears the burden of peace.

I understood the idea of bearing burdens—but in too limited a fashion. I saw only the physical burdens—the burns, amputations, bullet holes, deaths, PTSD…These scars mark hundreds of thousands of our veterans and I wholeheartedly believe they define their carriers as warriors. Nothing can change that.

What I didn't recognize was that there are other burdens as well. If having to wonder for the rest of my life whether I am eternally damned because I killed people isn't a burden, then I don't know what is.

My burden was hidden from everyone, including myself. The fact that it was unseen did nothing to reduce its weight. In some ways it multiplied it.

It came as a shock for me to realize that I had always tied my identity as a warrior to external things—medals, uniforms, physical toughness...

My concept of being a warrior had to do with how *others* saw me. As if a curtain was being pulled back, I started to comprehend what had been going on all along.

I began to see just how shallow, fragile and exposed that reliance upon others' opinions had made me. I'd thought that the label of 'warrior' was something that could be bestowed on me—and likewise taken away. Not anymore.

My Bronze Star and two Air Medals, all with combat distinguishing devices, made up a large part of my external membership badge to the warrior club. So did my uniforms, dirty and soiled boots, banged-up helmet and plaques on the wall. I'd thought that they proved I was a warrior. But they don't—they're just accoutrements.

What proves I am a warrior is the unanswerable question that hangs over my head. Living the rest of my life unsure if I'm already damned for what I've done is my burden. It is what I carry with me and it is mine alone to bear.

I bear the burden of peace.

Holy shit. It started to make sense.

I wasn't a puss for feeling screwed up about killing. Entertaining the question *"Good people don't kill. I killed. What does that make me?"* suddenly didn't feel like an admission of weakness anymore.

As I said before, there is no answer to my question. I'm okay with that. A certain calmness entered my life as I gained understanding of what was bothering me. I don't know what will happen to me after I die, but I also don't worry about it.

I have good days and bad, just like everyone else. The difference between my bad days now and my bad days before I started writing is this: Now I know the anger, irritation, jumpiness and annoyance are coming from somewhere else. It's not the four thousandth time my son has asked to go to the park, or the third time my daughter has tossed stuffed animals into the toilet today that upsets me. Whereas before I might have ignored their annoying behavior until I hit a breaking point and started shouting, now I see their innocence in relation to what's causing my anger. Instead of lashing out I consciously seek to diffuse it, to channel it away.

Several times as I was writing I discussed various flights with Lena. I was surprised by her reaction. Each time I thought I was just rehashing old information with her, assuming that I had told her this stuff before. I hadn't. I had told her the facts concerning the flights; she knew what I'd done and what had happened to me—but I had never told her how any of it made me feel. How could I have? Until I started writing I'd never let *myself* know how I'd felt. I'd just assumed she could read it in me.

Now that she knows what is going on in my head, she can read the warning signs. She knows when I'm getting antsy. She knows when I just need a break. She'll take the kids for a bit on the weekend, giving me time to go for a long run, go kayaking, or just run some errands by myself. Being alone is a great time for me to work through things, and that in and of itself is a positive development. There was a period when having time to think was the last thing I wanted.

I no longer seek to get 'over' my combat experiences. That was a fool's errand to begin with. They've had too great an impact on me to ever be forgotten—and they never should be. They make up a large component of who I am now and will play a major role in how I live from here on out.

I'm going to live the rest of my life as well as I can, according to my own understanding of what is good and right. If I screw it up, then I'll pay. If I get it right, then maybe instead of a dung beetle I'll be reincarnated as a Saudi prince.

Either way, my transgressions will not be passed along to my kids. My family will not suffer for my inability to come to grips with the actions of my past.

I'm aware of my burden now only as much as my own weight. It is part of me—and I'm strong enough to carry it. If that changes, if my burden grows and threatens to crush me, I'll be strong enough to ask for help. I have gained a lot by being able to honestly examine my emotions, but that doesn't mean I have it all figured out.

I have no idea where my life will go from here, but I move

forward with confidence instead of trepidation.

I no longer fear damaging my children—they will suffer their own trials in life but not because of me.

I don't fear the quiet anymore—the demons that used to torment me have lost their teeth.

I can allow my emotions free rein without apprehension—they will be appropriate and measured.

I will never stop being a warrior. By owning my burden I can be more than that though—I can be the husband, father and man my family deserves.

For now, that's enough.

EPILOGUE

JUST IN CASE there is any confusion, I want to be perfectly clear about who I am.

I don't wear a uniform anymore but I still consider myself a Marine. I never got an Eagle Globe and Anchor tattoo on my arm because it was already on my soul—where it will always remain.

I am a proud veteran of Operation Iraqi Freedom. I believe that I made the right decisions under difficult circumstances.

I wouldn't change any of them.

I killed when I had to. When I did take life I limited the scope of the violence I inflicted to the bare minimum. I'm confident that I killed only legal combatants and operated within the laws of war.

Regardless of the qualifiers, I am a killer. I will have to live with that for the rest of my life.

What follows are my opinions. I hold no advanced degrees, no scholarly knowledge that can 'prove' my ideas. All I have to offer are my two cents—one Marine's view of the challenges facing returning warriors and the role the warriors themselves can play in overcoming them.

When I started to narrow down the cause of my unease I did some reading. What I found written among some very good books—namely, LtCol Dave Grossman's *On Killing*, Bernard

Verkamp's *The Moral Treatment of Returning Warriors in Early Medieval and Modern Times* and Dr. Jonathan Shay's *Achilles in Vietnam* and *Odysseus in America*—opened my eyes to the burdens common to warriors throughout history.

I was amazed to learn that the medieval Catholic Church imposed penances on warriors returning from the Crusades. Initially I thought that was pretty screwed up. First the Church sends you across the world to fight in the name of religion. Then you suffer the horrors of combat. When, finally, you return home the same Church that sent you slaps three years of penances on you for the killing you did in their name?

What the fuck?

Then I thought about it some more. Maybe the Church wasn't seeking to punish these men. Maybe it was helping them. I think that the Church might have understood that the returning warrior bore some burdens for what he'd had to do in combat. Imposing penance was the Church's way of lifting them from his shoulders.

Only three years of penance and I'm free? Sign me up.

That wasn't the only interesting tidbit contained in those books. I came to realize that what I thought was unique to me was anything but—the warrior's burden has been widely accepted as normal by cultures throughout history.

Some ancient societies understood, better than we do, that the majority of returning warriors needed something to formalize their re-introduction to civil society. They used purification rituals, penance and other culturally based methods to welcome their warriors back from combat. They acknowledged that normal humans can't be hacking heads off one day, and the next be engaging in civil discourse as if nothing had happened. Unless you are a psychopath it doesn't work that way.

In the US, we seem to think that it does.

Our veterans, those who do not bear external wounds or obvious psychological ones, are expected to slip back into civil society without a hiccup. They find themselves stranded like I did—intent on returning to the person they'd been before combat and struggling with fundamental changes that make that impossible.

I held the popular misconception that people dealing with difficult events fall into one of two categories—all screwed up or untouched. That belief left me hanging in no-man's land. I wasn't suffering overtly, but in the words of Marsellus Wallace in *Pulp Fiction*, I was "pretty fuckin' far from okay."

I knew that I had been changed somehow, but the composition of that change eluded me. Then I read about the concept of bloodguilt.

The dictionary defines bloodguilt as "Guilt caused by murder or bloodshed." At first glance I read this with the eyes of a twice-a-year Catholic—it's the guilt I *should* feel for having killed. Then I re-read the definition. It wasn't saying that I should feel anything—guilt, horror, anguish, elation, rage or victory—for having killed. It simply put a label on a feeling that was already there.

I feel guilty for having killed. Simple as that. The men in my sights, the men I drove missiles through were just that—men. That they were on the other end of my sights was the only difference between us on a human level. I wish that I could see them as demented demons begging to be obliterated, but I can't. They were husbands, fathers, sons and brothers—and I killed them.

Yes, I believe some people deserve to die. Yes, I believe the world would be a better place if certain people were removed from the gene pool. I still paid a price for doing it.

The Mohawk definition of warrior, as vague as it is, resonates strongly with me for this reason. It speaks of the burdens borne by all warriors across time and culture—the universal price of being a warrior. It includes me in that definition expressly because of the pain I feel—not because I ignored it or toughed it out for so long.

If I had been a knight from the Crusades, I might have anticipated this feeling. If I had been a Mohawk brave, the concept of suffering for having spilled another's blood might have been a normal part of my emotional landscape. As a Marine though, thoroughly prepared as I was for the mechanics of killing, I didn't have a clue about how I should feel about it.

In the absence of thoughtful instruction, I sponged up popular culture's lessons on killing. What I should have understood to be a normal human reaction thus seemed a betrayal of all that I held dear.

I occupy a middle ground that I believe counts the majority of veterans among its population. It is a place where one can feel pretty screwed up inside while maintaining a façade of normalcy, a place of uncomfortable questions and disconcerting emotions.

Some will figure out their own way to deal with their burdens. Like me, they will still occupy the middle ground but at least they'll know why. Others will be so tormented by demons they cannot understand that they will self-destruct in search of relief. The lucky ones of this second group will get help. The unlucky will die.

I think most suffer silently. They live outwardly happy lives that occasionally get undercut by unresolved issues and emotions. Their kids learn to say things like "Daddy's in one of his moods" and walk on eggshells so as not to provoke him. The good times are wonderful but the bad times are terrifying. Do I have to mention that, to a kid, the good ones don't outweigh the bad?

This is not living. Not in the way veterans or their families deserve.

We veterans are welcomed home with open arms now, a striking difference from a few decades ago. Our society has come a long way toward understanding the difference between the warriors and the potentially disagreeable political decisions they are sworn to carry out. I am personally thankful for the warm reception I received when I got home.

Cutting edge advancements in psychological and physical care are also available to veterans. This, too, is a tremendous improvement over the societal and governmental treatment of veterans of past wars. I always had this safety net beneath me—and still do.

There's one problem though. I have to ask for it.

Our current system assumes a veteran suffers no lingering aftereffects of combat unless he or she says so. In effect, the veteran must do something they abhor—admit to feeling something they equate with weakness—in order to get access to help.

Why? The burdens are real, they are as old as combat itself. Why should modern veterans have to ask for help relieving them?

It seems to me that we could just as easily go the other way—assume every veteran bears burdens. If new warriors are educated on the near universal effects of combat on the human psyche—disassociated from era, weapons or location—then maybe they will be better able to recognize their specific burdens when the time is right.

At the same time, if our society can work out a way to allow each veteran an opportunity to address his or her burden—*after their service*—I believe each will be much more successful in post-service life.

One only has to look at the mental healthcare requirements of Vietnam-era veterans to see the potential cost of ignoring our most recent veterans' needs. Wouldn't it be better to prevent the crushing downward spiral of negative life choices rather than try to fix it after the fact?

None of this is new—books about the burdens of warriors, both fiction and non-fiction, could fill a library. I have to ask myself, as a relatively well-educated man, why did it take me so long to recognize them in myself? I read books, I was aware of the paralyzing uncertainty of combat, of the terrible decisions one has to make and live with. I didn't have stars in my eyes—I knew what I was getting into. So why couldn't I see my torment reflected off the pages? Why did I feel so *alone*?

Because the books were all about someone else's war— Vietnam stories were my dad, WWII stories were my grandfather and further back than WWII might as well have been fiction. The amazing literature produced by some of the veterans of those conflicts could not reach into my head and make me look into a mirror. I was unable to see the universality of my experiences echoed in the words of someone else's conflict—until I stumbled on Dr. Shay's books.

As I read *Odysseus in America* and *Achilles in Vietnam* I was struck by how much I could empathize with the emotional burdens carried by the Vietnam veterans Dr. Shay interviewed. The light came on in my head—this was what I'd been searching for.

Time and time again I read passages where Dr. Shay explained the genesis of a specific emotional response and then illustrated how warriors separated by 2700 years shared that response. I could understand those emotions. I'd felt them, lived them—and here they were, explained.

I waited for the load to lift off my shoulders, to feel vindicated for emotions I'd previously misunderstood. Here it was, proof that I wasn't alone—I waited for the release that knowledge should have provided.

It never came. Instead, I got upset.

Why? Why should I get upset when a brilliant psychiatrist and classical scholar clearly explained the universality of the warrior experience I felt but couldn't articulate?

Because each time Dr. Shay used a veteran's story to illustrate his point, I felt challenged to defend my reactions. Each vignette he used was so fantastic, so over the top terrifying or horrifying that any rational human being would shiver and think "how could you *not* be screwed up after experiencing that?"

I could relate to the feelings the veterans were having, yet my experiences ranked nowhere near theirs in horror, guilt or pure trauma. I felt like an idiot with a sunburn whining in the burn ward of a hospital. I felt so *weak* for feeling my discomfort in the face of such real suffering.

If I hadn't been willing to risk feeling weak in order to uncover the cause of my unease, the normalcy of my combat experiences— as compared to those described in Dr. Shay's books—would have prevented me from identifying with the pain contained in those pages.

I say this not as a criticism of Dr. Shay's work, but rather as an example of how much of the literature that deals with the challenges faced by veterans focuses solely on extremes. This is understandable—it is at the extremes that the clearest lines of explanation can be drawn. I don't live at the extremes though, and by definition, neither do the majority of veterans.

As of 2012, there are almost 23 million veterans in the United States. Several million of them served in Iraq and Afghanistan. Over 55,000 of these recent veterans have suffered physical wounds, up to 300,000 have suffered Traumatic Brain Injury (TBI) and between 220,000 and 600,000 are suffering from Post Traumatic Stress Disorder (PTSD). It is to our credit as a society that these men and women have the best chance in the history of warfare to recover and live fulfilling lives.

But these numbers are misleading when examining the human cost of war. Behind the diagnosed cases of physical and psychological wounds lie a multitude of undiagnosed ones. Like me, many veterans hide their wounds out of pride, fear and shame. Pride because we believe we should be able to handle anything, fear because we think our wounds exhibit weakness, and shame because others have suffered more yet appear to be fine. On a societal level, nothing is being done to help veterans in this middle ground deal with the burdens that poison their lives. There's a reason for that.

These are not physical wounds. They fall somewhere between a diagnosable disorder and 'fine'. They don't follow predictable biological processes that can be dealt with externally. The 'cure' cannot be administered en masse—each veteran must figure it out individually.

These wounds exist deep in the psyche of the warrior; they challenge the very structure of the soul. They strike in a place so unprotected by the modern definition of a warrior that many veterans would rather die than face them.

Heartbreakingly, many choose exactly that.

Ancient societies had rituals in place to address these wounds, ours does not. That doesn't mean we have to allow them to fester unattended. We, as veterans, can choose to face our burdens and, by doing so, gain the ability to move on with our lives.

I don't pretend to have a formula that will help everybody, nobody does. Just as the burdens are unique to each individual, so too will be the resolution. I also don't suggest that simple self-awareness can relieve the crippling symptoms of PTSD— that would be foolishness in the extreme. But the middle ground is real, and I think millions of veterans are unknowingly trapped there. Like me, they can achieve some measure of relief by taking time to reflect on difficult experiences and honestly assess where they stand. The specific steps of each individual's journey will be different and my story can offer only the most rudimentary roadmap. But there is a common start point.

The journey begins when the veteran admits to him- or herself that they are carrying some sort of burden. These burdens have been crushing souls for centuries—they are as old as war itself. There is no shame in acknowledging them, no weakness in feeling their weight. Yet we keep acting like there is.

I think the opposite is true. Our burdens, and the manner in which we carry them, define us as warriors. Just as true courage cannot exist without fear, a true warrior cannot be without a burden. Those of us who've served recently chose to do so. We chose to become warriors and I, for one, relished the external regalia of that honored profession. But the uniforms, medals and insignia are only external manifestations of the intangible strength that defines a warrior. We display the external symbols of a warrior with pride, but hide our inner torment as if it is shameful, as if it is weakness. As the warriors of our nation, it is within our power to reverse this misconception. But we will have to do it one at a time, through our example, not our words.

It is not realistic to think we, as veterans, will ever 'get over' our combat experiences. Nor should we seek to. They are part of us now and we've earned them. We chose to bear the burdens from those experiences by volunteering to serve, and now we bear the burden of peace.

The Mohawks were right. *That* is what makes us warriors.

ACKNOWLEDGMENTS

FIRST AND FOREMOST, I apologize for any mistakes or omissions of information in this book. I endeavored to write only that which I knew at the time, eschewing any details learned later. For the most part, names of units and actual locations are omitted because that information is not important to the telling of my story. What is important is that the reader feels the confusion, fatigue and excitement of flying a helicopter gunship in combat. In Iraq, my world was defined by voices on the radio and what I could see from 50 feet above the ground. It is into that world that I sought to place the reader.

The conversations related in this book are true and accurate to the best of my knowledge. Memories fade over time, however, so while parts of the book are not transcripts of actual conversations, they do reflect the information discussed and the general mood of those speaking. Some of the names have been changed.

I received support and encouragement from so many people throughout the writing process that I will inevitably forget to mention some of them. This is not a reflection of my level of appreciation, but rather of my poor note-taking skills and memory. That being said, I would like to thank Mary Gold, Dr. Gary Lamphere, Jennifer Lamphere, Kelley Hughes, David Lynch, Corey Aber and SgtMaj Carlton Kent for their editorial and promotional assistance.

I wish to thank the dedicated Marines and Sailors who gave

me safe aircraft to fly, refueled and rearmed me at all times of the day and night, and stood ready to come get me if the mission so required. Being a pilot is the easiest job in a squadron, made so by the legions of professional warriors with blistered hands, split knuckles and hydraulic-soaked coveralls who toil behind the scenes. Semper Fidelis, Devils.

To Gash, Weasel, IKE, BT, JoJo, Spock, Count and Fuse I thank you for being the best division mates a guy could have. I know exactly how lucky I am to have been fated to fly with you gentlemen.

This book would never have been completed if not for one man in particular—David Hazard from Ascent. David saw the importance of the message I was trying to convey before I did, and threw his considerable expertise into helping me develop my story. From teaching me the basics of storytelling, to guiding me through multiple edits and professionally producing the finished book, it is no exaggeration to say that his inputs were invaluable. Thank you very much for all you did, David.

Throughout my life, my parents have provided love and support that allowed me to step out with confidence. The further I travel into my own adventure in parenting, the more amazing their example of how to balance family, work and marriage is to me. Thank you, Mom and Dad.

My sister took time out of her busy work schedule, and put her own writing project on hold, to edit the entire manuscript and correct my atrocious misplacement of commas. Any portions of the book that do not flow nicely or seem garbled are probably places where I ignored her advice. Thank you, Ali.

I owe the greatest debt of gratitude to my wife, Lena. Her support and love made the positive ending for this book possible. It is through her that I have the opportunity to experience the best that life has to offer.

Made in the USA
Lexington, KY
23 November 2012